OXFORD READINGS IN FEMINISM

F   ASK

Reading

Battle   0118 9013100

Cave...

2.

14.

5.

Feminism and Masculinities

Edited by

Peter F. Murphy

UNIVERSITY PRESS

OXFORD
UNIVERSITY PRESS

Great Clarendon Street, Oxford OX2 6DP

Oxford University Press is a department of the University of Oxford.
It furthers the University's objective of excellence in research, scholarship,
and education by publishing worldwide in

Oxford New York

Auckland Bangkok Buenos Aires Cape Town Chennai
Dar es Salaam Delhi Hong Kong Istanbul Karachi Kolkata
Kuala Lumpur Madrid Melbourne Mexico City Mumbai Nairobi
São Paulo Shanghai Taipei Tokyo Toronto

Oxford is a registered trade mark of Oxford University Press
in the UK and in certain other countries

Published in the United States
by Oxford University Press Inc., New York

Introduction, Notes, and Selection © Peter F. Murphy

The moral rights of the authors have been asserted

Database right Oxford University Press (maker)

First published 2004

British Library Cataloguing in Publication Data

Data available

Library of Congress Cataloging in Publication Data

(Data applied for)

ISBN 0–19–926724–3

1 3 5 7 9 10 8 6 4 2

Typeset in Minion
by RefineCatch Limited, Bungay, Suffolk
Printed in Great Britain by
Ashford Colour Press Ltd., Gosport, Hampshire

Dedicated to Charlie Haynie (1935–2001)

Freedom Rider, radical, mentor, friend, and a very early activist in the American men's movement

Contents

Part II 1985–The Present

Notes on Contributors

SAMUEL ADU-POKU is an Assistant Professor of Art Education in the Department of Art at the Youngstown State University in Ohio, USA. He has been an instructor in art education and studio art, both in Ghana and Canada. His research interests are in the areas of gender studies, Africentric studies, multiculturalism, and art education.

LOUISE ARCHER is a Senior Research Fellow at the Institute for Policy Studies in Education, London Metropolitan University, England. Her research covers issues of 'race', ethnicity, gender, and social class, primarily in relation to young people and education. She is author of *'Race', Masculinity and Schooling: Muslim Boys and Education* (2003) and is co-author of *Higher Education and Social Class: Issues of Exclusion and Inclusion* (2002).

TIM CARRIGAN is deceased. Together with John Lee (see below) he was an activist in Gay Liberation and then in community affairs in South Australia and Sydney. They also worked together on a history of homosexual subcultures in Australia. Tim earned his Ph.D. in history at Adelaide University where he wrote a thesis on the history of gay theory, and he had a tutorship in sociology at Macquarie University, though he eventually left the academic world and became editor of a Sydney gay community newspaper.

KENNETH CLATTERBAUGH is a Professor of Philosophy and Adjunct Professor in Women Studies at the University of Washington, USA. He is the author of *Contemporary Perspectives on Masculinity: Men, Women, and Politics in Modern Society* (1997) as well as several articles dealing with men and masculinity.

BOB CONNELL is Professor of Education at the University of Sydney, Australia. He is author or co-author of several books: *Ruling Class Ruling Culture* (1977), *Making the Difference* (1982), *Gender and Power* (1987), *Schools and Social Justice* (1994), *Masculinities* (1995), *The Men and the Boys* (2001), and most recently *Gender* (2002). He is a contributor to research journals in sociology, education, political science, gender studies, and related fields. His current research concerns gender equity, social justice in education, globalization, and intellectuals.

BRIGID COSTELLO is a lecturer in digital media production in the School of Media and Communications at the University of New South Wales, Sydney, Australia. She has worked in the film and television industry as a producer, director, writer, and cinematographer. Since 1994 she has worked in new media production on the design and production of websites, games, and interactive CD-ROM titles.

ABBY L. FERBER is Associate Professor of Sociology and Director of Women's Studies at the University of Colorado at Colorado Springs, USA. She is the author of *White Man Falling: Race, Gender and White Supremacy* (1998); the American Sociological Association's *Hate Crime in America: What Do We Know?* (2000, with Valerie Jeness and Ryken Grattet); *Making a Difference: University Students of Color Speak Out* (2002, with Julia Lesage, Debbie Storrs, and Donna Wong); co-editor of *Privilege: A Reader* (2003, with Michael Kimmel); and editor of *Home Grown Hate: Gender and Organized Racism* (2003).

PAUL HOCH is, I believe, deceased. He published several books, among them *Academic Freedom in Action* (1970), *Rip Off the Game: The Exploitation of Sports by the Power Elite* (1973), and *The Newspaper Game: The Political Sociology of the Press* (1979).

MARJORIE KIBBY is a Senior Lecturer in Cultural Studies in the School of Social Sciences at the University of Newcastle, New South Wales, Australia, where she teaches courses that focus on the intersection of communication and culture. Her research interests include the construction and representation of gender, race, and class in the media, particularly masculinity and aboriginality in film and music. Her recent publications examine these themes in relation to information, community, and commerce on the Internet.

MICHAEL S. KIMMEL is a Professor of Sociology at the State University of New York at Stonybrook, USA, National Spokesperson for the National Organization for Men Against Sexism, and author and editor of several books and articles. His books include *Changing Men* (1987), *Men's Lives* (co-edited) (6th edn. 1987), *Men Confront Pornography* (ed.) (1990), *Against the Tide: Pro-Feminist Men in the United States, 1776–1990* (co-edited) (1992), *Manhood in America: A Cultural History* (1996), *The Politics of Manhood* (co-edited) (1996), and, most recently, *The Gendered Society* (2000). He founded and edits the flagship journal in the field (*Men and Masculinities*). His written work has appeared in dozens of magazines, newspapers, and scholarly journals, including the *New York Times Book Review*, the *Harvard Business Review*, *The Nation*, the *Village Voice*, the *Washington Post*, and *Psychology Today*.

GARY KINSMAN teaches in the Sociology Department at Laurentian University in Sudbury, Ontario, Canada. He is the author of *The Regulation of Desire: Homo and Hetero Sexualities* (1996), and many articles and book chapters on gender and sexual politics. He remains a queer liberation and socialist activist.

BOB LAMM is a freelance writer and teacher in New York City, USA. His political articles and personal essays have appeared in more than forty periodicals, among them the *New York Times*, *Publishers Weekly*, *Lillith*, *Solidarity*, the *Village Voice*, and the *Journal of Popular Film and Television*, as well as three anthologies. He has taught everything from nursery school to junior high and high school to college (Yale, Queens College, and the New School). Currently, he runs improv comedy workshops for beginners and non-performers at the City University of New York Graduate Center, Friends in Deed and elsewhere.

JOHN LEE is deceased. Together with Tim Carrigan (see above) he was an activist in Gay Liberation and then in community affairs in South Australia and Sydney. They also worked together on a history of homosexual subcultures in Australia.

PETER F. MURPHY is the Chair of the Department of English and Philosophy at Murray State University in Kentucky (USA). He is General Editor of a new book series from the University of Wisconsin Press, 'Critical Masculinities,' and the author of *Studs, Tools and the Family Jewels: Metaphors Men Live By* (2001). He edited, also, *Fictions of Masculinity: Crossing Cultures, Crossing Sexualities* (1994).

JOSEPH PLECK is one of the very early theorists of and activists in the American men's movement. He has published extensively in the area of men and mascu-linity. In addition to the collection of essays from which his essay comes, he co-edited (with Jack Sawyer) *Men and Masculinity* (1974), and wrote *The Myth of Masculinity* (1981) and *Working Wives, Working Husbands* (1985). He teaches at the University of Illinois at Urbana–Champaign, USA. His research focuses on fatherhood and on adolescent male sexual behavior.

EMMANUEL REYNAUD is Chief of the Social Security Department, Social Security Policy and Development Branch of the International Labour Organ-ization Geneva, Switzerland. He has published widely in the field of pension reform; among his many books are *International Perspectives on Supplementary Pensions* (1996) and *Social Dialogue and Pension Reform: United Kingdom, United States, Germany, Japan, Sweden, Italy, Spain* (2000).

JACK SAWYER is a social psychologist living in Berkeley, California, USA, and is president of the Parker Street Foundation. He is active in St Mark's Episcopal Church, the Parker Street Housing Cooperative, and local and national politics. He was formerly on the faculty of the University of Chicago and of Northwestern University.

ROBERT STAPLES is a Professor of Sociology at the University of California, San Francisco, USA, and is currently a Visiting Research Fellow at Monash University, Centre for Australian Indigenous Studies, in Melbourne, Australia. He has published over two hundred articles in popular and scholarly period-icals in the United States, Yugoslavia, Austria, Venezuela, Australia, and New Zealand, and has written or edited fifteen books. Among his books are *The Urban Plantation* (1987), *The Black Family: Essays and Studies* (1991), and *Black Families at the Crossroads* (1993). In addition, he is active in community groups as well as serving on the Board of Directors of the National Council of

Family Relations, the Sex Information and Education Council of the United States, and the Black World Foundation.

JOHN STOLTENBERG is a long-time radical feminist activist against sexual violence, and philosopher of gender, based in the USA. He is the author of *Refusing to Be a Man: Essays on Sex and Justice* (rev. edn, 2000), *The End of Manhood: Parables on Sex and Selfhood* (rev. edn, 2000), and *What Makes Pornography 'Sexy'?* (1994), as well as numerous articles and essays in several anthologies. For *Men Can Stop Rape*, he conceived and creatively directs the 'My Strength Is not for Hurting' media campaign. He has lived with the writer Andrea Dworkin since 1974.

ANDREW TOLSON is Principal Lecturer and Subject Leader in Media Studies at De Montfort University, England, where he teaches modules on Broadcast Talk and Political Communication and the Media, as well as contributing to core courses in Media and Cultural Studies. His main research interest is in broadcast talk (mediated verbal interaction) including work on interviewing, commentary, audience participation, and verbal presentation. He also has research interests in political communication and in gender studies (masculinity). His recent publications include *Mediations: Text and Discourse in Media Studies* (1996) and *Talk Shows: Discourse, Performance Spectacle* (2001).

PAUL WILLIS is a member of the professoriate at the University of Wolverhampton, England. During the 1980s he served as youth policy adviser to Wolverhampton Borough Council in the English Midlands. There he produced *The Youth Review* (1988), which formed the basis for youth policy in Wolverhampton and for the formation of the democratically elected Youth Council, both still functioning. He has held a variety of consulting posts including those at the English Arts Council (1992–3) and the Tate Gallery of the North (1995–6). His books include *Profane Culture* (1978), *Learning to Labour* (1981), *Common Culture: Symbolic Work at Play in the Everyday Cultures of the Young* (1990), *How Working Class Kids Get Work* (1998), and *The Ethnographic Imagination* (2001); and in 2000 he co-founded the Sage journal *Ethnography.*

CARL WITTMAN died of AIDS complications in 1986. He was a gay rights activist who attended Swarthmore College where he became involved in the civil rights movement. In 1963 he became one of the leaders of the radical left-wing Students for a Democratic Society (SDS). In 1974 he initiated the publication of the magazine *RFD*, and in 1981 he moved to Durham, North Carolina, USA, where he was one of the founders of the Durham Gay and Lesbian Health Project.

Acknowledgements

Once again, I want to begin by thanking my friend and wife, Sarah Gutwirth. Sarah's faith in the project and in me, coupled with her editing skills, improved this book immensely. My mother-in-law, Madelyn Gutwirth, provided invaluable historical references and critical insights.

Several people and groups at Murray State University contributed significant support. My Dean, Dr Sandra Jordan, allowed me the time away from my departmental chair's responsibilities to write when deadlines demanded it, and the 2003–2004 Presidential Fellowship from the Committee on International Studies and Research gave me both time and money to pursue the editing and writing full-time.

My research assistants worked long and hard to scan all of the articles into a computer, and to proofread the frequently inaccurate renditions. For their yeomen's work I wish to thank Kevin Link, who started the project, and Daniel B. Dietrich, B. J. Wilson, and Kristin Gillingham who stepped in toward the end to finish it. Their contributions were immeasurable.

All of the contributors to the collection deserve my thanks and two in particular warrant special acknowledgement: Michael Kimmel and Bob Lamm. Michael was more than generous with advice throughout the entire project, and Bob's immediate and warm friendship provided genuine enthusiasm for the project.

The series editors, Susan James and Teresa Brennan, deserve my deepest appreciation, and Ruth Anderson, my editor at Oxford University Press, merits my greatest thanks. Her advice, intelligence, and assistance only improved this collection of essays.

Within the extracts, editorial interpolations are given in italic type in square brackets. Where matter has been cut from the original to save space, this is indicated by an ellipsis in square brackets thus: [. . .].

Acknowledgements of essay sources include the following:

Adu-Poku, Samuel, 'Envisioning (Black) Male Feminism: A Cross-Cultural Perspective', *Journal of Gender Studies* 10(2) (July 2001), 157–67.

Archer, Louise, '"Muslim Brothers, Black Lads, Traditional Asians": British Muslim Young Men's Constructions of Race, Religion, and

Masculinity', *Feminism and Psychology* 11(1) (February 2001), 79–105.

Carrigan, Tim, Bob Connell and John Lee, 'Toward a New Sociology of Masculinity', *Theory and Society* 14(5) (September 1985), 551–604.

Clatterbaugh, Kenneth, 'What Is Problematic about Masculinities?' *Men and Masculinities* 1(1) (July 1998), 24–45.

Ferber, Abby L., 'Racial Warriors and Weekend Warriors: The Construction of Masculinity in Mythopoetic and White Supremacist Discourse', *Men and Masculinities* 3(1) (July 2000), 30–56.

Hoch, Paul, excerpts from *White Hero Black Beast: Racism, Sexism and the Mask of Masculinity* (London: Pluto Press, 1979).

Kibby, Marjorie and Brigid Costello, 'Displaying the Phallus: Masculinity and the Performance of Sexuality on the Internet', *Men and Masculinities* 1(4) (April 1999), 352–64.

Kimmel, Michael S., 'Masculinity as Homophobia: Fear, Shame and Silence in the Construction of Gender Identity', in Harry Brod and Michael Kaufman (eds.) *Theorizing Masculinities* (Thousand Oaks, CA: Sage, 1994), 119–41.

Kinsman, Gary, 'Men Loving Men: The Challenge of Gay Liberation', in Michael Kaufman (ed.) *Beyond Patriarchy: Essays by Men on Pleasure, Power and Change* (New York: Oxford University Press, 1987), 103–20.

Lamm, Bob, 'Learning from Women' (1975). Earlier versions of this essay appeared in *Morning Due: A Journal of Men Against Sexism* (Seattle), 2(2), 1976; and in Jon Snodgrass (ed.) *For Men Against Sexism: A Book of Readings* (Albion, CA: Times Change Press, 1977), 49–56.

Men's Free Press Collective, The 'Hopes and Dreams: Creating a Men's Politics', in Victor Seidler (ed.) *The Achilles Heel Reader: Men, Sexual Politics and Socialism* (London: Routledge, 1991), 17–32.

Pleck, Joseph H., 'Men's Power with Women, Other Men, and Society: A Men's Movement Analysis' (1977), in Elizabeth Pleck and Joseph H. Pleck (eds.) *The American Man* (Englewood Cliffs, NJ: Prentice-Hall, 1980), 417–33.

Reynaud, Emmanuel, excerpts from *Holy Virility: The Social Construction of Masculinity* (London: Pluto Press, 1983).

Sawyer, Jack, 'On Male Liberation' appeared originally in *Liberation* 15(6–8) (Aug.–Sept.–Oct. 1970), 32–3, and was then reissued in Joseph H. Pleck and Jack Sawyer (eds.) *Men and Masculinity* (Englewood, Cliffs, NJ: Prentice-Hall, 1974), 170–3.

Staples, Robert, excerpts from *Black Masculinity: The Black Male's Role in American Society* (Oakland, CA: The Black Scholars Press, 1982).

Stoltenberg, John, 'Toward Gender Justice' (1974) in Jon Snodgrass (ed.) *For Men Against Sexism: A Book of Readings* (Albion, CA: Times Change Press, 1977), 74–83.

Tolson, Andrew, excerpts from *The Limits of Masculinity: Male Identity and Women's Liberation* (New York: Harper & Row, 1977).

Willis, Paul, 'Shop Floor Culture, Masculinity and the Wage Form', in John Clarke, Charles Critcher, and Richard Johnson (eds.) *Working-Class Culture: Studies in History and Theory* (London: Hutchinson, 1979), 185–98.

Wittman, Carl, 'A Gay Manifesto', in Karla Jay and Allen Young (eds.) *Out of the Closets: Voices of Gay Liberation* (New York: Douglas, 1972), 330–42.

Introduction

Peter F. Murphy

Male authors of pro-woman and pro-feminist works span at least twenty-five hundred years and represent a vitally rich tradition. While much has been written about the overwhelming number of misogynist male authors, and complaints have been lodged against histories of feminism dominated by a few male writers, an intellectual history of male authors who have supported women's rights and causes is long overdue.[1]

This Introduction cannot, of course, provide such a wide-ranging history. Rather, my task here is to locate the essays in this collection within the broader context of that prolific heritage, even if this Introduction must, perforce, provide only an abridged overview of this critical tradition.

Men supporting women's rights begins at least as early as late fifth- and early fourth-century Greece when Aristophanes pens his play *Lysistrata* (411 BCE), and Plato writes the *Republic* (380 BCE). In both of these works, women assume roles of equality with men, and see themselves included in important political decisions and strategies. Lysistrata introduces the notion of women holding political power, and suggests that they would wield it more wisely and more judiciously than men have ever done, and in Book V of Plato's *Republic*, guardian women acquire the same education as men and are given equal opportunities to participate in the activities of the state. By introducing the idea that even some women could be educated, Plato initiates the subsequent and sustained debates over women being allowed an education, an issue that dominated feminist debate in the seventeenth century.[2]

In the first century CE, Plutarch (46–120 CE) compiles his *Mulierum virtutes* (trans. *The Virtues [or Bravery] of Women*), which provides one of the earliest catalogues of women's achievments,[3] a genre

1

adopted over the next several centuries by a variety of male authors as a means to praise famous women in history.

In the medieval period,[4] a proto-feminist consciousness arises, one that may be characterized even as an emerging feminist awareness. Christine de Pizan's (1365–85) ground-breaking feminist treatise, *The City of Ladies* (1405), initiates what Joan Kelly refers to as 'the four-century long debate known as the *querelle des femmes*' (5), the 'Woman question'.

In the midst of this newly articulated political awareness on the part of women, two important male writers join the debate: Giovanni Boccaccio (1313–75) and Geoffrey Chaucer (1343–1400), both of whom compiled catalogues of famous women as well. Boccaccio's unique (though not unproblematic) history of famous pagan women, *De claris mulieribus* (1355–9) (translated as *Concerning Famous Women* or just *Famous Women*), relies as much on a negative, insincere characterization of women as it does on what Virginia Brown describes as his 'praise of women's intellectual powers or their literary accomplishments or their moral virtues or their artistic creations' (xix).

Chaucer wrote his own version of the catalogue in *The Legend of Good Women* (1386), but his most famous contribution to a pro-woman position is, of course, 'The Wife of Bath's Tale'. Here Chaucer indicts the history of male misogynist writings by philosophers, theologians, and the medical profession while suggesting that women should have complete sovereignty over their lives (and their bodies).

The Renaissance witnesses the emergence of two significant philosophical traditions, both of which influence the deliberations about women's rights: Neoplatonism and humanism. The international spread of humanism across Europe in the fifteenth century saw the production of a truly international male response to the *querelle des femmes*, with the publication of works by men from Spain, France, and Italy. One of the first male authors from the Renaissance whose work can be described as pro-woman is the Spanish courtier Juan Rodriguez de la Camara. His treatise, *Triunfo de las donas* (trans. *The Triumph of Women*) appeared in 1438, and although a somewhat ambivalent work, according to Albert Rabil, Jr., Rodriquez 'argues not for the equality but for the superiority of women' (20). Within two years of Rodriquez's work, Martin Le Franc (1410–61) composed a long poem, *Le Champions des dames*, in which he defends 'women against their many detractors' and, not unlike Christine de Pisan, counters Jean de Meun's misogynist contributions to *The Romance of the Rose* (Rabil, Jr., 21).

Probably the earliest familiar male writer is Heinrich Cornelius Agrippa (1486–1535) whose *La Supériorité du sexe féminin* was published in 1509, the same year as Erasmus's *Praise of Folly*. Agrippa's treatise represents an important early proto-feminist work by a man who argues against the misogynist interpretations of women's capacities, roles, and rights. In a style that is both confrontational and ironic,[5] Agrippa counters the previous arguments against women posited by the medical profession, church fathers, legal system, philosophers, and statesmen.

Following closely on Agrippa's work, though written in the context of a debate with Juan Luis Vives, Desiderius Erasmus (1466–1536) pens *Encomium madrimonii* (1518), a treatise on equality in marriage, and five years later Vives publishes *On the Education of a Christian Woman*. Although, as Ian Maclean points out, both men insisted 'that ultimate authority resides with the husband' (40), the debate in which they participate reinforces the radical idea a woman may have any rights within the institution of marriage, an issue that recurs throughout much of the struggle over women's rights during the next century or more.

While there are several significant works written by men that follow closely upon Agrippa's treatise, the most important remains *The Defence of Good Women* by Sir Thomas Elyot (1490?–1546), published in 1545. Relying heavily on Agrippa's work, though written in the form of a Platonic dialogue, according to Diane Bornstein, Elyot's text introduces two new themes from the Renaissance: 'the education of women and the tendency for them to marry in their twenties' (x).

Approximately twenty-five years after Elyot publishes his treatise, Edmund Tilney (1536–1610) writes *The Flower of Friendship: A Brief and Pleasant Discourse of Duties in Marriage* (1568). Tilney's work both revives the discussion of friendship within marriage carried on by Erasmus and Vives fifty years earlier, and anticipates the writings of Poulain de la Barre (1647–1723).

While the seventeenth century is a period dominated by male misogynist texts, it is also a period that sees an eruption of pro-feminist work by men, especially French male writers. As early as 1632, Jacques Du Bosc publishes *L'Honneste Femme* (translated in 1639 as *The Compleat Woman*), but of even greater significance is François Poullain de la Barre's pro-feminist treatise, *The Woman as Good as the Man or, the Equality of Both Sexes*, published in 1673. This work earned for de la Barre the posthumous identification by Simone de Beauvoir as 'the leading feminist of the age' (cited in MacLean, 11).[6]

In *The Woman as Good as the Man*, de la Barre provides the first truly radical, uncompromising, and profoundly effective defence of women's equality at all levels of society. For de la Barre, custom and habit are understood to be the determining factors in the way we perceive gender difference, and only by exposing those prejudices can change occur to equalize relations between the sexes.

Across the Channel, the work of four Englishmen deserves acknowledgement: William Walsh's (1663–1708) 1691 *Dialogue concerning Women, Being a Defence of the Sex Written to Eugenia*, 'gave exposure to, as well as showed general concern with, the issue of women's place in society' (Smith, 193); John Dunton (1659–1733), the editor of the *Athenian Gazette* (1690–1) and the *Athenian Mercury* (1691–7), in which he wrote a column answering questions about women; the Poet Laureate Nahum Tate (1652–1715), whose *A Present for the Ladies* (1693), while no more original than Walsh's work, 'was perhaps the best proof of some establishment susceptibility to feminist concerns in the age' (Smith, 193); and Daniel Defoe (1660–1731), whose brief essay 'Project for an Academy of Women', published in 1697, argues for separate and equal education for women.

If the seventeenth century was a period dominated by French profeminist male authors, the eighteenth century can be seen as an epoch all but monopolized by them. With the exception of two Americans, Thomas Paine and Dr. Benjamin Rush, men's participation in the struggle for women's rights throughout the century is overshadowed by the French. Of the better-known French thinkers, Denis Diderot (1713–84), Charles Louis de Montesquieu (1689–1755), Paul Henri d'Holbach (1723–89), and Jean Intome Nicolas de Condorcet (1743–94) argued on behalf of the rights of women. Of particular note in the works of these men were such issues as birth control and constitutional rights, themes that emerge with significant power during the Enlightenment.[7]

In the first quarter of the century, Jacques-Phillipe de Varennes published an essay entitled *Les Hommes* (1727) that relies also on the egalitarian principle, insisting 'somewhat heretically on the equality of perfection in the souls of men and women, [and rejecting explicitly] the traditional confirmation of women's inferiority with regard to natural law and the will of God' (Williams, 339–40). At mid-century, between approximately 1750 and 1758, three other significant works by men were published. In 1750, Puissieux brings out what Williams refers to as 'the more overtly militant brochures' (Williams, 340). Three years later, and adhering to the tradition of clerics who had voiced support for women's rights, the Jesuit Philippe Joseph Caffiaux 'devoted four tomes to the *Défenses du beau sexe*, including, most usefully, a bibliography of contemporary feminist literature' (Willliams, 340).

Toward the end of the decade, in 1758, Pierre-Joseph Boudier de Villemert published his highly popular *L'Ami des femmes ou la philosophie du beau sexe*, in which he too 'advanced a theory of the complementary nature of the sexes' (Williams, 339).

While the works of Montesquieu, Holbach, and Condorcet remain at the forefront of men's involvement in the campaign for women's rights, their greater renown precludes the necessity to review their contribution at great length.

At the end of the century, in 1799, Louis Thérémin publishes *De la Condition des femmes dans la République*, a work that Madelyn Gutwirth describes as 'the most searching work by a man of this era about women' (381). Thérémin, according to Gutwirth, 'is for the most part egalitarian, observantly taking his own sex to task' (381),[8] and for this must be seen as a crucial advocate of women's rights. In many ways Thérémin initiates the depth and breadth of the struggle that erupts in the nineteenth century to make those theorized rights into a reality.

In Germany at about the same time, Theodor Gottlieb von Hippel (1741–96) writes one of the seminal texts in the history of profeminist men, *On Improving the Status of Women*, published in 1792.[9] Hippel argues closely and critically against the dominant ideology of the time, that women are irrational, unreasonable (or without reason altogether), and emotional. He attacks the whole notion that the subjection of woman was a punishment from God, and can be described best as a strong advocate of 'the restoration of natural and inalienable rights based on abstract principles of justice and equality' (Sellner, 34).

In America, Thomas Paine (1737–1809), Dr. Benjamin Rush (*c.* 1745–1813), and Charles Brockden Brown (1771–1810) voiced strong support for women's rights. Paine, according to Eleanor Flexner, 'was perhaps the first [American male] to describe, and condemn, the position of women' (14), while Rush identified the necessity for women to have access to a much better education as a key issue in the early years of the republic. Brockden Brown's fictional dialogue *Alcuin* (1789), provides what Michael Kimmel and Thomas Mosmiller describe as 'perhaps the most far-reaching vision of women's equality in the era before Seneca Falls . . . in which [is found] a sustained argument for the rights of women' (58).

Nineteenth-century Europe experienced the introduction of two radical political theories: liberalism and Marxism, both of which had a profound effect on the women's movement. In America, however, the one political struggle out of which the campaign for women's equality emerged was the abolitionist opposition to slavery, a movement inspired more by a radical Protestantism than by any political ideology. In Europe, the liberal utilitarianism of John Stuart Mill (1806–76) and the historical materialism of Friedrich Engels (1820–95) presented arguments in favour of women's rights, while in America abolitionist men such as Frederick Douglass (1817–95) and William Lloyd Garrison (1805–79) were early advocates of a woman's right to vote.

These four men represent only the most significant male voices, but by no means the only ones. Several other European, British, and American pro-feminist men joined the battle for women's rights. In Britain, for example, William Thompson (1775–1833) penned an appeal on behalf of women against men whom he saw as directly responsible for keeping women in a form of civil and domestic slavery, and Robert Owen (1771–1858), the utopian socialist, defended women's rights. In France, another utopian socialist, Charles Fourier (1772–1837), 'insisted in 1808 that "as a general thesis: *social progress and historic changes occur by virtue of the progress of women toward liberty . . . the extension of women's privilege is the general principle of all social progress*"' (Anderson and Zinsser, 371).[10] From Norway, Henrik Ibsen's (1828–1906) play *A Dolls' House* (1879) presents a plea for the emancipation of women, while in Germany, August Bebel develops the Marxist position, introduced by Engels, into an immensely popular book, *Women and Socialism* (1885).

In the United States, William E. Channing (1780–1842), an early and radical abolitionist, advocated women's suffrage, and Ralph Waldo Emerson (1803–82), the American transcendentalist, made the connection between abolitionism and women's rights in his speech before the Woman's Rights Convention in 1855. A lesser-known, but no less important, American pro-feminist male was Parker Pillsbury (1809–98). Working closely with Elizabeth Cady Stanton (1815–1902) and Susan B. Anthony (1820–1906), Pillsbury helped publish 'a radical woman's rights newspaper appropriately entitled, *The Revolution*' (Roberston, 33). Pillsbury also holds the rather crucial distinction of being one of the few, if not the only, male abolitionist who continued to defend a woman's right to vote in spite of the growing dominance of the issue of the struggle for the black freedmen's right to vote.

In Britain at this time, and throughout much of Europe, women were fighting for political and legal rights 'ranging from child custody to control of property, from equal public education to the vote' (Anderson and Zinsser, 338). In addition to political rights, feminists struggled for improved economic status and conditions. One male voice stands out loud and clear in these campaigns. John Stuart Mill's *The Subjection of Women* (1869) played a central role in articulating women's oppression and their need for political rights, but here, too, given the extent to which Mill's contribution to feminism is well documented further exegesis seems unnecessary. While Mill provides the liberal defence of women's equality before the law, Engels introduces the socialist position. Engels's *Origin of the Family, Private Property and the State* represents the earliest, though certainly not the only, socialist contribution to the discussion of women's rights. In addition to Engels, the work of several other socialist men deserve acknowledgement: August Bebel (1840–1913), Charles Fourier (1772–1837), V. I. Lenin (1870–1924), and even Karl Marx (1818–83) himself.

While in Europe feminists were debating the relevance of liberalism and socialism to the cause of women's rights, in the United States, the dominant feminist struggle centred on suffrage, but included several other issues and encompassed, at a minimum, the abolitionist movement.[11] American women's struggle for political rights predates the demand for the vote by at least twelve to fifteen years, however.

One of the earliest American male voices of the nineteenth century in defence of women's rights is John Neal. In a piece published in June 1843, Neal exclaims his sense of the injustice women experience just because they are women, and introduces the relationship between slavery and women's status in society.

The relationship between abolition and women's rights remained a complicated one from the earliest days of the struggle against slavery, especially (though not exclusively) as it pertained to men's advocacy on behalf of women. While some men, most notably John Greenleaf Whittier (1807–92) and Theodore Weld (1803–95), voiced concern that the demand for woman's rights would compromise the struggle against slavery, others remained staunch advocates of women's equality. When, for example, women were excluded from the World Anti-Slavery Convention in London (1840), William Lloyd Garrison (1805–79), 'registered his protest by refusing to be seated as a delegate in the main hall, and by remaining in the gallery with the women instead'; in addition, a less well-known black delegate, Charles Remond, refused to be seated (Flexner, fn. 1, 347).

In addition to Garrison, Douglass aligned himself (initially) with the women's rights movement. In 1848, the year of the first Woman's Rights Convention in the United States, Douglass was a strong supporter of Elizabeth Cady Stanton, and took the floor in support of women's rights. This is Douglass before the Civil War. After the Civil War, several male advocates of suffrage (in addition to Douglass, most notably there was Wendell Phillips) rejected women's demand for the vote taking the position that suffrage for the freed black man was a much greater priority.

The early years of the twentieth century have been referred to as the period of 'first-wave feminism', a time dominated by such political demands as equal pay and a focus on anti-war and anti-fascist activism. Maggie Humm observes that with women's victory in the struggle for suffrage accomplished, the women's movement 'narrowed to "welfare feminism" in the 1930s, 1940s and 1950s with campaigns for family allowances (Britain) and legal equalities (American League of Women)' (2).[12] First-wave feminists, that is, endorsed the franchise for women, equal opportunities in the professions, access to higher education, and the elimination of restrictions within marriage, and several men joined the struggle.

In the first quarter of the century, at least in the United States, several well-known radical men joined the struggle for a woman's right to an education and the vote.[13] In Britain, the radical peace advocate and eminent philosopher, Bertrand Russell (1872–1970), wrote a tract on *Marriage and Morals* (1929) in which he critiques the repressive nature of conventional sexual morality, while the American anthropologist and social critic Ashley Montagu (1905–99) argued against women's inferiority in his book *The Natural Superiority of Women* (1952). Written in the 1950s, Montagu's work takes on greater significance given the conservatism that dominated that period. As Rosemary Agonito points out in her prefatory remarks to an excerpt from Montagu's book, against several centuries of diatribes and at a historical juncture dominated by the desire to get women back into the home, Montagu maintained that 'the mass of scientific evidence contradicts this tradition at every turn and proves that women are physically and intellectually superior to men' (361).[14]

In this broad context, the work of the French philosopher Simone de Beauvoir (1908–86) provides a crucial transition to what becomes the radical feminism of the 1960s and 1970s. De Beauvoir's identification of woman as 'Other' helped articulate an understanding of the female as alienated from her humanity due to the objectification of woman intrinsic to patriarchy. De Beauvoir's crucial insight that women are complicit in their own oppression, both by accepting this reified characterization and by perpetuating it in their behaviour and in their writings, provided a radical catalyst for subsequent generations of feminists.

Out of de Beauvoir's insights, and as a result of the issues and struggles of the women involved in first-wave feminism, emerged what has come to be called 'second-wave feminism'. As Humm suggests, 'the belief that patriarchal power is invisible as well as visibly sexist, that it is a dynamic of our daily lives and not merely a dynamic of electoral politics, informs the demands of current feminism' (13), especially as manifest in what second-wave feminism terms sexual politics. At its core, second-wave feminism sees women's reproductive rights as the central factor in their oppression, and thus focuses on birth control, childcare, parenting, androgyny, pornography, and lesbianism.

In the context of the New Left, the civil rights movement, and opposition to the war in Vietnam, the women's liberation movement emerged. Feminists expanded their struggle to address personal and individual issues, out of which came the crucial realization that 'the personal is political'. When the personal, emotional, sexual experiences of women's lives gained significance as legitimate social concerns with political consequences, men were forced to examine their own socially constructed roles as men. While the second half of the twentieth century saw the continued involvement of several men as advocates of women's rights, one significant difference between the work of these men (as well as the work by men that precedes the twentieth century), is that in the 1970s men turn the feminist lens upon themselves as men.

The realization that who we are as individuals constitutes a political construction, coupled with the creation of consciousness-raising groups, inspired a crucial change in the relationship between feminism and men in the 1960s and 1970s. At that historical juncture, feminism became more a critical perspective through which men could scrutinize masculinity, and less a call for men to act solely as advocates for women's causes (though the latter remains an important component of the 'pro-feminist men's movement', with men organizing against pornography, violence against women, rape, and gay-bashing).[15]

No longer is masculinity the known, unexamined, natural phenomenon that it had been taken to be. Beginning in the 1960s, men start to apply feminism to an examination of their own lives as men in a patriarchal society. While many of these analyses evoked reactionary answers, and (at least in the United States) several remained liberal at best,[16] out of these initial engagements a more radical position emerged, especially from Britain.

Men were not alone in this feminist analysis of masculinities. Several women contributed invaluable insights into the discourse of 'men's studies', a 'feminist masculinity', and the 'male condition', and in this dialogue with women, the investigation of what it means to be a man in a patriarchal society became more subtle, more layered, more radical.

This brings us to the present work, a collection of essays and excerpts from books and periodicals that span approximately the last thirty-five years, from 1970 to 2001. These works include both out-of-print and recently published essays representing the investigation of masculinity from a feminist perspective during the second wave of feminism. They focus specifically on the ways in which a feminist analysis provides insights into the social, cultural, and political construction of manhood. The collection is not, that is, a general review of the investigation of masculinity from a broadly conceived academic perspective. The primary thematic structure relies on examples of works that have applied a feminist analysis to investigate masculinity in its myriad manifestations. Thus, the book represents the feminist interrogation of masculinity in which feminism becomes a politically radical methodology. In this way, it is less about masculinity studies or men's studies or about helping to define a new academic field, and more about what feminism has to tell us about being a man.

In many ways, this collection is autobiographical, especially Part I. The impetus behind the book in general, and the selections from the first fifteen years, comes out of a sense that these no-longer-available works are important and should be read and taught. For me, growing up in the 1960s and having my life changed significantly from reading Shulamith Firestone's *Dialectic of Sex* in 1971, and Simone de Beauvoir's *The Second Sex* shortly thereafter, the essays in Jon Snodgrass's anthology provided male companions to me and other men at a time when the dominant voices in feminism were those of women. Andrew Tolson's somewhat orthodox Marxist analysis also resonated with my own immersion in Marxism at the time, and the books by Paul Hoch and Emmanuel Reynaud were inspirational and affirming to me at a time when my understanding of what it meant to be a man was still very much in its formative stage.

The pieces in Part II come out of my desire to include the most current scholarship in the field of feminist masculinities while at the same time trying to identify essays that might be seen as in conversation with the work that was being done in the 1970s and 1980s. The essays in Part II, that is, build on this heritage and introduce new voices in the debate.

While I have organized the collection chronologically, I want to discuss the essays relationally. The chapters, that is, can be considered under four broad categories: general theoretical essays (Sawyer; Pleck; the excerpts from *For Men against Sexism* (Stoltenberg; Lamm); Tolson; the excerpt from *The Achilles Heel Reader*; Hoch; Reynaud; Carrigan *et. al.*; Kimmel; Clatterbaugh); works on gay liberation (Wittman; Kinsman); examinations of black masculinity (Staples; Archer; Adu-Poku); and essays that examine other specific topics such as working-class masculinity, the Internet, and white men's power groups (Willis; Kibby and Costello; Ferber). These categories are neither rigid nor exclusive. All of the essays, for example, contribute to the critical theoretical lens through which masculinities can be interrogated, and certainly the excerpts from Tolson, the editorial from *Achilles Heel*, and the pieces by Stoltenberg, Hoch, and Reynaud could be included with those on gay liberation. The general rubrics, however, allow for an overview that moves from the general to the specific, from the theoretical to the 'practical', from the past to the present.

The collection begins with Jack Sawyer's 1970 essay from *Liberation* magazine, 'On Male Liberation', a 'classic' essay from the earliest years of the pro-feminist American men's movement. Sawyer's essay helped to define the subsequent development of the discourse of men's studies and the men's movement in general.

The two essays from Jon Snodgrass' book, *For Men Against Sexism*, represent some of the more radical work being done by men in the first half of 1970s. John Stoltenberg's article was originally a speech given to the Gay Academic Union in New York City in the autumn of 1974 and Bob Lamm's was a speech to the Queens College Women's Studies Union on 28 October 1975. Stoltenberg locates male bonding and men's need to oppress women as much in the gay men's liberation camp as in the heterosexual male community. While the sexual politics of heterosexual men or 'how they affect the gender class of women', are quite clearly to keep women oppressed, gay men are not innocent of a similar alignment. This insight reinforces Stoltenberg's demand for men to repudiate masculinity, and his call for men to 'betray the presumptions of their own gender class—conspicuously, tactically, and uncompromisingly'.

Bob Lamm's exposé on why and what men can and must learn from women describes the lessons he garnered from the two occasions he taught a course on 'Men, Masculinity, and Sexism'. First and foremost, Lamm learned the importance for men to listen to women—not just pretending to listen to them, but really, truly paying attention to what they have to say and thinking about their comments and insights. Second, Lamm learned about rape. And third, Lamm learned that contrary to popular belief (at least the popular belief of most men), men are not indispensable in women's lives. These early lessons resonate throughout much of the subsequent work by pro-feminist male theorists and activists.

Joseph Pleck's article, published originally in 1977, represents the work of an early and ground-breaking participant in what was, at the time, an emerging anti-sexist men's movement. Pleck analyses male power relationships in the context of patriarchy, which he sees as a dual system in which men oppress women, and in which men oppress themselves and each other. His interest in the world of men's work, where most American men, far from being power-wielders, find themselves relatively powerless, inspired subsequent work, as did his analysis of the psychological reasons why American males seek power over women.

Andrew Tolson, the first British author in the book, represents one of the marked differences between the more liberal, and at times, psychologizing focus of the American contribution and the more political, overtly socialist analysis of British writers. In his book *The Limits of Masculinity: Male Identity and Women's Liberation*, published in 1977, Tolson relies on a personal account of one man's struggle against sexism, while at the same time interrogating that experience through a Marxist lens. Grounded in his participation in a men's group, a personal/political arrangement that emerged directly out of the consciousness-raising groups feminists created in the 1960s, Tolson examines what he sees as the 'inter-related conventions' of masculinity.

The 'editorial' from *Achilles Heel*, a pro-feminist men's journal begun in 1978 by Victor Seidler, Andy Metcalf, and several others, responds in many ways to Tolson's acknowledgment that the personal is indeed political. Written by men with extensive experience in both socialist struggles and in men's groups, the editorial collective sought to construct alignments with the women's movement and the gay movement 'in the struggle against sexual oppression'.

In his book *White Hero Black Beast: Racism, Sexism and Mask of Masculinity*, Paul Hoch argues that the relationship between sexism and racism is the key to the chauvinist mind and to the tendency for men to oppress women and members of cultures they presume to be inferior. Synthesizing the radical insights of Marxism with those of psychoanalysis, Hoch identifies an intimate relationship between 'the predominant Western conception of manhood and that of racial (and species) domination'.

Consistent with the work of Tolson and the *Achilles Heel* collective, Hoch wants to expand the concept of sex role to embrace both a historical and a social class dimension. In addition, and at the centre of Hoch's treatise, lies an understanding of masculinity as an interracial competition for women, a fear of impotence and homosexuality, and the victory of the white hero over the black beast. These important insights reveal the structure of masculinity as a mask, a cult, a social ritual.

Emmanuel Reynaud's *Holy Virility: The Social Construction of Masculinity*, was published originally in France in 1981. Reynaud addresses the fundamental question of what being a 'man' within patriarchy means and how power can be redistributed between the genders. For Reynaud, the close interrelationship between a man's mutilation of his body and his oppression of women culminates in an intense homophobia quite similar to Hoch's notion of the repressed 'woman within' that men deny and degrade.

In 'Toward a New Sociology of Masculinity', published originally in 1985, the authors provide a helpful review of what they refer to as the 'Book on Men' period of the men's movement. They stress the absence in most of these early works of any attempt to engage the relationship of heterosexual men's liberation with gay men's liberation. In contrast to these previous works, the authors provide an outline of an analysis of masculinity designed to introduce a new and radical sociology of masculinity that rests on their innovative (though contested) concept of a masculine hegemony.

Michael Kimmel's essay represents a preliminary working out of a theoretical chapter in a book that became *Manhood in America: A Cultural History*. His analysis of masculinity as homophobia applies Connell's concept of hegemony to the ideologically dominant 'image of masculinity of those men who hold power'.

For Kimmel, masculinity is not static, it is historical; and it is 'defined more by what one is not rather than who one is'. Men define themselves, that is, 'in opposition to a set of "others"—racial minorities, sexual minorities, and, above all, women'.

Echoing Hoch's thesis of the intimate connection between sexism and racism, Kimmel shows how the 'hyphenated' American male (e.g., Italian-, Jewish-, African-, Native-, Asian-, gay), are designated as both emasculated and as hypermasculine. This dichotomy echoes the mask of masculinity that Hoch describes; for Kimmel the myth of the sexually aggressive man who is also a 'violent rapacious beast', represents the demon 'against whom "civilized" men must take a decisive stand and thereby rescue civilization'.

Kenneth Clatterbaugh's interrogation of what exactly is meant by the term 'masculinities' poses difficult questions for many of the essays included in this collection, and even the title of this book itself. Responding in many ways to Connell's idea of the 'hegemony of masculinity', and Kimmel's 'image of masculinity' as 'young, white, northern, heterosexual, Protestant father of college education, fully employed, of good complexion, and recent record in sports', Clatterbaugh focuses on the confusion that results from the use of the highly ambiguous terms 'masculinity' and 'masculinities'. As a philosopher, Clatterbaugh brings to his analysis a logically consistent scrutiny of the contradictions apparent in much of the recent literature on masculinities. He finds, for example, a recurrent tangle of equivocation in the concept of masculinity, and points out that 'all inferences that use masculinity in one sense in the premise and another in the conclusion are fallacies of equivocation'.

As he explores the significance of several different conceptions of masculinity, Clatterbaugh demands a clarity in our writing and our thinking about men, manhood, masculinity, and masculinities. Without this kind of precision, according to Clatterbaugh, we will never be able to create the kind of critical and sustainable discipline that is required to generate a legitimate and progressive political change in the construction of men and manhood.

Another area in need of clarification is the relationship of the men's movement to gay liberation, a connection introduced in the early 1970s by Carl Wittman in his decisive call-to-arms, 'A Gay Manifesto'. Published originally in the 22 December 1969–7 January 1970 issue of the San Francisco *Free Press* as 'Refugees from Amerika: A Gay Manifesto', Wittman's piece inspired young gay men at the time to embrace their homosexuality and join the gay liberation movement.[17]

Wittman's use of feminism as a primary lens through which to understand the oppression of homosexuals, and the extent to which the women's liberation movement provides important insights into the oppression of gay men, initiates a history of pro-feminist gay male discourse that resonates for the next thirty-five years (and, hopefully, beyond). By locating the source of women's oppression and gay oppression in the same social and cultural systems, Wittman maintains that at the heart of both the gay liberation movement and the women's liberation movement lay the political critique of sexism and male supremacy.

Gary Kinsman's essay on gay liberation, published eighteen years after 'A Gay Manifesto', picks up on many of the points raised by Wittman in his initial call for gay rights. Kinsman, for example, comments on how 'socially organized power relations among and between men based on sexuality, race, class, or age have been neglected', while at the same time presenting a radical vision for the politics of gay liberation. He identifies heterosexism and heterosexual privilege as two defining components of our lives as men and as women, and he asserts that if gay liberation is to be successful it 'must challenge not only the institutionalization of heterosexuality as a social norm but also the institution of masculinity'. In addition, he examines the significance of the 'gay ghetto' as both a liberatory space and an oppressive one.

Unlike Wittman, though, Kinsman locates his critique as much in the contradictions inherent in the 'men's movement' as in the institution of heterosexuality. Kinsman, that is, stresses the necessity for straight men who are 'interested in seriously transforming their lives . . . [to] begin to ask what the experience of gay men can bring into view for them'.

Kinsman's observation that 'power relations among and between men based on . . . race . . . [has] been neglected', is countered to some extent by the work of Robert Staples. In his book *Black Masculinity: The Black Male's Role in American Society*, Staples provides one of the earliest positive, critical engagements with feminism by a black male scholar. In examining the relationship between male sexism and black feminism, Staples never loses sight of the fact that black men 'represent one of the most powerless groups in America'. While this in no way exonerates black men for their sexist behaviour, it introduces an important dimension to and distinction between the sexism of black men and that of white men. For Staples, then, the central issue that any radical analysis of gender has to consider is the relationship between sexism and racism.

Thus, for Staples, the necessity for feminists to work from a perspective that is more 'global rather than visceral and racially nationalistic' is paramount to understanding better 'why black men exhibit these symptoms of sexism'. This insight, coupled with his assertion that 'unwittingly, many do not realize the high price that they pay for their sexism', anticipates several of the issues both the women's movement and pro-feminist men will turn their attention to later in the decade in which Staples's book appears.

Published almost twenty years after Staples's book on black masculinity, the essays by Louise Archer and Samuel Adu-Poku share Kinsman's earlier view that issues around black masculinity remain largely undertheorized, despite the growth of academic interest in masculinity. For these authors, when black masculinity in general, and a black male feminism in particular, are examined, what frequently occurs is a conflation of race and gender where the subtleties of each identity are lost.

Countering the tendency of previous scholarship to position Muslim masculinity as 'problematic', Archer strives to elucidate the ways in which these young men 'construct their own identities' by enacting and subverting definitions of power. By showing 'the fluidity and range of identities constructed by the young men', Archer hopes to 'counter dominant (negative) public stereotypes/discourses of young Muslim men in Britain'.

Adu-Poku's essay builds on issues raised by Staples almost twenty years earlier, particularly the question of black men's presence in feminism, and the tensions that sometimes result from that interaction. Exploring the intersections of race and gender and the construction of different 'masculinities', Adu-Poku argues that speaking autobiographically and from a cross-cultural perspective provides a means of addressing the challenges of misappropriation in envisioning (black) male feminism.

Echoing Staples's call for men and women to work together if we are to embrace the feminist insight that we either 'make our own history or remain victims of it', Adu-Poku endorses the forging of a productive alliance between women and pro-feminist (black) males through a collective action that can advance the struggle against sexism, racism, and systematic power imbalances in society.

Another area of masculinities that has been all but ignored is the experiences of blue-collar workers. Paul Willis's ethnography of working-class masculinity counters that tendency, while complementing the efforts of the *Achilles Heel* collective in their desire to understand better the personal/subjective dimension of male workers. Relying on first-hand observations by men who participate in what Willis calls 'male cultures of work', he examines the construction of 'a crude pride' and 'the mythology of *masculine* reputation—to be strong and to be known for it', that permeates shop-floor culture. The various ways in which men try to gain control over the work process exhibited in the particular use of language and humour informs much of Willis's work. In addition, how and why men resist the repetitive, dehumanizing, task-oriented work in the factory may provide insights into relevant strategies, policies, and demands that might be usefully employed by the trade union movement.

In their article on the performance of masculinity on the Internet, Marjorie Kibby and Brigid Costello break new ground in the feminist analysis of masculinities. They examine adult-video conferencing sites powered specifically by CU-SeeMe software, where men present sexualized bodies as objects of the gaze through an interactive medium that enables, while it limits, the possibility for men of the passive and the feminine. Within this unstable subject/object framework, according to the authors, the men construct a masculine subjectivity and a male sexual identity that is both an affirmational community performance and an individual erotic display. In this broad context, the essay examines, specifically, the impact of men's use of this technology on the objectification of women in pornography, the active and passive modes of sexual gratification, and the role of penile display in the construction of male sexuality. At the same time, though, 'as a type of interactive pornography, CU-SeeMe provides the opportunity for both men and women to construct positions that are simultaneously the subject and the object of the consuming gaze'.

Abby L. Ferber's essay represents an important and powerful indictment of the close relationship between two seemingly very different groups: the purportedly 'progressive' mythopoetic men's movement, and the fascistic hate groups of the white supremacist movement. Based on a close examination of the writings by leaders of both groups, Ferber traces the ways they construct gender in essentialist terms, depict contemporary American men as demasculinized, blame contemporary social problems on this demasculinization, and seek to help men rediscover their lost 'true masculinity' and to reassert their rightful authority. According to Ferber, both movements encourage white men to see themselves as victims and argue that (white) men are the truly oppressed minority in today's world. Both movements, that is, are primarily concerned with revalidating a reactionary male identity.

The collection of essays in this book represents, at the very least, an antidote to the conservative and reactionary attempts to both leave masculinity unexamined and to reassert its central, privileged,

17

empowered place in patriarchal, capitalist society. In their comprehensive history of women's roles from prehistory to the present, Bonnie Anderson and Judith Zinsser maintain that 'through "small deeds" and daring conceptions, through political actions and personal confrontations, feminists have gradually brought about the rejection of traditions which have restricted women's and men's lives for centuries' (431). In some small way, I hope that this anthology contributes to that struggle.

Notes

1. Timothy F. Sellner's observation notwithstanding, that 'the role played by men in this movement, both as theoretician and active participant, is now for the most part known to us' (19), the full history of males writing in support of women's rights has not been written. Indeed, I would argue, this tradition is not well known at all.

   My initial research has identified a minimum of 250 male advocates of women's rights. For the American contribution alone, see Michael S. Kimmel and Thomas E. Mosmiller (eds.), *Against the Tide: Pro-Feminist Men in the United States 1776–1990: A Documentary History*, which includes works by about 120 American men. In addition, the website 'Sunshine for Women' has an essay on-line as well as a bibliography that lists another thirty or so names. These sources do not include all of the male historians who have written comprehensive and sympathetic histories of women's movements or biographies of individual feminist women, and works by feminists translated by men. Since 1960, the field of feminist masculinities has burgeoned, probably doubling the number of male writers who pre-date the last forty years.

2. Such a notable feminist as Juliet Mitchell characterized Plato as 'a proto-feminist' philosopher, one whose work anticipates that of feminist women in the seventeenth century (97).

3. For a history of catalogues of women from antiquity to the Renaissance, see Glenda McLeod.

4. For the brief historical contexts for each period I discuss in this Introduction, especially those on the medieval period, the Renaissance, and the seventeenth and eighteenth centuries, I have relied extensively on Sandra M. Gilbert and Susan Gubar.

5. As Rabil points out, though, contemporary critics have described Agrippa's style in terms of flippancy, paradox, and jest. For the former see Ian Maclean's *Renaissance Notion of Woman*, and for the latter two see Linda Woodbridge's *Women and the English Renaissance* (Rabil, 30–1; fnn. 61 and 62).

6. Michael A. Seidel attests also to de la Barre's significance to feminism when he points out that Pierre Bayle, in his *Dictionnaire*, cited Poullain 'as among the three most important feminist writers of the age' (499).

7. In his informative survey of feminism during the French enlightenment, David Williams provides a helpful overview of several male authors who wrote in support of women's rights.

8. Thérémin is not without contradiction, however. According to Gutwirth, 'he nevertheless falls in with the dominant constructs of gender as he finds women both better than men and yet more hideous when depraved than members of his own sex' (381).
9. The other work, *On Marriage*, has a somewhat complicated history. The first two editions (those of 1774 and 1775) followed a fairly traditional idea about male supremacy in marriage, 'and in fact contain some censorious comments on the manners and behavior of the female sex'. The third edition of 1792, on the other hand, 'actively advocates the emancipation of women, and equality in marriage' (Sellner, 27).
10. Quoted from the original, *Théorie des quartre movements et des destinées generales*, cited in Susan Groag Bell and Karen M. Offen (eds.), *Women, the Family, and Freedom: The Debate in Documents*, vol. 1, *1750–1880*, p. 41. Italics are in the Anderson and Zinsser text.
11. For information on the nineteenth-century American women's movement, and in particular the suffrage movement, I have relied extensively on DuBois and Flexner.
12. For an overview of twentieth-century feminism I have relied on Humm, Evans, and Anderson and Zinsser.
13. Again, I have relied on the invaluable documentary history edited by Michael S. Kimmel and Thomas E. Mossmiller.
14. Montagu's position is not unproblematic, however. There is a tendency in his work to emphasize a woman's dedication to child-rearing and the nurturing of children that borders closely on an essentialism. His defence of women's rights, however, especially at the time he was writing, should not be ignored.
15. For example, men organized in opposition to rape and joined Take Back the Night rallies and marches, they developed radical therapy programs for men guilty of wife-battering, they actively opposed pornography, and they supported gay rights.
16. For more on this see my review essay in *Feminist Studies*.
17. Allen Young states unequivocally that 'reading it moved [him] to take a big step and attend his first gay liberation meeting' (Jay and Young, xlv).

Works cited

Agonito, Rosemary (ed.), *History of Ideas on Woman: A Source Book* (New York: G. P. Putnam's Sons, 1978).

Anderson, Bonnie S. and Judith P. Zinsser, *A History of Their Own: Women in Europe from Prehistory to the Present*, vol. 2 (New York: Harper & Row, 1988).

Bell, Susan Groag and Karen M. Offen (eds.), *Women, the Family, and Freedom: The Debate in Documents*, vol. 1, *1750–1880* (Stanford, CA: Stanford University Press, 1983).

Bornstein, Diane, 'Introduction', in *The Feminist Controversy of the Renaissance* (Delmar, NY: Scholar's Facsimiles & Reprints, 1980), v–xiii.

DuBois, Ellen Carol, *Feminism and Suffrage: The Emergence of An Independent Women's Movement in America, 1848–1869* (Ithaca, NY: Cornell University Press, 1978).

Evans, Richard J., *The Feminists: Women's Emancipation Movements in Europe, America, and Australasia, 1840–1920* (New York: Harper & Row, 1977).

Flexner, Eleanor, *Century of Struggle: The Woman's Rights Movement in the United States* (Cambridge, MA: Harvard University Press, 1968).

Gilbert, Sandra M. and Susan Gubar, 'Literature of the Middle Ages and the Renaissance', and 'Literature of the Seventeenth and Eighteenth Centuries', in *The Norton Anthology of Literature by Women* (New York: W. W. Norton, 1985), 1–15 and 39–58, respectively.

Gutwirth, Madelyn, *The Twilight of the Goddesses: Women and Representation in the French Revolutionary Era* (New Brunswick, NJ: Rutgers University Press, 1992).

Humm, Maggie (ed.), *Modern Feminisms: Political, Literary, Cultural* (New York: Columbia University Press, 1992).

Jay, Karla and Allen Young (eds.), *Out of the Closets: Voices of Gay Liberation* (New York: New York University Press, 1992).

Kelly, Joan, 'Early Feminist Theory and the *Querelle des Femmes*, 1400–1789', *Signs* 8 (Autumn 1982), 4–28.

Kimmel, Michael S. and Thomas E. Mosmiller (eds.), *Against the Tide: Pro-Feminist Men in the United States, 1776–1990: A Documentary History* (Boston, MA: Beacon Press, 1992).

MacLean, Gerald M., 'Introduction' to de la Barre, François Poullain, in *The Woman as Good as the Man or, the Equality of the Sexes* [1673] (Detroit, MI: Wayne State University Press, 1988), 11–52.

Maclean, Ian, *The Renaissance Notion of Woman: A Study of the Fortunes of Scholasticism and Medical Science in European Intellectual Life* (Cambridge: Cambridge University Press, 1980).

McLeod, Glenda, *Virtue and Venom: Catalogs of Women from Antiquity to the Renaissance* (Ann Arbor, MI: University of Michigan Press, 1991).

Mitchell, Juliet, *Women: The Longest Revolution* (New York: Random House, 1984).

Murphy, Peter F., 'Toward a Feminist Masculinity: A Review Essay', *Feminist Studies* (Summer 1989), 351–61.

Rabil, Jr., Albert, 'Agrippa and the Feminist Tradition', in Agrippa, Henricus Cornelius, *Declamation on the Nobility and Preeminence of the Female Sex* [1529] (Chicago, IL: University of Chicago Press, 1996), ix–xxviii.

Robertson, Stacey M., ' "Aunt Nancy Men": Parker Pillsbury, Masculinity, and Women's Rights Activism in the Nineteenth-Century United States', *American Studies* 37 no. 2 (1996), 33–60.

Seidel, Michael A., 'Poulain de la Barre's *The Woman as Good as the Man*', *Journal of the History of Ideas* 35 no. 3 (July–September 1974), 499–508.

Sellner, Timothy F., 'Introduction' to von Hippel, Theodore Gottlieb, in *On Improving the Status of Women* [1792] (Detroit, MI: Wayne State University Press, 1979), 19–49.

Smith, Hilda L., *Reason's Disciples: Seventeenth-Century English Feminists* (Urbana, IL: University of Illinois Press, 1982).

Sunshine for Women website, *http://www.pinn.net/~sunshine/main.html*

Williams, David, 'The Politics of Feminism in the French Enlightenment', in Peter Hughes and David Williams (eds.), *The Varied Pattern: Studies in the Eighteenth Century* (Toronto: A. M. Hakkert, 1971), 333–51.

Woodbridge, Linda, *Women and the English Renaissance: Literature and the Nature of Womankind* (Urbana, IL: University of Illinois Press, 1986).

Part I. 1970–1985

On Male Liberation

Jack Sawyer*

Male liberation calls for men to free themselves of the sex-role stereotypes that limit their ability to be human. Sex-role stereotypes say that men should be dominant; achieving and enacting a dominant role in relations with others is often taken as an indicator of success. 'Success,' for a man, often involves influence over the lives of other persons. But success in achieving positions of dominance and influence is necessarily not open to every man, since dominance is relative and hence scarce by definition. Most men in fact fail to achieve the positions of dominance that sex-role stereotypes ideally call for. Stereotypes tend to identify such men as greater or lesser failures, and in extreme cases, men who fail to be dominant are the object of jokes, scorn, and sympathy from wives, peers, and society generally.

One avenue of dominance is potentially open to any man, however—dominance over a woman. As society generally teaches men they should dominate, it teaches women they should be submissive, and so men have the opportunity to dominate women. More and more, however, women are reacting against the ill effects of being dominated. But the battle of women to be free need not be a battle against men as oppressors. The choice about whether men are the enemy is up to men themselves.

Male liberation seeks to aid in destroying the sex-role stereotypes that regard 'being a man' and 'being a woman' as statuses that must be achieved through proper behavior. People need not take on restrictive roles to establish their sexual identity.

A major male sex-role restriction occurs through the acceptance of a stereotypic view of men's sexual relation to women. Whether or not men consciously admire the Playboy image, they are still influenced by the implicit sex-role demands to be thoroughly competent and self-assured—in short, to be 'manly.' But since self-assurance is part of the

---

* Reprinted with permission of Simon & Schuster Adult Publishing Group, from *Men and Masculinity*, edited by Joseph H. Pleck and Jack Sawyer. Copyright © 1974 Prentice-Hall, Inc.

stereotype, men who believe they fall short don't admit it, and each can think he is the only one. Stereotypes limit men's perception of women as well as of themselves. Men learn to be highly aware of a woman's body, face, clothes—and this interferes with their ability to relate to her as a whole person. Advertising and consumer orientations are among the societal forces that both reflect and encourage these sex stereotypes. Women spend to make themselves more 'feminine,' and men are exhorted to buy cigarettes, clothes, and cars to show their manliness.

The popular image of a successful man combines dominance both over women, in social relations, and over other men, in the occupational world. But being a master has its burdens. It is not really possible for two persons to have a free relationship when one holds the balance of power over the other. The more powerful person can never be sure of full candor from the other, though he may receive the kind of respect that comes from dependence. Moreover, people who have been dependent are coming to recognize more clearly the potentialities of freedom, and it is becoming harder for those who have enjoyed dominance to maintain this position. Persons bent on maintaining dominance are inhibited from developing themselves. Part of the price most men pay for being dominant in one situation is subscribing to a system in which they themselves are subordinated in another situation. The alternative is a system in which men share, among themselves and with women, rather than strive for a dominant role.

In addition to the dehumanization of being (or trying to be) a master, there is another severe, if less noticed, restriction from conventional male sex roles in the area of affect, play, and expressivity. Essentially, men are forbidden to play and show emotion. This restriction is often not even recognized as a limitation, because emotional behavior is so far outside the usual range of male activity.

Men are breadwinners, and are defined first and foremost by their performance in this area. This is a serious business and results in an end product—bringing home the bacon. The process area of life—activities that are enjoyed for the immediate satisfaction they bring—are not part of the central definition of men's role. Yet the failure of men to be aware of this potential part of their lives leads them to be alienated from themselves and from others. Because men are not permitted to play freely, or show affect, they are prevented from really coming in touch with their own emotions.

If men cannot play freely, neither can they freely cry, be gentle, nor show weakness—because these are 'feminine,' not 'masculine.' But a fuller concept of humanity recognizes that all men and women are potentially both strong and weak, both active and passive, and that these and other human characteristics are not the province of one sex.

The acceptance of sex-role stereotypes not only limits the individual but also has bad effects on society generally. The apparent attractions of a male sex role are strong, and many males are necessarily caught up with this image. Education from early years calls upon boys to be brave, not to cry, and to fight for what is theirs. The day when these were virtues, if it ever existed, is long past. The main effect now is to help sustain a system in which private 'virtues' become public vices. Competitiveness helps promote exploitation of people all over the world, as men strive to achieve 'success.' If success requires competitive achievement, then an unlimited drive to acquire money, possessions, power, and prestige is only seeking to be successful.

The affairs of the world have always been run nearly exclusively by men, at all levels. It is not accidental that the ways that elements of society have related to each other has been disastrously competitive, to the point of oppressing large segments of the world's population. Most societies operate on authoritarian bases—in government, industry, education, religion, the family, and other institutions. It has been generally assumed that these are the only bases on which to operate, because those who have run the world have been reared to know no other. But women, being deprived of power, have also been more free of the role of dominator and oppressor; women have been denied the opportunity to become as competitive and ruthless as men.

In the increasing recognition of the right of women to participate equally in the affairs of the world, then, there is both a danger and a promise. The danger is that women might end up simply with an equal share of the action in the competitive, dehumanizing, exploitative system that men have created. The promise is that women and men might work together to create a system that provides equality to all and dominates no one. The women's liberation movement has stressed that women are looking for a better model for human behavior than has so far been created. Women are trying to become human, and men can do the same. Neither men nor women need be limited by sex-role stereotypes that define 'appropriate' behavior. The present models for men and women fail to furnish adequate opportunities for human development. That one-half of the human race should be dominant and the other half submissive is incompatible with a notion of freedom. Freedom requires that there not be dominance and submission, but that all individuals be free to determine their own lives as equals.

27

2 A Gay Manifesto

Carl Wittman*

San Francisco is a refugee camp for homosexuals. We have fled here from every part of the nation, and like refugees elsewhere, we came not because it is so great here, but because it was so bad there. By the tens of thousands, we fled small towns where to be ourselves would endanger our jobs and any hope of a decent life; we have fled from blackmailing cops, from families who disowned or 'tolerated' us; we have been drummed out of the armed services, thrown out of schools, fired from jobs, beaten by punks and policemen.

And we have formed a ghetto, out of self-protection. It is a ghetto rather than a free territory because it is still theirs. Straight cops patrol us, straight legislators govern us, straight employers keep us in line, straight money exploits us. We have pretended everything is OK, because we haven't been able to see how to change it—we've been afraid.

In the past year there has been an awakening of gay liberation ideas and energy. How it began we don't know; maybe we were inspired by black people and their freedom movement; we learned how to stop pretending from the hip revolution. Amerika in all its ugliness has surfaced with the war and our national leaders. And we are revulsed by the quality of our ghetto life. Where once there was frustration, alienation, and cynicism, there are new characteristics among us. We are full of love for each other and are showing it; we are full of anger at what has been done to us. And as we recall all the self-censorship and repression for so many years, a reservoir of tears pours out of our eyes. And we are euphoric, high, with the initial flourish of a movement.

We want to make ourselves clear: our first job is to free ourselves; that means clearing our heads of the garbage that's been poured into them. This article is an attempt at raising a number of issues, and presenting

* Reprinted with permission of Karla Jay.

some ideas to replace the old ones. It is primarily for ouselves, a starting point of discussion. If straight people of good will find it useful in understanding what liberation is about, so much the better.

It should also be clear that these are the views of one person, and are determined not only by my homosexuality, but my being white, male, middle-class. It is my individual consciousness. Our group consciousness will evolve as we get ourselves together—we are only at the beginning.

I. ON ORIENTATION

1. *What homosexuality is*: Nature leaves undefined the object of sexual desire. The gender of that object is imposed socially. Humans originally made homosexuality taboo because they needed every bit of energy to produce and raise children: survival of species was a priority. With overpopulation and technological change, that taboo continued only to exploit us and enslave us.

As kids we refused to capitulate to demands that we ignore our feelings toward each other. Somewhere we found the strength to resist being indoctrinated, and we should count that among our assets. We have to realize that our loving each other is a good thing, not an unfortunate thing, and that we have a lot to teach straights about sex, love, strength, and resistance.

Homosexuality is *not* a lot of things. It is not a makeshift in the absence of the opposite sex; it is not hatred or rejection of the opposite sex; it is not genetic; it is not the result of broken homes except inasmuch as we could see the sham of American marriage.

Homosexuality is the capacity to love someone of the same sex

2. *Bisexuality*: Bisexuality is good; it is the capacity to love people of either sex. The reason so few of us are bisexual is because society made such a big stink about homosexuality that we got forced into seeing ourselves as either straight or non-straight. Also, many gays got turned off to the ways men are supposed to act with women and vice-versa, which is pretty fucked-up. Gays will begin to turn on to women when 1) it's something that we do because we want to, and not because we should, and 2) when women's liberation changes the nature of heterosexual relationships.

We continue to call ourselves homosexual, not bisexual, even if we do make it with the opposite sex also, because saying 'Oh, I'm Bi' is a copout for a gay. We get told it's OK to sleep with guys as long as we sleep with women too, and that's still putting homosexuality down. We'll be gay until everyone has forgotten that it's an issue. Then we'll begin to be complete.

3. *Heterosexuality*: Exclusive heterosexuality is fucked up. It reflects a fear of people of the same sex, it's anti-homosexual, and it is fraught with frustration. Heterosexual sex is fucked up, too; ask women's liberation about what straight guys are like in bed. Sex is aggression for the male chauvinist; sex is obligation for the traditional woman. And among the young, the modern, the hip, it's only a subtle version of the same. For us to become heterosexual in the sense that our straight brothers and sisters are is not a cure, it is a disease.

II. ON WOMEN

1. *Lesbianism*: It's been a male-dominated society for too long, and that has warped both men and women. So gay women are going to see things differently from gay men; they are going to feel put down as women, too. Their liberation is tied up with both gay liberation and women's liberation.

This paper speaks from the gay male viewpoint. And although some of the ideas in it may be equally relevant to gay women, it would be arrogant to presume this to be a manifesto for lesbians.

We look forward to the emergence of a lesbian liberation voice. The existence of a lesbian caucus within the New York Gay Liberation Front has been very helpful in challenging male chauvinism among gay guys, and anti-gay feelings among women's liberation.

2. *Male chauvinism*: All men are infected with male chauvinism—we were brought up that way. It means we assume that women play subordinate roles and are less human than ourselves. (At an early gay liberation meeting one guy said, 'Why don't we invite women's liberation—they can bring sandwiches and coffee.') It is no wonder that so few gay women have become active in our groups.

Male chauvinism, however, is not central to us. We can junk it much more easily than straight men can. For we understand oppression. We have largely opted out of a system which oppresses women daily—our egos are not built on putting women down and having them build us up. Also, living in a mostly male world we have become used to playing different roles, doing our own shit-work. And finally, we have a common enemy: the big male chauvinists are also the big anti-gays.

But we need to purge male chauvinism, both in behavior and in thought among us. Chick equals nigger equals queer. Think it over.

3. *Women's liberation*: They are assuming their equality and dignity and in doing so are challenging the same things we are: the roles, the exploitation of minorities by capitalism, the arrogant smugness of straight white male middle-class Amerika. They are our sisters in struggle.

Problems and differences will become clearer when we begin to work together. One major problem is our own male chauvinism. Another is uptightness and hostility to homosexuality that many women have—that is the straight in them. A third problem is differing views on sex: sex for them has meant oppression, while for us it has been a symbol of our freedom. We must come to know and understand each other's style, jargon and humor.

III. ON ROLES

1. *Mimicry of straight society*: We are children of straight society. We still think straight: that is part of our oppression. One of the worst of straight concepts is inequality. Straight (also white, English, male, capitalist) thinking views things in terms of order and comparison. A is before B, B is after A; one is below two is below three; there is no room for equality. This idea gets extended to male/female, on top/on bottom, spouse/not spouse, heterosexual/homosexual, boss/worker, white/black, and rich/poor. Our social institutions cause and reflect this verbal hierarchy. This is Amerika.

We've lived in these institutions all our lives. Naturally we mimic the roles. For too long we mimicked these roles to protect ourselves—a survival mechanism. Now we are becoming free enough to shed the roles which we've picked up from the institutions which have imprisoned us.

'Stop mimicking straights, stop censoring ourselves'

2. *Marriage*: Marriage is a prime example of a straight institution fraught with role playing. Traditional marriage is a rotten, oppressive

institution. Those of us who have been in heterosexual marriages too often have blamed our gayness on the breakup of the marriage. No. They broke up because marriage is a contract which smothers both people, denies needs, and places impossible demands on both people. And we had the strength, again, to refuse to capitulate to the roles which were demanded of us.

Gay people must stop gauging their self-respect by how well they mimic straight marriages. Gay marriages will have the same problems as straight ones except in burlesque. For the usual legitimacy and pressures which keep straight marriages together are absent, e.g. kids, what parents think, what neighbors say.

To accept that happiness comes through finding a groovy spouse and settling down, showing the world that 'we're just the same as you' is avoiding the real issues, and is an expression of self-hatred.

3. *Alternatives to marriage*: People want to get married for lots of good reasons, although marriage won't often meet those needs or desires. We're all looking for security, a flow of love, and a feeling of belonging and being needed.

These needs can be met through a number of social relationships and living situations. Things we want to get away from are: 1) exclusiveness, propertied attitudes toward each other, a mutual pact against the rest of the world; 2) promises about the future, which we have no right to make and which prevent us from, or make us feel guilty about, growing; 3) inflexible roles, roles which do not reflect us at the moment but are inherited through mimicry and inability to define equalitarian relationships.

We have to define for ourselves a new pluralistic, role free social structure for ourselves. It must contain both the freedom and physical space for people to live alone, live together for a while, live together for a long time, either as couples or in larger numbers; and the ability to flow easily from one of these states to another as our needs change.

Liberation for gay people is defining for ourselves how and with whom we live, instead of measuring our relationship in comparison to straight ones, with straight values.

4. *Gay 'stereotypes'*: The straights' image of the gay world is defined largely by those of us who have violated straight roles. There is a tendency among 'homophile' groups to deplore gays who play visible roles—the queens and the nellies. As liberated gays, we must take a clear stand. 1) Gays who stand out have become our first martyrs. They came out and withstood disapproval before the rest of us did.

2) If they have suffered from being open, it is straight society whom we must indict, not the queen.

5. *Closet queens*: This phrase is becoming analagous [*sic*] to 'Uncle Tom.' To pretend to be straight sexually, or to pretend to be straight socially, is probably the most harmful pattern of behavior in the ghetto. The married guy who makes it on the side secretly; the guy who will go to bed once but who won't develop any gay relationships; the pretender at work or school who changes the gender of the friend he's talking about; the guy who'll suck cock in the bushes but who won't go to bed.

If we are liberated we are open with our sexuality. Closet queenery must end. *Come out.*

But in saying come out, we have to have our heads clear about a few things: 1) Closet queens are our brothers, and must be defended against attacks by straight people; 2) The fear of coming out is not paranoia; the stakes are high: loss of family ties, loss of job, loss of straight friends—these are all reminders that the oppression is not just in our heads. It's real. Each of us must make the steps toward openness at our own speed and on our own impulses. Being open is the foundation of freedom: it has to be built solidly; 3) 'Closet queen' is a broad term covering a multitude of forms of defense, self-hatred, lack of strength, and habit. We are all closet queens in some ways, and all of us had to come out—very few of us were 'flagrant' at the age of seven! We must afford our brothers and sisters the same patience we afforded ourselves. And while their closet queenery is part of our oppression, it's more a part of theirs. They alone can decide when and how.

....

IV. ON OPPRESSION

....

It is important to catalog and understand the different facets of our oppression. There is no future in arguing about degrees of oppression. A lot of 'movement' types come on with a line of shit about homosexuals not being oppressed as much as blacks or Vietnamese or workers or women. We don't happen to fit into their ideas of class or caste. Bull! When people feel oppressed, they act on that feeling. We feel oppressed. Talk about the priority of black liberation or ending imperialism over and above gay liberation is just anti-gay propaganda.

1. *Physical attacks*: We are attacked, beaten, castrated and left dead time and time again. There are half a dozen known unsolved slayings

in San Francisco parks in the last few years. 'Punks,' often of minority groups who look around for someone under them socially, feel encouraged to beat up on 'queens,' and cops look the other way. That used to be called lynching.

Cops in most cities have harassed our meeting places: bars and baths and parks. They set up entrapment squads. A Berkeley brother was slain by a cop in April when he tried to split after finding out that the trick who was making advances to him was a cop. Cities set up 'pervert' registration, which if nothing else scares our brothers deeper into the closet.

One of the most vicious slurs on us is the blame for prison 'gang rapes.' These rapes are invariably done by people who consider themselves straight. The victims of these rapes are us and straights who can't defend themselves. The press campaign to link prison rapes with homosexuality is an attempt to make straights fear and despise us, so they can oppress us more. It's typical of the fucked-up straight mind to think that homosexual sex involves tying a guy down and fucking him. That's aggression, not sex. If that's what sex is for a lot of straight people, that's a problem they have to solve, not us.

2. *Psychological warfare*: Right from the beginning we have been subjected to a barrage of straight propaganda. Since our parents don't know any homosexuals, we grow up thinking that we're alone and different and perverted. Our school friends identify 'queer' with any non-conformist or bad behavior. Our elementary school teachers tell us not to talk to strangers or accept rides. Television, billboards and magazines put forth a false idealization of male/female relationships, and make us wish we were different, wish we were 'in.' In family living class we're taught how we're supposed to turn out. And all along the best we hear about homosexuality is that it's an unfortunate problem.

3. *Self-oppression:* As gay liberation grows, we will find our uptight brothers and sisters, particularly those who are making a buck off our ghetto, coming on strong to defend the status quo. This is self-oppression: 'don't rock the boat'; 'things in SF are OK'; 'gay people just aren't together'; 'I'm not oppressed.' These lines are right out of the mouths of the straight establishment. A large part of our oppression would end if we would stop putting ourselves and our pride down.

4. *Institutional oppression*: Discrimination against gays is blatant, if we open our eyes. Homosexual relationships are illegal, and even if these laws are not regularly enforced, they encourage and enforce closet queenery. The bulk of the social work/psychiatric field looks

upon homosexuality as a problem, and treats us as sick. Employers let it be known that our skills are acceptable only as long as our sexuality is hidden. Big business and government are particularly notorious offenders.

The discrimination in the draft and armed services is a pillar of the general attitude toward gays. If we are willing to label ourselves publicly not only as homosexual but as sick, then we qualify for deferment; and if we're not 'discreet' (dishonest) we get drummed out of the service. Hell, no, we won't go, of course not, but we can't let the army fuck over us this way, either.

V. ON SEX

1. *What sex is*: It is both creative expression and communication: good when it is either, and better when it is both. Sex can also be aggression, and usually is when those involved do not see each other as equals; and it can also be perfunctory, when we are distracted or preoccupied. These uses spoil what is good about it.

I like to think of good sex in terms of playing the violin: with both people on one level seeing the other body as an object capable of creating beauty when they play it well; and on a second level the players communicating through their mutual production and appreciation of beauty. As in good music, you get totally into it—and coming back out of that state of consciousness is like finishing a work of art or coming back from an episode of an acid or mescaline trip. And to press the analogy further: the variety of music is infinite and varied, depending on the capabilities of the players, both as subjects and as objects. Solos, duets, quartets (symphonies, even, if you happen to dig Romantic music!) are possible. The variations in gender, response, and bodies are like different instruments. And perhaps what we have called sexual 'orientation' probably just means that we have not yet learned to turn on to the total range of musical expression.

2. *Objectification*: In this scheme, people are sexual objects, but they are also subjects, and are human beings who appreciate themselves as object and subject. This use of human bodies as objects is legitimate (not harmful) only when it is reciprocal. If one person is always object and the other subject, it stifles the human being in both of them. Objectification must also be open and frank. By silence we often assume or let the other person assume that sex means commitments: if

it does, OK; but if not, say it. (Of course, it's not all that simple: our capabilities for manipulation are unfathomed—all we can do is try.)

Gay liberation people must understand that women have been treated exclusively and dishonestly as sexual objects. A major part of their liberation is to play down sexual objectification and to develop other aspects of themselves that have been smothered so long. We respect this. We also understand that a few liberated women will be appalled or disgusted at the open and prominent place that we put sex in our lives; and while this is a natural response from their experience, they must learn what it means for us.

For us, sexual objectification is a focus of our quest for freedom. It is precisely that which we are not supposed to share with each other. Learning how to be open and good with each other sexually is part of our liberation. And one obvious distinction: objectification of sex for us is something we choose to do among ourselves, while for women it is imposed by their oppressors.

3. *On positions and roles*: Much of our sexuality has been perverted through mimicry of straights, and warped from self-hatred. These sexual perversions are basically anti-gay:

'I like to make it with straight guys'
'I'm not gay, but I like to be "done"'
'I like to fuck, but don't want to be fucked'
'I don't like to be touched above the neck'

This is role playing at its worst; we must transcend these roles. We strive for democratic, mutual, reciprocal sex. This does not mean that we are all mirror images of each other in bed, but that we break away from roles that enslave us. We already do better in bed than straights do, and we can be better to each other than we have been.

4. *Chickens and studs*: Face it, nice bodies and young bodies are attributes, they're groovy. They are inspiration for art, for spiritual elevation, for good sex. The problem arises only in the inability to relate to people of the same age, or people who don't fit the plastic stereotypes of a good body. At that point, objectification eclipses people, and expresses self-hatred: 'I hate gay people, and I don't like myself, but if a stud (or chicken) wants to make it with me, I can pretend I'm someone other than me.'

A note on exploitation of children: kids can take care of themselves, and are sexual beings way earlier than we'd like to admit. Those of us who began cruising in early adolescence know this, and we were doing the cruising, not being debauched by dirty old men. Scandals such as the one in Boise, Idaho—blaming a 'ring' of homosexuals for perverting their youth—are the fabrications of press and police and politicians. And as for child molesting, the overwhelming amount is done by straight guys to little girls: it is not particularly a gay problem, and is caused by the frustrations resulting from anti-sex puritanism.

5. *Perversion*: We've been called perverts enough to be suspect of any usage of the word. Still many of us shrink from the idea of certain kinds of sex: with animals, sado/masochism, dirty sex (involving piss or shit). Right off, even before we take the time to learn any more, there are some things to get straight:

1. we shouldn't be apologetic to straights about gays whose sex lives we don't understand or share;

2. it's not particularly a gay issue, except that gay people probably are less hung up about sexual experimentation;

3. let's get perspective: even if we were to get into the game of deciding what's good for someone else, the harm done in these 'perversions' is undoubtedly less dangerous or unhealthy than is tobacco or alcohol;

4. while they can be reflections of neurotic or self-hating patterns, they may also be enactments of spiritual or important phenomena: *e.g.* sex with animals may be the beginning of interspecies communication: some dolphin-human breakthroughs have been made on the sexual level: *e.g.* one guy who says he digs shit during sex occasionally says it's not the taste or texture, but a symbol that he's so far into sex that those things no longer bug him; *e.g.* sado/masochism, when consensual, can be described as a highly artistic endeavor, a ballet the constraints of which are the thresholds of pain and pleasure.

VI. ON OUR GHETTO

We are refugees from Amerika. So we came to the ghetto—and as other ghettos, it has its negative and positive aspects. Refugee camps are better than what preceeded them, or people never would have come. But they are still enslaving, if only that we are limited to being ourselves there and only there.

Ghettos breed self-hatred. We stagnate here, accepting the status quo. The status quo is rotten. We are all warped by our oppression, and in the isolation of the ghetto we blame ourselves rather than our oppressors.

Ghettos breed exploitation. Landlords find they can charge exorbitant rents and get away with it, because of the limited area which is safe to live in openly. Mafia control of bars and baths in NYC is only one example of outside money controlling our institutions for their profit. In San Francisco the Tavern Guild favors maintaining the ghetto, for it is through ghetto culture that they make a buck. We crowd their bars not because of their merit but because of the absence of any other social institution. The Guild has refused to let us collect defense funds or pass out gay liberation literature in their bars—need we ask why?

Police or con men who shake down the straight gay in return for not revealing him; the bookstores and movie makers who keep raising prices because they are the only outlet for pornography; heads of 'modeling' agencies and other pimps who exploit both the hustlers and the johns—these are the parasites who flourish in the ghetto.

San Francisco—ghetto or free territory. Our ghetto certainly is more beautiful and larger and more diverse than most ghettos, and is certainly freer than the rest of Amerika. That's why we're here. But it isn't ours. Capitalists make money off us, cops patrol us, government tolerates us as long as we shut up, and daily we work for and pay taxes to those who oppress us.

To be a free territory, we must govern ourselves, set up our own institutions, defend ourselves, and use our own energies to improve our lives. The emergence of gay liberation communes and our own paper is a good start. The talk about a gay liberation coffee shop/dance hall should be acted upon. Rural retreats, political action offices, food cooperatives, a free school, unalienating bars and after hours places— they must be developed if we are to have even the shadow of a free territory.

VII. ON COALITION

Right now the bulk of our work has to be among ourselves—self educating, fending off attacks, and building free territory. Thus basically we have to have a gay/straight vision of the world until the oppression of gays is ended.

But not every straight is our enemy. Many of us have mixed identities, and have ties with other liberation movements: women, blacks, other minority groups; we may also have taken on an identity which is vital to us: ecology, dope, ideology. And face it: we can't change Amerika alone.

Who do we look to for coalition?

1. *Women's liberation*: Summarizing earlier statements, 1) they are our closest ally; we must try hard to get together with them; 2) a lesbian caucus is probably the best way to attack gay guys' male chauvinism, and challenge the straightness of women's liberation; 3) as males we must be sensitive to their developing identities as women, and respect that; if *we know what our* freedom is about, *they* certainly know what's best for *them*.

2. *Black liberation*: This is tenuous right now because of the uptightness and supermasculinity of many black men (which is understandable). Despite that, we must support their movement, particularly when they are under attack from the establishment; we must show them that we mean business; and we must figure out who our common enemies are: police, city hall, capitalism.

3. *Chicanos*: Basically the same problem as with blacks: trying to overcome mutual animosity and fear, and finding ways to support them. The extra problem of super up-tightness and machismo among Latin cultures, and the traditional pattern of Mexicans beating up 'queers,' can be overcome: we're both oppressed, and by the same people at the top.

4. *White radicals and ideologues*: We're not, as a group, Marxist or Communist. We haven't figured out what kind of political/economic system is good for us as gays. Neither capitalist or socialist countries have treated us as anything other than *non grata* so far.

But we know we are radical, in that we know the system that we're under now is a direct source of oppression, and it's not a question of getting our share of the pie. The pie is rotten.

We can look forward to coalition and mutual support with radical groups if they are able to transcend their anti-gay and male chauvinist patterns. We support radical and militant demands when they arise, *e.g.* Moratorium, People's Park; but only as a group; we can't compromise or soft-peddle our gay identity.

Problems: because radicals are doing somebody else's thing, they tend to avoid issues which affect them directly, and see us as jeopardizing their 'work' with other groups (workers, blacks). Some years ago a dignitary of SDS on a community organization project announced at an initial staff meeting that there would be no homosexuality (or dope) on the project. And recently in New York, a movement group which had a coffee-house get-together after a political rally told the gays to leave when they started dancing together. (It's interesting to note that in this case, the only two groups which supported us were women's liberation and the Crazies.)

Perhaps most fruitful would be to broach with radicals their stifled homosexuality and the issues which arise from challenging sexual roles.

5. *Hip and street people*: A major dynamic of rising gay liberation sentiment is the hip revolution within the gay community. Emphasis on love, dropping out, being honest, expressing yourself through hair and clothes, and smoking dope are all attributes of this. The gays who are the least vulnerable to attack by the establishment have been the freest to express themselves on gay liberation.

We can make a direct appeal to young people, who are not so up tight about homosexuality. One kid, after having his first sex with a male, said, 'I don't know what all the fuss is about; making it with a girl just isn't that different.'

The hip/street culture has led people into a lot of freeing activities: encounter/sensitivity, the quest for reality, freeing territory for the people, ecological consciousness, communes. These are real points of agreement and probably will make it easier for them to get their heads straight about homosexuality, too.

6. *Homophile groups*: 1) Reformist or pokey as they sometimes are, they are our brothers. They'll grow as we have grown and grow. Do not attack them in straight or mixed company. 2) Ignore their attack on us. 3) Cooperate where cooperation is possible without essential compromise of our identity.

CONCLUSION: AN OUTLINE OF IMPERATIVES FOR GAY LIBERATION

1. Free ourselves: come out everywhere; initiate self defense and political activity; initiate counter community institutions.

2. Turn other gay people on: talk all the time; understand, forgive, accept.

3. Free the homosexual in everyone: we'll be getting a good bit of shit from threatened latents: be gentle, and keep talking and acting free.

4. We've been playing an act for a long time, so we're consummate actors. Now we can begin *to be*, and it'll be a good show!

3 Toward Gender Justice

John Stoltenberg*

THE HETEROSEXUAL MODEL

I want to begin by describing certain features of the patriarchal society in which we live, certain features I will call *the heterosexual model*.

In this model, men are the arbiters of human identity. From the time they are boys, men are programmed by the culture to refer exclusively to other men for validation of their self-worth. A man's comfort and well-being are contingent upon the labor and nurture of women, but his identity—his 'knowledge of who he is'—can only be conferred and confirmed by other men.

Under patriarchy, women are not reliable witnesses to a man's worthiness, except in bed—and there as a class, not as individuals. Thus if a particular women does not esteem a man's genital functioning, he has the right to turn to another woman who does, without loss of phallic worth.

Women are programed to refer to men for their identities as well, but the program is seriously stacked against them. In the heterosexual model, a woman's 'knowledge of who she is' cannot be separate from her relation to an individual man. The only validation of her self-worth to which she is entitled is whatever identity she gets from being supportive to, and the property of, a man.

Under patriarchy, men are the arbiters of identity for both males and females, because the cultural norm of human identity is, by definition, male identity—*masculinity*. And, under patriarchy, the cultural norm of male identity consists in power, prestige, privilege, and prerogative *as over and against* the gender class women. That's what masculinity is. It isn't something else.

---

* Adapted from a speech to a conference of the Gay Academic Union in New York City, 29 November 1974. Reprinted with permission of John Stoltenberg.

Attempts have been made to defend this norm of masculinity as having a natural basis in male sexual biology. It has been said, for example, that male power in the culture is a natural expression of a biological tendency in human males toward sexual aggression. But I believe that what is true is the reverse. I believe that masculinist genital functioning is an expression of male power in the culture. I believe that male sexual aggression is entirely learned behavior, taught by a culture that men entirely control. I believe, as I will explain, that there is a *social process* by which patriarchy confers power, prestige, privilege, and prerogative on people who are born with cocks, and that there is a *sexual program* promoted by the patriarchy (not Mother Nature) for how those cocks are supposed to function.

The social process whereby people born with cocks attain and maintain masculinity takes place in *male bonding*. Male bonding is institutionalized learned behavior whereby men recognize and reinforce one another's bona fide membership in the male gender class and whereby men remind one another that they were not born women. Male bonding is political and pervasive. It occurs whenever two males meet. It is not restricted to larger all-male groupings. It is the form and content of each and every encounter between two males. Boys learn very early that they had better be able to bond. What they learn in order to bond is an elaborate behavioral code of gestures, speech, habits and attitudes, which effectively exclude women from the society of men. Male bonding is how men learn from each other that they are entitled under patriarchy to power in the culture. Male bonding is how men get that power, and male bonding is how it is kept. Therefore, men enforce a taboo against unbonding—a taboo which is fundamental to patriarchal society.

The subsequent program for male sexual behavior, patriarchy's prototype for male genital functioning, is, of course, *the fuck*: the hard cock, the vaginal penetration, the tense pelvic thrusting, and the three-second ejaculation. Authentic sensations get unlearned. What gets learned, and therefore what gets felt, is genital operability.

But men learn that they have power, prestige, and privilege in the culture long before they ever learn how to fuck. And then, I believe, what each man learns on his own is that in order for his genitalia to work this way reliably—that is, to operate in intimacy in the way that is commensurate with what the man knows of his power and prerogative in the culture—he must claim over his partner a corresponding advantage. There must be for him, in the erotic encounter itself, some real or imagined disparity of power and prerogative between himself and whomever he fucks. Otherwise he can't do it. He can't accomplish the program—the sexual program for expressing his cultural attributes— his attributes obtained by belonging to a gender class that has defined itself as supreme.

Men who fuck differ only in the form of that power disparity which they require between themselves and whomever they would choose to fuck. Some men rape, some men marry, and so forth.

At the slightest hint that there could be between the partners a common dignity, a reciprocity of moral concern, or any justice what-soever—in that moment prototypical male genital functioning fails; in that moment, it goes numb.

Men who are programed to make genital assertions of their mascu-linity in erotic encounters with women know privately but well what an unreliable gauge of masculinity their genital programing really is. Far more reliable are their non-erotic bonds with other men—where power, prestige, privilege, and pride are actually gauged and exchanged; and where the culture's norm of masculinity originates and prospers.

THE SEXUAL POLITICS OF GAY MALE LIBERATION

Patriarchy, then, is grounded in a cultural norm of masculinity perpetuated by the sexual politics of heterosexual men. Their sexual politics—how they affect the gender class of women—are quite clearly to keep women oppressed. And their masculinity—their power in the culture as over and against the women they oppress—derives from their bonds with other men, not from their erotic activities. What-ever men do in the name of their so-called heterosexual orientation is an assertion of that power, not how they obtain it. The only way a genital male could be disenfranchised from that power, which under patriarchy is his birthright, is by failing to bond well enough with other men—not through any failure on his part to exercise some heterosexual standard of genital functioning.

Why, then, has *homosexuality* in men been grounds for denying some males full access to the birthright of their gender class? In the Judeo-Christian tradition of patriarchy, there is a stricture on male-male assfucking. Historically, the prohibition has been against that act, not against men who behave together with affection which reinforces their affinity. An early version of this injunction is written in Leviticus 18 : 22 (*The Jerusalem Bible*): 'You must not lie with a man as with a woman. This is a hateful thing.' Significantly, this dictum occurs in the context of a catalogue of conjugal rules which ritualize and institutionalize two main themes: the property rights of men over the bodies of women, and an absolute loathing of female carnality. Similarly, wherever else there have been laws on the books against male-male assfucking, those laws are tucked in among legislation, enacted and enforced by men, to execute their purpose of maintaining the powerlessness of women. The law against sodomy between males is not a discrete phenomenon. It is a thread in a legal fabric which systematically oppresses women. And in this context, patriarchy's aversion to sodomy between males is a necessary expression of the taboo against unbonding, since to assfuck a genital male is to 'lie with' him 'as with a woman,' and since under patriarchy, the way to lie with a woman is to make a genital assertion of male power in the culture, over and against her body in particular. A man violates the taboo against unbonding if he asserts that power disparity genitally *between himself and another male.* I believe therefore that the cultural bias against male homosexuality stems directly from these two facts: That patriarchy requires that men maintain their brotherhood through a common contempt of women; and that the male homosexual act is construed as a threat to the male-male bond, since there is the implication that one of the partners gets fucked as a woman.

Recently, in the history of patriarchy's relentless advance, there has occurred a movement for homosexual liberation. The main argument for this movement, as adduced by genital males, seems to me to be this: That laws against the male homosexual act should be repealed; that males who engage in it should be free to do so without fear of censure or economic liability; that the male homosexual act, if performed between two consenting genital males, ought to be construed by both partners *and by the culture* as a valid form of male bonding; and that all the rights, privileges, and powers belonging to genital males by virtue of their membership in the male gender class should belong as well to men who assfuck other men and to those men whose asses get fucked. In other words, the claim that male homosexuals are fully entitled to male civil liberties is based on the presumption that the male assfuck is a special expression of a co-equal power bond between men; that the male assfuck is not an assertion of a power disparity between the partners, since neither partner, prior to the act, is as powerless in the culture as a woman, and since each partner, after the act, can take his place in the culture with his masculinity intact.

To summarize, the relationship between cultural 'homophobia' and male 'gay pride' is as follows: Under patriarchy, both the basic prohibition against male homosexuality and the basic argument for male homosexual liberation are expressions of the same sexual politics—namely, the accreditation of men by contracting to vilify women.

These same sexual politics are evinced in certain factions of the male homosexual movement that have solicited the support of lesbian women. The Gay Academic Union and the National Gay Task Force are two such organizations, initiated by men and enlisting lesbian participation on the pretext of a novel ruse: that the predicaments of gay men and lesbian women in society are analogous; that gay men and lesbian women are disenfranchised from power in the culture for the same reason and in the same way. This is conspicuously not the case. The struggle of lesbian women is against the whole of institutionalized misogyny. The dilemma of gay men is merely to prove that they are not women. The struggle of lesbian women is against all forms of male power over their lives: the male capitalists who decide when women are needed in the labor force and when they are not; the male courts who decree lesbian women are not fit to rear their children; the male professors who would teach them reverence for great men; male rapists, male pornographers, male psychiatrists, male gynecologists; and all of the laws, customs, and habits which define women as the carnal chattel of men, which deny women absolute control of their own bodies and lives. The dilemma of gay men, on the other hand, is how to get cultural confirmation of their masculinity, how to come out and be one of the guys, how to have full access to all the powers, prestige, prerogatives, and privileges that other men have over and against women.

It is no accident that certain gay males are promoting the notion of a lesbian and gay male coalition. Such a notion is absolutely in the best interests of gay males, especially gay males in the professions, who have an economic stake in male supremacy and who persist in believing that the only real issue is homosexual liberation. Gay males consistently make no commitment to the struggle of women against male power over their lives. Such a commitment would contradict the objective of male homosexual liberation, which is to secure for gay males their birthright to power in the culture over women. Gay males may pay lip service to the issues of discrimination against women, or gay males may make token adjustments within their organizations to grant women 'more equality,' but these are solicitous and reactionary stratagems, intended to let women know they are 'welcome,' or intended to keep women from leaving, because the fact is that these men have a specific political need to belong to an organization in which women are present. An all-male organization merely serves the personal needs of gay men within it to acknowledge and esteem one another's masculinity. Patriarchy permits gay men to obtain masculinist power in this way, by bonding with other men, organizationally, professionally, and personally. But patriarchy prohibits gay men from exercising that power over other genital males. Masculinist power is for use against women. Men are not supposed to treat men the way they treat women. That is at the center of the gay male appeal to straight men for acceptance, and that is at the center of the gay male need to have women in their organizations. Because if the truth were revealed that the impulse of most gay men *is* to treat selected genital males as if they were women, then the entire credibility of the movement for male homosexual liberation would be impugned. Under patriarchy, the acceptable exercise of masculinist power requires the presence of the gender class that by definition is powerless —women. Thus, an organization in which women are present provides exactly the form gay men require in order to assert their masculinist power, and by asserting it, to demonstrate to the culture that they are not in fact faggots, that they are not in fact women, but that clearly they are the men and they have power over and against the women.

REPUDIATING MASCULINITY

In order to end the system of patriarchy, the very sexual identities of males will have to change. A male is no less complicitous in that system by being homosexual than by being heterosexual, or vice versa. A male is complicitous in that system by reason of his investment in *masculinity*, a norm of human identity that is consistent with and derived from his privileged irresponsibility to women. Under patriarchy, a commitment to the maintenance of masculinity *in any form* is a commitment to sexist injustice.

The form of men's consciousness raising is but a new manifestation of male bonding. Whether composed of straight men or gay men, these groups are defined in every detail by the culturally programed urgency of men to bond, in order to confer and confirm their masculinity, which is their power in the culture over and against women. The patriarchal taboo against unbonding circumscribes the 'consciousness' of all-male groups in a very political way, since effective male bonding requires that a genital male not respect the life of a woman so much as he respects his own and that of his fellows. In the context of men's consciousness-raising groups, therefore, it is formally taboo to comprehend and take seriously women's emerging political analysis, except in a self-interested or reactionary way. To take seriously in one's 'consciousness' the fact of sexist injustice would have to mean for men, as it does already for many women, *a total repudiation of masculinity*. All 'men's liberation,' which in form and content is masculinity-*confirming*, is thus an escalation and permutation of masculinist aggression. And its victims, ultimately, are women, whether or not they are taken to bed.

Masculinity is not, as some have said, a vague set of 'qualities' (such as 'ambition,' 'strength,' 'courage,' or 'competitiveness'). Nor is masculinity an abstract 'role,' which can be 'played' or 'not played,' or which any two people can take turns at. What is denoted by the word masculinity derives from the objective reality, the fact of our lives under patriarchy, that all members of the gender class of males are entitled to obtain their sense of self by postulating the selflessness of the gender class of women, their sense of worth by asserting female worthlessness, and their power in the culture by maintaining the powerlessness of women. Masculinity is that sense of self, that sense of worth, that right to power that accrues to every male on account of the global subjugation of women. Thus masculinity, that cultural construct of human identity, is antithetical to gender justice. And, in short: masculinity is immoral.

What is required is moral commitment to struggle for gender justice. That means that genital males must find a form for taking responsibility to the lives of women.

There are many apparently 'sensitive,' 'compassionate,' and 'sympathetic' men around—men who present themselves as being in favor of social justice but who act in their lives as if they would sooner die than relinquish the prerogative that they got by being born male. It has been men like these who, through the political left, have given us their masculinist visions for social change and who, through the arts, psychiatry, and philosophy, have described for us the great male themes of modern life: alienation, estrangement, anguish, and dread—all out of that typical man's sensibility which holds his male self to be at the center of the knowable universe. Many such men have said that their male hurt and their male pain would be tempered if only men would learn to cry more, or feel more, or trust other men more, or have better sex. Many such men would prefer to make self-interested emotional accommodations rather than moral commitment. I think the grim reality at this point in human history is that not very many genital males have access to a moral conscience which has not been gender-linked along with the rest of their sexual and social programing.

But I believe that there are a few genital males who are persuaded that what is wrong with the culture is its sexist injustice and that what is wrong with their lives is their complicity in it. And I imagine that those few genital males might commit themselves to these two projects:

One. I imagine that a genital male could begin, with a kind of humility, to read and study feminist texts, a study which if full-time could take a year or longer. I think it is not possible to take seriously women's lives if one is ignorant of what it means to bear the real brunt of masculinist aggression. And there is much information which women have written which absolutely gives the lie to all those catch-phrases of men's liberation, such as 'Men are victims, too.' It is time genital males understood that the road to gender justice is not paved with self-indulgent aphorisms about 'the essential personhood of men and women.' The fact is that men's lives and women's lives are different because, from birth, men and women live under absolutely different cultural conditions. And genital males cannot presume to understand the conditions under which women are forced to live their lives by imaginary analogies to the privileged woes of men. [. . .]

Two. At the same time, I imagine that a genital male could begin to live as a conscientious objector to all the scenarios of male bonding—to refuse to cooperate with all the patterns of expectation that, whenever two males meet, they are to respect one another's masculinity and condone one another's power over women. And I imagine that during this period of conscientious bond-breaking a genital male might discover to what an appalling extent male friendships and alliances are based on the private understanding that 'we are men, not women, and therefore we are preferred.' I don't underestimate the shock that will come with this recognition: when a genital male discovers that seemingly innocuous exchanges between himself and another genital male can turn in an instant into a tacit pact against women, and that all he was ever programed to long for in relationships with men connects at its very center to a process that keeps women oppressed. What is necessary is for genital males to betray the presumptions of their own gender class—conspicuously, tactically, and uncompromisingly. The alternative, as I see it, is to betray every woman who has ever said she is not free.

48

I think these are two ways a genital male could begin to live differently: by studying feminist texts and by resisting masculinist bonds.
And I think that these two ways are merely a beginning.

Eventually, perhaps, some genital males could share in the struggle
against sexist injustice as honest allies of feminist women. But at this
point in time, this much is clear: None of us can presume that we have
yet done enough in our own lives to eradicate our allegiance to masculinity. Unless we change, we cannot claim to be comrades with women.
Until we change, the oppressor is us.

[*A 'Suggested Beginning Reading List for Genital Males' was dropped
from the end of the essay.*]

4 Learning from Women

Bob Lamm*

I want to begin by stating how much of a pleasure and an honor it is for me to be speaking here at the invitation of the Women's Student Union. Sometimes, when speakers make these declarations, it's a matter of form and courtesy. But it's a very special honor for me to be here, because I owe a very great debt to the women I've known at Queens College—many of whom have worked with the Women's Student Union, with Queens Women Against Rape, and on the Women's Festivals. Officially, in many cases, I was the teacher for these women. But, in reality, they were *my* teachers, and I come here today to try to express a little of what I've learned from them. Despite all my male and professorial resistance, they taught me quite a bit about their lives and oppression as women, about feminism, and about my own sexism.

When I began teaching courses on 'Men, Masculinity, and Sexism' at Queens in the summer of 1974, I was very much impressed with my own qualifications for teaching. I thought I knew a whole lot about men's lives and about masculinity. And (although I was too clever to say this out loud) I thought I knew a whole lot about women's lives.

The truth is that I knew virtually nothing about the reality of women's lives. The truth is that I came here with no serious background in feminist literature. The truth is that I had no understanding of how absurd and sexist it was for a man to teach a course on men and masculinity without a good grasp of feminist literature. The truth is that I had no idea of how much I didn't know.

And the most *glaring* truth is this one: there's nothing unusual about what I've just said. It's quite common. This afternoon, once two o'clock comes and classes begin again, a whole lot of male professors

* This essay is drawn from a speech delivered to the Queens College Women's Student Union on 28 October 1975. Reproduced with permission of Bob Lamm. Copyright © Bob Lamm 2003.

are going to start telling women students about their lives as women. Some male professors may call this teaching process biology or psychology or history or literature or anthropology. I would call such teaching what many feminists have called it—*male supremacy*. This so-called educating goes on in every part of this college, and in every part of the world except for the few small bits of turf that feminists have managed to fight for and win.

Thus, there was nothing unique about my coming in to teach a course about sexism without much understanding of women's lives or feminism. But something unique did happen to me after I started teaching here. Unlike many male professors at Queens College, I didn't get away with my act so easily. Lo and behold—there were a lot of strong, eloquent, angry women in my classes who weren't awed by my professorial power or by my radical politics. And these women changed my life.

My course on 'Men, Masculinity, and Sexism' in the summer of 1974 was intense and explosive. It lasted six weeks, three nights a week—but it felt like a year. The students in the class—both women and men—were among the most honest people I've ever met in my life. As a result, the class included moments of risky and revealing self-disclosure. It was also the scene of bitter and shattering political fights. Women in the course, speaking out of their anger as victims of a sexist society, wouldn't sit by quietly and be insulted and patronized. Men in the course, speaking out of their fear and hostility to feminist challenge, wouldn't sit by quietly and listen to attacks on their patriarchal privileges.

One thing I learned was the importance of men *listening* to women, *listening* to women's feelings and anger, and fighting off our potential for serious backlash. I had repeated conferences with a few male students, and found myself telling them again and again to listen to the women in the class. Not to freak out, not to strike back in anger, but instead to work hard at hearing what the women were saying.

The more I found myself in that role, the more I realized how little I myself listened to what the women were saying. The more I observed the backlash and misogyny of male students, the more I had to notice my own backlash and misogyny. And, as I moved increasingly away from a mediating teacher role to active personal involvement in the class, some of my own woman-hating anger began to emerge right in front of me. By the end of the course, it was clear, as one male student wrote, that I was just another fucked-up, insecure man—only with more power than the male students.

During the first week of the class a woman student asked if she could present a special session on rape—a subject that my course syllabus did not cover. I reacted favorably and we set up the class for the next week. Now, at first, my consent may seem like an enlightened act, but it wasn't. It was an act of uninformed male liberalism. I had no idea of the political and educational importance of having a class on rape in a course on men and masculinity. I was simply being amiable or cooptive, depending on your point of view.

My misunderstanding of rape went something like this. I perceived rape to be a serious crime, somewhere between mugging and murder. I was vaguely aware that men were the perpetrators—and women the victims—of this particular crime. But I never considered the political implications of these obvious facts, or the connection between rape and our norms of masculinity.

My mental image of rape was of a sex crime, of what men continue to call a 'crime of passion.' My image of rape victims contained a subconscious suspicion: what kind of women would *get themselves* into that kind of position? Thus, I had in my head every vicious, woman-hating stereotype that society promotes about rape, right down to blaming the rape victim rather than the rapist for the crime. I had no understanding of the politics of rape—or of how my own power and privilege as a man might have some bearing on the continual rape of women by men in our society.

Women students changed all that. The class on rape and the discussions which followed shattered all of my traditional male prejudices about rape. Women students taught me that rapists are not peculiar, abnormal men. Rapists are very normal masculine men. There is no exact profile of a 'typical rapist' because rapists come in all sizes and shapes, all races and nationalities, all ages and social classes. Many are white middle-class husbands and fathers.

Women students taught me that rape is neither a sex crime nor a crime of passion. Rape is often premeditated. And rape is a crime of *violence* rather than sex. It is a crime of violence against women. It is an attack by men on women's bodies, on women's feelings, on women's very existence. Women students taught me that rape is not an isolated, brutal crime against women. It is only one small part of a systematic pattern of male violence against women in America. Some women are raped in their homes or in the streets by men whom we call 'strangers.' Some women are raped in their homes or in the streets by men we call psychiatrists, doctors, college professors, friends, lovers, husbands, and fathers.

Women students taught me that rape can involve psychological as well as physical coercion. Many men, if asked 'Have you ever raped a woman?' would quickly respond in the negative. But what if the question were, 'Have you ever, at any time, in any way, through direct physical attack or subtle psychological manipulation, coerced a woman into close physical contact?' How many men could easily answer *no* to that question?

Thus, women students taught me that rape is something in which I myself am deeply implicated—directly in my relationships with women but also indirectly since I benefit from the male privilege that legitimizes rape. For rape is one of the most savage and yet one of the most accurate metaphors for how men relate to women in this society. It is a political crime committed by men as a class against women as a class. Rape is an attempt by men to keep all women in line. It is a clear expression of the hatred of women that pervades our society and our visions of masculinity.

One final thing I learned about rape was about rape jokes and warnings. Every time that a man calls a woman a 'bitch,' the threat of rape lies behind his hostility. Every time a man calls a woman a 'witch,' he reminds her of the slaughter of millions of women whose independence and medical knowledge threatened male dominance. And every time a man makes a joke about rape or wife-beating, he issues a warning to women. But, if I learned anything at all from women students, I learned this: rape is no joke.

My second course on 'Men, Masculinity, and Sexism' took place in the spring of 1975. It was as intense as the first but in a very different way. When women spoke out in the first class, men responded out of self-righteous indignation and all hell broke loose. In the second class, when women spoke out, men evaded the issue and pretended to be sympathetic. This made honest interaction impossible. The eventual result was that the six women students in the class decided to split. They came in one afternoon and announced that they were holding their own separate class for women for the last six weeks of the semester.

The women spent those weeks meeting on their own without students or a male teacher. Their final papers unanimously proclaimed what a valuable experience the all-women's class had been. As one student wrote, 'Our common bonds as women enabled us to discuss topics with our feelings. We can express our thoughts openly because of the oppression we share. We don't have to *prove* what we say is valid. We trust each woman's words and respect her feelings.' Every woman wrote about this class in similarly glowing terms, even those who had been most hesitant at the time of the split.

Now, as a male teacher whose women students all left his class, what did I learn from this experience? Before the course I already had some understanding of why women wanted their own space to control as they saw fit. Because of this, I accepted and supported the women's split and didn't try to stop it. But talking to the women students at the end of the term, and reading their final papers, taught me some vital lessons about the value and necessity of women's space. And when I say 'women's space,' I mean this in a very general way. I mean space and time that women exist in and control without male presence or dominance. I mean women's classes, women's studies programs, women's centers, women's self-help clinics, women's consciousness-raising groups, women's coffeehouses, women's bookstores, women's newspapers, women's music, women's communes, women's farms, and, of course, women loving other women. When I speak of the importance of women's space, I'm speaking of all these things and a whole lot more.

I don't need to dwell too long on an obvious point: men in this society have *no concept* of the importance and beauty and necessity of women controlling their own space, their own bodies, their own lives. Every bit of our socialization as men tells us that we're indispensable, that women simply can't get along without us. We're told that women can only find love from a man. We're told that women have nothing to say or to give to each other.

But here's what I learned as a male teacher. The best college course I've ever been formally responsible for—the very best—was the one where I wasn't there, where I gave no professorial direction, where women controlled their own classroom time.

And that says something very crucial to me, something that men had better begin to learn. The notion that men are indispensable to women is the worst kind of lie. Not only can women function and grow quite well without us being there; in many situations, women can function and grow *much more easily* without us being there. So if men really want to help women—as we always claim—one concrete step is often to get out of the way. Women students in my class learned more from each other than they ever could have if I was there. That fact crashes rather heavily into my male ego and my professorial conceit—but it's true and it won't go away. And it helps me to understand a little better that word that frightens and angers men so much: *separatism.*

Which brings me to a final point about the split. I *did* have ultimate power; I could have stopped the split but chose not to. I could have threatened those six women with no credit or with flunking grades or other academic perils. As long as male teachers have that kind of power over women's lives, it doesn't matter all that much whether they choose to use it or not. Things will be different only when women in the academic world—and in the rest of society—don't have to answer to *any* man, even one that is supposedly sympathetic.

[*A section on masculinity and sport has been omitted.*]

I've tried to touch on some of what I've learned from women and from feminism. Needless to say, I'm still very much at the beginning, and the same is true of every man in this society. Each of us, if we're serious about learning from women and dealing with our sexism, has a lifetime project ahead. If we sincerely want to learn and change, we've got to start reading every available bit of women's writing and feminist literature. This includes women's novels, poetry, history, political literature, autobiographies, biographies, newspapers, journals, and the like.

Also, if we sincerely want to learn and change, we've got to try to shut up and listen to women. This is still the hardest thing for me to do, and yet it is the most essential. In a conversation, men rarely let women get a word in; and if a woman talks, a man usually interrupts; and even if a man doesn't interrupt, men don't listen anyway. We're too busy mentally formulating our next bit of oratory. If we want to learn and change, we've got to begin by listening to women and trying to really hear them.

Beyond that, I'm not sure what to say. I know it may seem bizarre or suspicious for a man to speak this way. I know that every time a man says anything halfway reasonable about sexism, it can simply be one more male game—one more way of trying to manipulate women and control women's lives.

But I honestly wish that things were different. I wish I could live in a society where women *truly* were free, where male supremacy seemed so perverse as to be totally unimaginable, where the kind of masculine sickness that still shapes my personality didn't exist. I wish I could live in a society where all of us here really could be friends and respect one another, and be apart or together as any of us saw fit. I wish I could live in a society where a Women's Student Union wasn't under pressure to include a male speaker on its program, where a speaking program *of women only* and *for women only* was considered fully legitimate and appropriate and beautiful.

I know all of these things are very far off, but I hope that they're possible someday. Too many men have ruined too many women's lives already. I've seen more than enough, and I've done more than enough, and I want it to stop.

5   Men's Power with Women, Other Men, and Society: A Men's Movement Analysis

Joseph H. Pleck*

My aim in this paper is to analyze men's power from the perspective afforded by the emerging anti-sexist men's movement. In the last several years, an anti-sexist men's movement has appeared in North America and in the Western European countries. While it is not so widely known as the women's movement, the men's movement has generated a variety of books, publications, and organizations,[1] and is now an established presence on the sex role scene. The present and future political relationship between the women's movement and the men's movement raises complex questions which I do not deal with here, though they are clearly important ones. Instead, here I present my own view of the contribution which the men's movement and the men's analysis make to a feminist understanding of men and power, and of power relations between the sexes. First, I will analyze men's power over women, particularly in relation to the power that men often perceive women have over them. Then I will analyze two other relationships men are implicated in—men's power with other men, and men's power in society more generally—and suggest how these two other power relationships interact with men's power over women.

....

MEN'S POWER OVER WOMEN, AND WOMEN'S POWER OVER MEN

....

It is becoming increasingly recognized that one of the most fundamental questions raised by the women's movement is not a question about women at all, but rather a question about men: why do men

* Reprinted with permission of Simon & Schuster Adult Publishing Group, from *The American Man*, edited by Elizabeth H. Pleck and Joseph H. Pleck. Copyright © 1980 by Prentice-Hall, Inc.

oppress women? There are two general kinds of answers to this question. The first is that men want power over women because it is in their rational self-interest to do so, to have the concrete benefits and privileges that power over women provides them. Having power, it is rational to want to keep it. The second kind of answer is that men want to have power over women because of deep-lying psychological needs in male personality. These two views are not mutually exclusive, and there is certainly ample evidence for both. The final analysis of men's oppression of women will have to give attention equally to its rational and irrational sources.

I will concentrate my attention here on the psychological sources of men's needs for power over women. Let us consider first the most common and common-sense psychological analysis of men's need to dominate women, which takes as its starting point the male child's early experience with women. The male child, the argument goes, perceives his mother and his predominantly female elementary school teachers as dominating and controlling. These relationships *do* in reality contain elements of domination and control, probably exacerbated by the restriction of women's opportunities to exercise power in most other areas. As a result, men feel a lifelong psychological need to free themselves from or prevent their domination by women. The argument is, in effect, that men oppress women as adults because they experienced women as oppressing them as children.

According to this analysis, the process operates in a vicious circle. In each generation, adult men restrict women from having power in almost all domains of social life except child-rearing. As a result, male children feel powerless and dominated, grow up needing to restrict women's power, and thus the cycle repeats itself. It follows from this analysis that the way to break the vicious circle is to make it possible for women to exercise power outside of parenting and parent-like roles and to get men to do their half share of parenting.

There may be a kernel of truth in this 'mother domination' theory of sexism for some men, and the social changes in the organization of child care that this theory suggests are certainly desirable. As a general explanation of men's needs to dominate women, however, this theory has been quite overworked. This theory holds women themselves, rather than men, ultimately responsible for the oppression of women— in William Ryan's phrase, 'blaming the victim' of oppression for her own oppression.[2] The recent film *One Flew Over the Cuckoo's Nest* presents an extreme example of how women's supposed domination of men is used to justify sexism. This film portrays the archetypal struggle between a female figure depicted as domineering and castrating, and a rebellious male hero (played by Jack Nicholson) who refuses to be emasculated by her. This struggle escalates to a climactic scene in which Nicholson throws her on the floor and nearly strangles her to death—a scene that was accompanied by wild cheering from the audience when I saw the film. For this performance, Jack Nicholson won the Academy Award as the best actor of the year, an indication of how successful the film is in seducing its audience to accept this act of sexual violence as legitimate and even heroic. The hidden moral message of the film is that because women dominate men, the most extreme forms of sexual violence are not only permissible for men, but indeed are morally obligatory.

To account for men's needs for power over women, it is ultimately more useful to examine some other ways that men feel women have power over them than fear of maternal domination.[3] There are two forms of power that men perceive women as holding over them which derive more directly from traditional definitions of adult male and female roles, and have implications which are far more compatible with a feminist perspective.

The first power that men perceive women having over them is *expressive power*, the power to express emotions. It is well known that in traditional male–female relationships, women are supposed to express their needs for achievement only vicariously through the achievements of men. It is not so widely recognized, however, that this dependency of women on men's achievement has a converse. In traditional male–female relationships, men experience their emotions vicariously through women. Many men have learned to depend on women to help them express their emotions, indeed, to express their emotions for them. At an ultimate level, many men are unable to feel emotionally alive except through relationships with women. A particularly dramatic example occurs in an earlier Jack Nicholson film *Carnal Knowledge*. Art Garfunkel, at one point early in his romance with Candy Bergen, tells Nicholson that she makes him aware of thoughts he 'never even knew he had.' Although Nicholson is sleeping with Bergen and Garfunkel is not, Nicholson feels tremendously deprived in comparison when he hears this. In a dramatic scene, Nicholson then goes to her and demands: 'you tell him his thoughts, now you tell me my thoughts!' When women withhold and refuse to exercise this expressive power for men's benefit, many men, like Nicholson, feel abject and try all the harder to get women to play their traditional expressive role.

A second form of power that men attribute to women is *masculinity-validating* power. In traditional masculinity, to experience oneself as masculine requires that women play their prescribed role of doing the things that make men feel masculine. Another scene from *Carnal Knowledge* provides a pointed illustration. In the closing scene of the movie, Nicholson has hired a call girl whom he has rehearsed and coached in a script telling him how strong and manly he is, in order to get him sexually aroused. Nicholson seems to be in control, but when she makes a mistake in her role, his desperate reprimands show just how dependent he is on her playing out the masculinity-validating script he has created. It is clear that what he is looking for in this encounter is not so much sexual gratification as it is validation of himself as a man—which only women can give him. As with women's expressive power, when women refuse to exercise their masculinity-validating power for men, many men feel lost and bereft and frantically attempt to force women back into their accustomed role.

As I suggested before, men's need for power over women derives both from men's pragmatic self-interest and from men's psychological needs. It would be a mistake to overemphasize men's psychological needs as the sources of their needs to control women, in comparison with simple rational self-interest. But if we are looking for the psychological sources of men's needs for power over women, their perception that women have expressive power and masculinity-validating power over them are critical to analyze. These are the two powers men perceive women as having, which they fear women will no longer exercise in their favor. These are the two resources women possess which men fear women will withhold, and whose threatened or actual loss leads men to such frantic attempts to reassert power over women.

Men's dependence on women's power to express men's emotions and to validate men's masculinity have placed heavy burdens on women. By and large, these are not powers over men that women have wanted to hold These are powers that men have themselves handed over to women, by defining the male role as being emotionally cool and inexpressive, and as being ultimately validated by heterosexual success.

There is reason to think that over the course of recent history—as male–male friendship has declined, and as dating and marriage have occurred more universally and at younger ages—the demands on men to be emotionally inexpressive and to prove masculinity through relating to women have become stronger. As a result, men have given women increasingly more expressive power and more masculinity-validating power over them, and have become increasingly dependent on women for emotional and sex role validation. In the context of this increased dependency on women's power, the emergence of the women's movement now, with women asserting their right not to play these roles for men, has hit men with special force.

It is in this context that the men's movement and men's groups place so much emphasis on men learning to express and experience their emotions with each other, and learning how to validate themselves and each other as persons, instead of needing women to validate them emotionally and as men. When men realize that they can develop themselves the power to experience themselves emotionally and to validate themselves as persons, they will not feel the dependency on women for these essential needs which has led in the past to so much male fear, resentment, and need to control women. Then men will be emotionally more free to negotiate the pragmatic realignment of power between the sexes that is underway in our society.

MEN'S POWER WITH OTHER MEN

After considering men's power over women in relation to the power men perceive women having over them, let us consider men's power over women in a second context: the context of men's power relationships with other men. In recent years, we have come to understand that relations between men and women are governed by a sexual politics that exists outside individual men's and women's needs and choices. It has taken us much longer to recognize that there is a systematic sexual politics of male–male relationships as well. Under patriarchy, men's relationships with other men cannot help but be shaped and patterned by patriarchal norms, though they are less obvious than the norms governing male–female relationships. A society could not have the kinds of power dynamics that exist between women and men in our society without certain kinds of systematic power dynamics operating among men as well.

One dramatic example illustrating this connection occurs in Marge Piercy's recent novel *Small Changes*. In a flashback scene, a male character goes along with several friends to gang-rape a woman. When his turn comes, he is impotent; whereupon the other men grab him, pulling his pants down to rape *him*. This scene powerfully conveys one form of the relationship between male–female and male–male sexual politics. The point is that men do not just happily bond together to oppress women. In addition to hierarchy over women, men create hierarchies and rankings among themselves according to criteria of 'masculinity.' Men at each rank of masculinity compete with each other, with whatever resources they have, for the differential payoffs that patriarchy allows men.

Men in different societies choose different grounds on which to rank each other. Many societies use the simple facts of age and physical strength to stratify men. The most bizarre and extreme form of patriarchal stratification occurs in those societies which have literally created a class of eunuchs. Our society, reflecting its own particular preoccupations, stratifies men according to physical strength and athletic ability in the early years, but later in life focuses on success with women and ability to make money.

In our society, one of the most critical rankings among men deriving from patriarchal sexual politics is the division between gay and straight men. This division has powerful negative consequences for gay men and gives straight men privilege. But in addition, this division has a larger symbolic meaning. Our society uses the male heterosexual–homosexual dichotomy as a central symbol for *all* the rankings of masculinity, for the division on *any* grounds between males who are 'real men' and have power and males who are not. Any kind of powerlessness or refusal to compete becomes imbued with the imagery of homosexuality. In the men's movement documentary film *Men's Lives*,[4] a high school male who studies modern dance says that others often think he is gay because he is a dancer. When asked why, he gives three reasons: because dancers are 'free and loose,' because they are 'not big like football players,' and because 'you're not trying to kill anybody.' The patriarchal connection: if you are not trying to kill other men, you must be gay.

Another dramatic example of men's use of homosexual derogations as weapons in their power struggle with each other comes from a document which provides one of the richest case studies of the politics of male–male relationships to yet appear: Woodward and Bernstein's *The Final Days*. Ehrlichman jokes that Kissinger is queer, Kissinger calls an unnamed colleague a psychopathic homosexual, and Haig jokes that Nixon and Rebozo are having a homosexual relationship. From the highest ranks of male power to the lowest, the gay–straight division is a central symbol of all the forms of ranking and power relationships which men put on each other.

The relationships between the patriarchal stratification and competition which men experience with each other and men's patriarchal domination of women are complex. Let us briefly consider several points of interconnection between them. First, women are used as *symbols of success* in men's competition with each other. It is some-times thought that competition for women is the ultimate source of men's competition with each other. For example, in *Totem and Taboo* Freud presented a mythical reconstruction of the origin of society based on sons' sexual competition with the father, leading to their murdering the father. In this view, if women did not exist, men would not have anything to compete for with each other. There is consider-able reason, however, to see women not as the ultimate source of male–male competition, but rather as only symbols in a male contest where real roots lie much deeper.

The recent film *Paper Chase* provides an interesting example. This film combines the story of a small group of male law students in their first year of law school with a heterosexual love story between one of the students (played by Timothy Bottoms) and the professor's daugh-ter. As the film develops, it becomes clear that the real business is the struggle within the group of male law students for survival, success, and the professor's blessing—patriarchal struggle in which several of the less successful are driven out of school and one even attempts suicide. When Timothy Bottoms gets the professor's daughter at the end, she is simply another one of the rewards he has won by doing better than the other males in her father's class. Indeed, she appears to be a direct part of the patriarchal blessing her father has bestowed on Bottoms.

Second, women often play a *mediating* role in the patriarchal strug-gle among men. Women get together with each other, and provide the social lubrication necessary to smooth over men's inability to relate to each other non-competitively. This function has been expressed in many myths, for example, the folk tales included in the Grimms' col-lection about groups of brothers whose younger sister reunites and reconciles them with their king-father, who had previously banished and tried to kill them. A more modern myth, James Dickey's *Deliver-ance*, portrays what happens when men's relationships with each other are not mediated by women. According to Carolyn Heilbrun,[5] the central message of *Deliverance* is that when men get beyond the bounds of civilization, which really means beyond the bounds of the civilizing effects of women, men rape and murder each other.

A third function women play in male–male sexual politics is that relationships with women provide men a *refuge* from the dangers and stresses of relating to other males. Traditional relationships with women have provided men a safe place in which they can recuperate from the stresses they have absorbed in their daily struggle with other men, and in which they can express their needs without fearing that these needs will be used against them. If women begin to compete with men and have power in their own right, men are threatened by the loss of this refuge.

Finally, a fourth function of women in males' patriarchal competition with each other is to reduce the stress of competition by serving as an *underclass*. As Elizabeth Janeway has written in *Between Myth and Morning*,[6] under patriarchy women represent the lowest status, a status to which men can fall only under the most exceptional circumstances, if at all. Competition among men is serious, but its intensity is mitigated by the fact that there is a lowest possible level to which men cannot fall. One reason men fear women's liberation, writes Janeway, is that the liberation of women will take away this unique underclass status of women. Men will not risk falling lower than ever before, into a new underclass composed of the weak of both sexes. Thus, women's liberation means that the stakes of patriarchal failure for men are higher than they have been before, and that it is even more important for men not to lose.

Thus, men's patriarchal competition with each other makes use of women as symbols of success, as mediators, as refuges, and as an underclass. In each of these roles, women are dominated by men in ways that derive directly from men's struggle with each other. Men need to deal with the sexual politics of their relationships with each other if they are to deal fully with the sexual politics of their relationships with women.

Ultimately, we have to understand that patriarchy has two halves which are intimately related to each other. Patriarchy is a *dual* system, a system in which men oppress women, and in which men oppress themselves and each other. At one level, challenging one part of patriarchy inherently leads to challenging the other. This is one way to interpret why the idea of women's liberation so soon led to the idea of men's liberation, which in my view ultimately means freeing men from the patriarchal sexual dynamics they now experience with each other. But because the patriarchal sexual dynamics of male–male relationships are less obvious than those of male–female relationships, men face a real danger: while the patriarchal oppression of women may be lessened as result of the women's movement, the patriarchal oppression of men may be untouched. The real danger for men posed by the attack that the women's movement is making on patriarchy is not that this attack will go too far, but that it will not go far enough. Ultimately, men cannot go any further in relating to women as equals than they have been able to go in relating to other men as equals—an equality which has been so deeply disturbing, which has generated so many psychological as well as literal casualties, and which has left so many unresolved issues of competition and frustrated love.

MEN'S POWER IN SOCIETY

Let us now consider men's power over women in a third and final context, the context of men's power in the larger society. At one level, men's social identity is defined by the power they have over women and the power they can compete for against other men. But at another level, most men have very little over their own lives. How can we understand this paradox?

The major demand to which men must accede in contemporary society is that they play their required role in the economy. But this role is not intrinsically satisfying. The social researcher Daniel Yankelovich[7] has suggested that about 80% of U.S. male workers experience their jobs as intrinsically meaningless and onerous. They experience their jobs and themselves as worthwhile only through priding themselves on the hard work and personal sacrifice they are making to be breadwinners for their families. Accepting these hardships reaffirms their role as family providers and therefore as true men.

Linking the breadwinner role to masculinity in this way has several consequences for men. Men can get psychological payoffs from their jobs which these jobs never provide in themselves. By training men to accept payment for their work in feelings of masculinity rather than in feelings of satisfaction, men will not demand that their jobs be made more meaningful, and as a result jobs can be designed for the more important goal of generating profits. Further, the connection between work and masculinity makes men accept unemployment as their personal failing as males, rather than analyze and change the profit-based economy whose inevitable dislocations make them unemployed or unemployable.

Most critical for our analysis here, men's role in the economy and the ways men are motivated to play it have at least two negative effects on women. First, the husband's job makes many direct and indirect demands on wives. In fact, it is often hard to distinguish whether the wife is dominated more by the husband or by the husband's job. Sociologist Ralph Turner writes: 'Because the husband must adjust to the demands of his occupation and the family in turn must accommodate to his demands on behalf of his occupational obligations, the husband appears to dominate his wife and children. But as an agent of economic institutions, he perceives himself as controlled rather than as controlling.'[8]

Second, linking the breadwinner role to masculinity in order to motivate men to work means that women must not be allowed to hold paid work. For the large majority of men who accept dehumanizing jobs only because having a job validates their role as family breadwinner, their wives' taking paid work takes away from them the major and often only way they have of experiencing themselves as having worth. Yankelovich suggests that the frustration and discontent of this group of men, whose wives are increasingly joining the paid labor force, is emerging as a major social problem. What these men do to sabotage women's paid work is deplorable, but I believe that it is quite within the bounds of a feminist analysis of contemporary society to see these men as victims as well as victimizers.

One long range perspective on the historical evolution of the family is that from an earlier stage in which both wife and husband were directly economically productive in the household economic unit, the husband's economic role has evolved so that now it is under the control of forces entirely outside the family. In order to increase productivity, the goal in the design of this new male work role is to increase men's commitment and loyalty to work and to reduce those ties to the family that might compete with it. Men's jobs are increasingly structured as if men had no direct roles or responsibilities in the family—indeed, as if they did not have families at all. But paradoxically, at the same time that men's responsibilities in the family are reduced to facilitate more efficient performance of their work role, the increasing dehumanization of work means that the satisfaction which jobs give men is, to an increasing degree, *only* the satisfaction of fulfilling the family breadwinner role. That is, on the one hand, men's ties to the family have to be broken down to facilitate industrial work discipline; but on the other hand, men's sense of responsibility to the family has to be increased, but shaped into a purely economic form, to provide the motivation for men to work at all. Essential to this process is the transformation of the wife's economic role to providing supportive services, both physical and psychological, to keep him on the job, and to take over the family responsibilities which his expanded work role will no longer allow him to fulfill himself. The wife is then bound to her husband by her economic dependency on him, and the husband in turn is bound to his job by his family's economic dependence on him.

A final example from the film *Men's Lives* illustrates some of these points. In one of the most powerful scenes in the film, a worker in a rubber plant resignedly describes how his bosses are concerned, in his words, with 'pacifying' him to get the maximum output from him, not with satisfying his needs. He then takes back this analysis, saying that he is only a worker and therefore cannot really understand what is happening to him. Next, he is asked whether he wants his wife to take a paid job to reduce the pressure he feels in trying to support his family. In marked contrast to his earlier passive resignation, he proudly asserts that he will never allow her to work, and that in particular he will never scrub the floors after he comes home from his own job. (He correctly perceives that if his wife did take a paid job, he would be under pressure to do some housework.) In this scene, the man expresses and then denies an awareness of his exploitation as a worker. Central to his coping with and repressing his incipient awareness of his exploitation is his false consciousness of his superiority and privilege over women. Not scrubbing floors is a real privilege, and deciding whether or not his wife will have paid work is a real power, but the consciousness of power over his own life that such privilege and power give this man is false. The relative privilege that men get from sexism, and more importantly the false consciousness of privilege men get from sexism, play a critical role in reconciling men to their subordination in the larger political economy. This analysis does not imply that men's sexism will go away if they gain control over their own lives, or that men do not have to deal with their sexism until they gain this control. I disagree with both. Rather, my point is that we cannot fully understand men's sexism or men's subordination in the larger society unless we understand how deeply they are related.

To summarize, a feminist understanding of men's power over women, when men have needed it, and what is involved in changing it, is enriched by examining men's power in a broader context. To understand men's power over women, we have to understand the ways in which men feel women have power over them, men's power relationships with other men, and the powerlessness of most men in the larger society. Rectifying men's power relationship with women will inevitably both stimulate and benefit from the rectification of these other power relationships.

Notes

1. See, for example, Deborah David and Robert Brannon, eds., *The Forty-Nine Percent Majority: Readings on the Male Role* (Reading, Mass.: Addison-Wesley, 1975); Warren Farrell, *The Liberated Man* (New York: Bantam Books, 1975); Marc Feigen Fasteau, *The Male Machine* (New York: McGraw-Hill, 1974); Jack Nichols, *Men's Liberation: A New Definition of Masculinity* (Baltimore: Penguin, 1975); John Petras, ed., *Sex: Male/Gender: Masculine* (Port Washington, N.J.: Alfred, 1975); Joseph H. Pleck and Jack Sawyer, eds., *Men and Masculinity* (Englewood Cliffs, N.J.: Prentice-Hall, 1974). See also the *Man's Awareness Network (M.A.N.) Newsletter*, a regularly updated directory of men's movement activities, organizations, and publications, prepared by a rotating group of men's centers (c/o Knoxville Men's Resource Center, P.O. Box 8060, U.T. Station, Knoxville, Tenn. 37916); the Men's Studies Collection, Charles Hayden Humanities Library, Massachusetts Institute of Technology, Cambridge, Mass. 02139.

2. William Ryan, *Blaming the Victim* (New York: Pantheon, 1970).

3. In addition to the mother domination theory, there are two other psychological theories relating aspects of the early mother–child relationship in men's sexism. The first can be called the 'mother identification' theory, which holds that men develop a 'feminine' psychological identification because of their early attachment to their mothers and that men fear this internal feminine part of themselves, seeking to control it by controlling those who actually are feminine, i.e., women. The second can be called the 'mother socialization' theory, holding that since boys' fathers are relatively absent as sex role models, the major route by which boys learn masculinity is through their mothers' rewarding masculine behavior, and especially through their mothers' punishing feminine behavior. Thus, males associate women with punishment and pressure to be masculine. Interestingly, these two theories are in direct contradiction, since the former holds that men fear women because women make men feminine, and the latter holds that men fear women because women make men masculine. These theories are discussed at greater length in Joseph H. Pleck, 'Men's Traditional Attitudes toward Women: Conceptual Issues in Research,' in *The Psychology of Women: Future Directions in Research*, ed. Julia Sherman and Florence Denmark (New York: Psychological Dimensions, 1978).

4. Available from New Day Films, P.O. Box 315, Franklin Lakes, N.J. 07417.

5. Carolyn G. Heilbrun, 'The Masculine Wilderness of the American Novel,' *Saturday Review* 41 (January 29, 1972), 41–4.

6. Elizabeth Janeway, *Between Myth and Morning* (Boston: Little, Brown, 1975); see also Elizabeth Janeway, 'The Weak are the Second Sex,' *Atlantic Monthly* (December, 1973), 91–104.

7. Daniel Yankelovich, 'The Meaning of Work,' in *The Worker and the Job*, ed. Jerome Rosow (Englewood Cliffs, N.J.: [*Prentice-Hall*] 1974).

8. Ralph Turner, *Family Interaction* (New York: Wiley, 1968), p. 282.

6 The Limits of Masculinity

Andrew Tolson*

I have mentioned, in my introductory chapter, the feminist practice of 'consciousness-raising', and have suggested its significance for men. In this final chapter I want to examine this suggestion, in the light of my experience as a member of a men's group. I want to argue that the experience of masculinity, in its social dimensions and historical shifts, can be clarified within a consciousness-raising group. The small group, ideally, provides a bridge between (often inarticulate, undefined) personal experience, and a collective, social context in which it is shared and can be analysed.

I am not claiming that there are any necessary parallels between men's groups, and the politics of Women's Liberation. In this sense, since it is a feminist political practice, to talk about 'men's consciousness-raising' is perhaps misleading. I retain the definition in this account, partly because it was adopted by our group in Birmingham; and partly because it does, still, capture the process of 'becoming conscious' (a growing 'self-consciousness') of murky, unconscious areas in personal experience. This, however, is not a feminist consciousness—constructed from a position of social subordination. Men remain 'subjects', in dominance, of a patriarchal culture. Whereas for women 'becoming conscious' is therefore a *political* struggle (with negative self-images, and *against* the power of men); for men it is more a way of gaining some self-distance *within* the dominant culture.

The Birmingham men's group met once a week for two years (1973–5). During this time there was a fluctuating membership of a dozen or so, but there was a core of five. None of us had met before; and though we were all middle class, our 'middle classness' differed— ranging from the son of a clergyman, to the son of a garage proprietor.

* Reprinted with permission of Andrew Tolson and Taylor and Francis Books Ltd., from *The Limits of Masculinity: Male Identity and Women's Liberation*, by Andrew Tolson.

We were all in our twenties, and lived in different areas of Birmingham. Three had had a university education, and two were still students. One, after five years as a draughtsman, was on the 'dole'; one, who had left school at fifteen, was a production designer in a large engineering firm; and one was a bookshopkeeper. One (myself) was single, four were married, three were fathers with young children.

But none of us really knew what we wanted from a men's group. Domestic pressure, it seemed, had propelled us this far—together with unconscious dissatisfactions with our work, our relations with our parents, our masculine identities. Our personalities reflected the diversity of our backgrounds—some (noticeably the 'students') being openly assertive and articulate; others (the 'workers') remaining wary and unfathomable. How could we unscramble this mixture of experience?

Initial uncertainties were compounded by difficulties of communication. Perhaps everyone is reticent about talking about themselves. And though our meetings were held in people's homes, and were informal, there was an inevitable routine of introductions and building confidence. We began to discover that we had no language of feeling. We were trapped in public, specialized languages of work, learned in universities or factories, which acted as a shield against deeper emotional solidarities. When we talked about ourselves and our experiences, these would be presented through the public languages, in abstract, formal ways. The factory manager actually talked about himself as if he 'functioned', like a machine. The student-philosopher spoke about his 'bad faith', and his struggle to 'be authentic'. And the man on the dole, in this context, kept silent—and was perceived to be incoherent, swept along by a fluid, introspective experience.

Within the group we evolved a practice of 'self-deconstruction'. One person would speak about himself, his perspectives, in particular situations (work, family life, sexual relationships) and the others, at first, would just listen. Listening, without interrupting, was the first thing we had to learn to do. The experience of speaking, at length, to other men about your life, was itself disconcerting. You began to feel detached from your own 'persona'. There was an element of unintentional self-parody, and speakers would often have to re-think, or deny what they had said: 'Well, it wasn't quite like that'; or, 'Perhaps that's only partly true.' The self-detachment achieved through speaking began to give meaning to the notion of 'consciousness-raising'. For it became possible to say the unsayable, to open up closed areas of identity.

For the group as a whole, self-parody was a basic mutual acceptance—beyond the role-playing, and the debating techniques, of traditional masculinity. Each individual was allowed to assume a formal identity ('academic', 'worker', 'drop-out') only in so far as he began to move beyond it. At times 'self-deconstruction' was directly encouraged, by ruthless questioning, and by focusing on the position of the individual within the group itself. Anything which had been overlooked, or seemed ambiguous, or simply did not 'ring true', was re-presented for the speaker's own clarification: 'What did you mean when you said x?'; 'I don't understand how x fits in with y,' etc. In this way, talking about your experience involved simultaneously questioning its apparent coherence, and reformulating it from a many-sided perspective.

Out of this process we began to develop an 'inter-personality'—an experience of which the focus was not a single individual, but the group itself. In part, this grew out of a structure of overlapping personal accounts. Each person's life contained some masculine experiences that were familiar to us all, and one of the most important sources of confidence was a look of recognition: 'Yes, I've felt that too'; 'I've had a similar experience.' Particularly important here were discussions of sexuality—as we recounted male fantasies of women, and feelings of sexual desire. It seemed that the splits in our heads—images of power and submissiveness—were expressive of ambivalent behaviour—moments of aggression and sensitivity. Was this a common masculine syndrome?

And through the technique of 'self-deconstruction', we began to discover each other's limitations. Listening to people's self-presentations involves building imaginary pictures of their lives—projecting yourself into their personal worlds. As we grew to know each other, the 'look of recognition' could be placed, not simply as a response to a person's 'character', but as an awareness of the contradictions of his identity. The questions we asked became leading questions—worrying away at repeated rationalizations, taking on a direction dictated by the individual himself. Not only did this allow an exploration of personal intuitions; it was also the foundation for a kind of group empathy—a mutual responsiveness.

For one of our preoccupations had to be the nature of the group itself: what it was doing as an entity, the different positions of group members, who was dominating (by defining the topics or asking the questions) and who was silent, who responded to whom, in what way. At times it was a kind of encounter group—as we talked about each other, touched each other, spent weekends together. The physical side

of things—how we presented ourselves by sitting, dressing, gesturing
—became as important as the verbal.

We had formed, in effect, a kind of peer-group. And as with any
peer-group culture the intensity of individual involvement was rooted
in an esoteric collective identity. This identity was amorphous, chaotic,
and is impossible, in detail, to recall. Our conversations developed
loosely, were easily side-tracked, involved hours of the most minute
observations. What emerged from the group therefore, was not so
much a 'theory of masculinity', as a rather vague, somewhat incoherent 'perspective'. None of us could really say why, but we were beginning to experience our immediate world in a fresh, exciting way. It was
possible, by being silent oneself, and watchful, to begin to perceive the
nuances of social interaction. At least this was a step beyond the blind
self-confidence of traditional masculinity. It also seemed important, in
a world dictated by career-schedules, to slow down, to make more
flexible routines—cooking, cleaning, being with children. To some
extent our group evolved a respect for inarticulacy; and encouraged
the open expression of previously-tabooed feelings—what made us
angry, what made us cry.

One 'theme' that did crystallize out of our men's group, was the
recurring problem of couple relationships. For everyone, an immediate reason for his joining the group was the feminist challenge to male
sexuality; and in part, the group acted as a therapeutic forum for a
struggle encountered within sexual relationships. Our meetings were
dominated by accounts of conflicts, jealousies, and reconciliations. In
almost every respect our experience was ambivalent. We were in
favour of women's independence, but felt threatened by it. We wanted
to renounce our aggressive role, but felt bound to it. We were tired of
disputes and petty squabbles, but had no power to stop them. Even
though we were searching for a unified sexuality, we still felt impelled
to 'perform'—and to watch ourselves performing. These emotional
complexes seemed to us to be inherent within 'nuclear' relationships.
The 'nuclear family' was a trap, both for women and for men, because
it demanded *polarized* gender-roles: 'assertive'/'submissive'; 'decisive'/
'uncertain'; 'detached'/'dependent'; etc. However 'complementary'
these may seem to be, they are, at a deeper level, devisive—a potential
source of friction.

One of the aspects of the group that I found particularly exciting
was the way our 'perspective' had formed. For my education had given
me an academic language deceptive in its apparent flexibility, with
which I could seize on aspects of experience, but could not express

their total, personal significance. In the group I was forced to learn the difference between analysis and abstraction—that it is not enough, for example, when discussing 'conscience', to talk blithely on about the 'super-ego'. Fears of making initiatives, of 'stepping out of line', are supported by intellectual rationalization, and lack of personal disclosure. I realized that the social theories I had learned applied to the society of which I was a part; that I was defined by the ideologies I criticized. So there was a continual attempt to find links between ideas and experiences—criticizing the ideas if they collapsed, or did not seem to fit, the complexities of experience.

But at a certain point in the group's development, the process of 'consciousness-raising' seemed to achieve a kind of 'resolution'. On one level, there remained a persistent problem of being unable to 'reconcile' different individual perspectives. Our masculine identities, though shared, were to some extent divergent—the products of varying kinds of work and family background. Against this variation, the collective dynamic of the group (and this may be a particular feature of men's groups, where 'chauvinist' tendencies are always present) itself became an analytic barrier. Individual accounts became predictable, the humour 'matey', the supportive atmosphere a little too cosy. At this point, which our group reached after about a year of meetings, 'consciousness-raising' faced a problem of further development. With the crystallization of a group 'perspective', the limits of inter-personality were reached.

In the Birmingham men's group (and we were by no means unique in this respect) this problem of further development was never fully articulated. We were faced with a complex question of self-definition, both of our social position as men, and of the political implications of our practice—which were not clearly recognized at the time. In retrospect, and in very general terms, I think two implicit considerations can be differentiated; for it is both necessary for us to comprehend the significance of 'consciousness-raising' as an activity (in part, we need a theory of consciousness, which defines the process of 'becoming conscious'—through individual awareness and interpersonal relationships—in terms which go beyond our immediate situation); and, second, because masculinity is social, rooted in the organization of work and family life, we are forced to recognize its practical implications. Without an attempt to change our lives, our critique of masculinity will remain one-sided.

The production of a theory of consciousness remains a specialized task, beyond the scope of any particular group—and I can only attempt to outline some preliminary definitions. I think we need to understand more about the relationship between social experience and the structures that define that experience. The process of 'consciousness-raising' seems to support the Marxist theory[1] that within a social formation (which is ultimately determined by relations of production) there are two kinds of defining structure: not only social institutions (school, legal system, mass media, etc., constituting a 'State Apparatus'); but also 'general ideologies' (located in types of ritual, and language). Social consciousness is as much structured by the 'codes' of a general ideological discourse, as it is by institutional boundaries and rules of behaviour. Patriarchy is a 'general ideology' substantially carried by codes of speech ('Wait till your father gets home') and by inherited rituals and customs (like 'initiation cere-monies' at work). Through language, patriarchy remains a powerful source of definition, even when the primary institution in which it is located—the family—has lost many of its former functions to the capitalist state. The language of patriarchy is communicated, for the most part, *unconsciously*, in early childhood, before the indi-vidual learns ways of speaking associated with the 'State Apparatus' as such.

I can offer little more than a sketch. Part of the problem is that patriarchal ideology, which defines the experience as masculinity, is extraordinarily diverse and detailed. I think this is possibly because, as an unconscious language, patriarchy permeates all the 'official' def-initions of state institutions. It is in this language that the power of men is enshrined. It is the social language of which 'man', as such, is the subject: an assertive language of politics and the market-place; a rational language which makes definitions and connections—the lan-guage of abstraction. It is also in the silences of this language that a repressed masculinity is imprisoned—as abstraction formalizes a man's identity, as rationality represses irrationality.

Becoming conscious of masculinity thus not only involves transforming social institutions, but also understanding the language of patriarchy. And 'consciousness-raising' is, perhaps, an activity appropriate to linguistic transformation. It requires learning a new way of speaking, which needs to accompany the deconstruction of masculinity.

An emphasis on language, in the analysis of patriarchy, has been an important focus of the Women's Movement. A new appreciation of the 'politics of language' has perhaps been the substantial contribu-tion of feminist theory (in the works of Sheila Rowbotham and Juliet

Mitchell for example) to traditional definitions of class struggle. As Sheila Rowbotham puts it:

The underground language of people who have no power to define and determine themselves in the world develops its own density and precision. It enables them to sniff the wind, sense the atmosphere, defend themselves in a hostile terrain. But it restricts them by affirming their own dependence upon the words of the powerful. It reflects their inability to break out of the imposed reality through to a reality they can define and control for themselves ... On the other hand, the language of theory—removed language—only expresses a reality experienced by the oppressors. It speaks only for their world from their point of view. Ultimately a revolutionary movement has to break the hold of the dominant group over theory, it has to structure its own connections.[2]

The Women's Liberation Movement has shown how becoming conscious of social contradictions involves a reappropriation of dominant languages, and a vocal liberation of their repressed silences.

But here, from the 'masculine' point of view, it is necessary to re-examine the 'reality experienced by the oppressors'. There is a sense in which feminist analysis sometimes tends to reduce the complexity of the 'dominant' world. Men do, of course, inherit patriarchal identities, and reproduce these identities in their own lives. The language of patriarchy thus perpetuates the oppression of women. As we have seen however, patriarchy operates by giving to men a family-based image of *work*, which is then reaffirmed by a work-based masculine culture. It is because of his status as a *worker*, that a man is able to possess, not only his wages, but also the language of buying and selling that dominates public life. And it is possession of this cultural power that provides him with some kind of explanation for the grind of alienated labour. It is thus crucial that, subjectively, such an explanation 'fits' his experience of working; and objectively, that his patriarchal aspirations are rewarded by the economic mode of production.

In these ways, the experience of consciousness-raising points towards a complex analysis of the operations of ideology. And it is necessary to understand how 'becoming conscious' of these operations provides a basis for their subsequent transformation. Ideology possesses concrete significance because it defines social consciousness; and if the ideological mechanism is itself a focus of struggle, it must be adequately theoretically described. Ideology can neither be represented in abstraction, as 'above' social determinations; nor can it be reduced to the passive 'reflection' of material life. One task of social theory is to comprehend the *dialectics* of meaning—partly pre-given and partly created—through which 'general ideologies' are constituted.

This understanding of patriarchy, as an ideological imposition, implies a further set of practical, and 'political' questions. For if the experience of masculinity is socially prestructured, how can it be changed? What is the defining power of patriarchy in the routines of daily existence? Again, in the Birmingham men's group, our answers to these questions remained far from satisfactory. A common interest in 'sexual politics' seemed to provide a starting-point—and we attempted, by analogy with the Women's Movement, to construct for ourselves a combination of 'personal' and 'political' projects. At the local level we helped in a preschool play-group run by Women's Liberation,[3] and made some, individual gestures towards restructuring sex-roles. Nationally, we participated in 'Men Against Sexism'—a bi-annual conference of men's groups, which published a newsletter, and developed a national network. From 1973–5 there were about forty such groups in various cities throughout the country.

But in all our practical activities, we faced an immediate contradiction. As men, as the agents of a patriarchal culture, we remained the dominant gender. In a certain sense, we were imperialists in a rebellion of slaves—concerned, defensively, about the threat to our privilege. The very notion of 'men's politics' was paradoxical. We had no experience of sexual oppression, violence, jokes at our expense. There were no issues to unite us—no basis for action against a system that already operates in our favour. This paradox was driven home by gay men at Men Against Sexism conferences. Above all, we had not 'come out'— we remained heterosexual, embarrassed at being thought gay, typical liberal men.

In the confusion of our position, these charges touched a core. We hoped to contribute to sexual politics—but were, apparently by definition, disqualified. The political contradiction was reflected in practical uncertainty, as we remained disabled by our masculinity. We tried to publicize ourselves—by speaking at meetings and to the local press —but failed to produce a consistent self-definition. We continued to explore personal projects—collective childcare, a 'denucleated' family life-style—but these remained within a 'progressive' middle-class culture. It would perhaps be wrong to entirely underestimate these activities: some did crystallize as 'alternative' institutions—the play-group, a food co-op, a radical press. With the support of the group some individuals succeeded in changing jobs, living in collective houses, achieving some independence from the family. But all these remained personal, or at least local, solutions to general social questions. And always, as 'straight men' we were wary and peripheral, in relation to their outcome.

Moreover, it is crucial, both for our tentative development and our subsequent demise, that we failed to confront our political position. For even though we did recognize, intuitively, the truth of the gay accusation—we preferred to avoid its implications. We continued to interpret our personalized practices through the politics of feminism. We continued to speak of 'men's liberation'; and to assume that we could parallel, even complement, the activities of Women's Liberation. By this token we internalized the masculine paradox—defining ourselves in terms of sexual oppression, as the guilty, oppressive agency—but we avoided the logical outcome. We held on, wishfully, to a kind of negative ideal, a self-destructive utopia.

As long as we adopted this contradictory definition, our confusion was inevitable. In the first place, we could not comprehend the transition from the small group to a wider political basis. Consciousness-raising remains a vitally necessary experience—but practical solutions to the problems it poses cannot be 'experientially' found. As it has been the purpose of this book to show, the experience of individual men is constituted by a whole social system of work and domestic life. And the transformation of this system, including its 'gender-roles', must remain a collective responsibility.

Equally however, and perhaps more significantly, we failed to appreciate the limits of masculinity itself. This is a difficult observation, but one I want finally to make—because I think straight men must recognize, openly, the truth of the gay and feminist position. Not only are different gender-identities ('feminine', 'gay', 'masculine') distinctively irreducible; they also fundamentally contradict, and do not simply 'complement' each other. The relation between the sexes cannot be 'symmetrical': it is incongruent—and, as men have had to learn, is constructed in terms of social *power* ('oppression'). To simply deny, or vaguely wish to 'relinquish', the reality of this power is to fall victim to a liberal myopia. And to assume that men can, unproblematically, experience 'men's liberation'—that there are any analogies with gay or feminist politics—is, in the end, an illusion. It is perhaps understandable that in the first, exciting years of the new feminism 'progressive' men should have shared this illusion. But men's 'consciousness' is not women's consciousness—and men's 'consciousness-raising' shows the impossibility of a 'men's politics'.

To reach this conclusion is not however, simply 'negative'. Discovering the political limits of masculinity is not a recipe for inactivity. Men can, I think, with a limited sphere, develop a supportive role which does not 'incorporate' feminist and gay initiatives. It is important that men should continue to participate in childcare and nursery education (crèches, play-groups, etc.) where their very presence challenges sex-role expectations. Some men may involve themselves in 'community' action—working with tenants' organizations, squatting, building play-centres, and free schools—which often co-exist with explicit feminist activities. Often, it seems, the most successful men's groups have been related to neighbourhood centres or newspapers—where sexual politics is part of an involvement in local political work.

And in particular, men who are convinced of the importance of sexual politics must, I think, begin to find ways of articulating their position. For socialist men especially, it is necessary to challenge a prevailing left-wing sectarianism which relegates questions of personal and family life to peripheral status—as 'women's issues'. Feminists and gays have themselves criticized the chauvinism of the left—its dogmatic formulas, its predictable 'party-lines'. Both groups have initiated a far-reaching debate with a male-dominated socialist tradition. It is vital that 'men against sexism' begin to take a constructive position within this debate—supporting the attention to personal experience, and the critique of socialist dogmatism, which sections of the Women's Movement have especially pioneered.[4]

I hope that this book has contributed to that possibility. I have tried to establish that masculinity, and men's personal experiences, are necessarily socially constructed. And I have argued that a man's gender-identity is interwoven with the ideology of 'free-individuality' which supports the system of capitalist wage-labour. If, as with Tom, the pressures of work become too great; or, as with Bill, a man faces the threat of redundancy—the reversal is both socio-economic and personal. In personal terms, the loss of social power is experienced as a crisis of gender-identity. If it is true that the 'solutions' to personal problems cannot themselves be 'personal' (for they symptomatically point to a complex social structure)—it is not, by the same token, simply 'idealist', or 'diversionary' to recognize the personal level. The challenge to socialist men is to understand masculinity as a social problem—and thus to work together for a non-sexist socialist society.

Notes

1. Readers familiar with his work will recognize the terminology of Louis Althusser. I have here adopted, somewhat eclectically, his thesis on 'Ideology and Ideological State Apparatuses', as developed in *Lenin and Philosophy and other Essays* (New York: Monthly Review Press, 1971).

2. Sheila Rowbotham, *Women's Consciousness, Man's World* (Harmondsworth: Penguin, 1973), pp. 32–3.

3. For a summary, and critical account of the Birmingham Women's Liberation Playgroup, including extensive discussion of problems of men and childcare, see *Out of the Pumpkin Shell* (Birmingham, 1975), a pamphlet published by Birmingham Women's Liberation.

4. Again, the classic texts are those of Sheila Rowbotham (*Woman's Consciousness, Man's World*; Harmondsworth: Penguin, 1973), and Juliet Mitchell (*Woman's Estate*; New York: Pantheon, 1971). The key periodicals are, for socialist feminism, *Red Rag* (22, Murray Mews, London W1); and for the relationship between gay liberation and socialism, *Gay Left* (c/o 36a, Craven Road, London W2).

7 Hopes and Dreams: Creating a Men's Politics

Men's Free Press Collective [*of* Achilles Heel]*

....
BY WAY OF AN INTRODUCTION . . .
....

This journal [*Achilles Heel*] has been produced by a working collective of socialist men who have been involved in men's groups and men's politics for some time. For all of us it is a process of making public a very private and very important experience—that of consciously redefining and changing the nature of our relationships with women and with each other as men. In making this experience public and in beginning to develop an analysis around it, we are in a sense 'coming out' politically as men and realigning ourselves with the women's and gay movements in the struggle against sexual oppression.

This isn't the first time such a venture has been attempted. A series of publications under the general title *Brothers Against Sexism* came out between 1972 and 1974, spurred on by the energy of a number of national conferences of men's groups that met over that period. Between the summers of 1975 and 1977 an internal news-sheet called 'Men's News' has been circulated among London groups (and in Manchester at least a similar local newsletter has been produced).

Inasmuch as the men's movement has been an important part of our own histories over the past five or six years we see this journal as a development within the history of men's publications and we hope to incorporate and explore some of the lessons and experiences of the past few years. At the same time, this is a new venture based pretty squarely in our own particular experience of men's politics and quite consciously committed to the development of what we see as an essential connection between socialism and sexual politics.

* Reprinted with permission of Victor Seidler and Taylor and Francis Books Ltd., from *The Achilles Heel Reader*, edited by Victor Seidler (1971).

Differences

Among the members of this collective perceptions differ as to how this connection can best be made by men—differences themselves based on diverging views of what socialism is and how we can most effectively contribute to its creation. That individuals differ about such things seems inevitable, but nevertheless important for us to state inasmuch as we do not see collectivity and individuality as mutually exclusive creatures. We feel that many of the problems of the Left at the moment flow from a confusion of socialism with an imposed collectivity around a set of 'correct' ideas. Our differences have emerged to some extent around the kind of material we should publish. [. . .] Mainly the differences have been to do with how we see men responding politically to the women's and gay movements, in particular whether or not there is a political basis for the growth of an autonomous men's movement, whether or not such a movement does in fact exist, whether it makes any sense for men to organize separately on the basis of being men.

These are difficult questions and have been at the heart of men's groups' historic ambivalence about asserting themselves publicly as an organized political presence. We have no solutions, but obviously we hope over the next few months to air the whole discussion of what men's politics is and what it could grow to become, and within that what kind of connections can be made between men's things and the organized and non-organized left. Simply to get such discussions down on paper (discussion which so far has taken the form of many excited but always incomplete and unrecorded conversations) is one of the main goals of the journal for now. [. . .]

Writing personally

In [*our*] discussions a number of issues came up, a couple of which we thought we should lay out in this introduction. The first is to do with the problem of language and vocabulary, the problem of how to write. It has been vitally important to all of us over the past few years to delve deeply into our inner lives and to consciously explore and develop our sense of ourselves as emotional, sensual and spiritual beings capable of a whole range of experience which our society on the whole denies to men. Part of this development has been a turning away from the abstractness and theoretical expertise which in our pasts as male socialists has tended to be central to our identities. It has been increasingly important to us to root our ideas in our own experience of life and to acknowledge people's personal lives as central to their being and thereby integral to the growth of a socialist society.

None of us wish to deny the importance of theory and generalization but at the same time we have developed an aversion to the abstraction and rhetoric in which so much theory on the left seems to have got stuck. In writing the editorial we have come up against the problem of wanting to generalize without being abstract. We feel the need for new ways of expressing ourselves and haven't yet found them. For the journal as a whole we hope that finding new ways of talking about things will be integral to the direction it will take. At the same time we see it as key in terms of an editorial policy that this will be a place where short stories, poems, interviews and all kinds of personal accounts can sit comfortably alongside more theoretical discussion.

The second issue to come up was the need to make clear that we have no pretensions to represent the men's movement. The six of us are in men's groups (two separate groups) at the moment and have been involved in left and sexual politics in different ways for several years, we were all part of the political transformations of the sixties— students' politics, the May Events in France, VSC and the growth of the 'new' new left of that period (some of us have longer political histories that encompass CND). In the 1970s we have been involved in socialist cultural work and working-class community and factory politics as members of East London Big Flame, the International Marxist Group and a libertarian Marxist group based in Brixton.

Over the past few years feminism has been the most important source of self-discovery and political change for us, slowly transforming our understandings of ourselves as political men, and our convictions about socialism and political organizing. Within this process of dissolution something new has taken root and begun to sprout. We don't know how it's going to grow and we have no desire to pre-empt any such growth with neat analyses and plans of action. We do, however, have a sense of shared history and shared perspective from which to attempt new beginnings. Many men in and out of men's groups will disagree with us—as will plenty of women in and out of the women's movement. It's important, then, to say that we do not speak for anyone but ourselves, though we would like to speak to as many people as possible and launch a publication that is as open as possible to contribution and discussion by people interested in sexual politics and socialism in general and men's politics in particular.

CREATING A MEN'S POLITICS

In the society in which we live, men are by and large brought up to be powerful, aggressive, competitive and tough or manipulative; and not to show feelings—particularly of weakness. As children, the world is hard on our inborn softness: we learn to endure pain, and to expect rewards and approval for our obedience. We learn to respect the authority that controls these rewards, and so we assume authority over others—particularly authority over women, whom we learn to see as inferior. We expend a lot of energy comparing ourselves with or proving ourselves to other men—and by extension, to ourselves. If we are working class we are placed in jobs that are by and large unsatisfying; if we are middle class we are placed in jobs which isolate us and in which we are forced to manipulate others. We are taught to look for our emotional satisfactions in one place alone—the family.

In the world we appear confident. We are supposed to be able to 'handle' things. But our inner lives, denied so early, are often deeply insecure and weak. If we crack up we tend to kill ourselves, commit suicide, rather than ask for help and end up in mental hospitals, as women tend to do. In most working- and middle-class families the roles are defined: men are the breadwinners, women are the homemakers. Our duty, internalized as self-fulfillment, is to work; to provide money for our families, who depend on us. In return we expect our families to love us and to nourish us, our wives to look after us. We make a bargain. It seems fair. It seems the 'natural' order of things. But it is not fair. It is not natural. We are usually the prisoners of work we do not or cannot enjoy. And we turn our homes into prisons for the women who, in isolation, bring up our children. Where we once expected and dreamed of an atmosphere of mutual love we find deep mutual resentment. Every so often, particularly in our sexual relationships, we become aware of the width of the gulf between ourselves and the women we had assumed we were close to.

Out of women's unpaid labour in the home, we, the labourers, are serviced for our work, and a new generation of labourers are given life and prepared for their future. Out of our total labours, at home and at work, surplus value is produced, profits are made, the system finds the means to its own renewal.

This, then, briefly and incompletely, is the sexual division of labour in capitalism—and the patriarchal relations that are concomitant with that division. Along with class divisions, the divisions between men

83

and women structure all our relationships, from the most public to the most intimate.

Masculinity in crisis

But the system we have described is not static. Even to talk about a system and to allot men and women fixed roles within it can be misleading. The roles we have described are increasingly contradictory and under pressure. Or, to put it another way, masculinity is in crisis. In part the roots are economic: in working-class homes more and more women have been forced out into poorly paid jobs—both to make up the family income and to escape the isolation and drudgery of the home. Similarly, middle-class women have been pulled into higher education in order to meet the demands of the rapidly expanding (until 1974) caring and teaching professions to find that they are by and large expected to combine their new career with household serfdom in wifedom and motherhood. Out of the pressures and contradictions of this double employment the modern women's movement has been born.

In the same period, men's work is deskilled and downgraded. Craft jobs, and the power over the work process that goes with them, are gradually phased out. Work is increasingly unpleasant. We are ... more and more at the service of the machinery we are supposed to control. We work for money, for the means to survival. Pride in work disappears, to be replaced by pride in consumption. Unemployment and low wages threatened our status as providers. Even our subsistence is made insecure. Local authority housing destroys our communities and undermines our status as homebuilders. Our alienation from our jobs, from our communities, our isolation, unrecognized, creates expectations of the family that cannot be fulfilled. In fear, we punish others, often the closest to us, for our own powerlessness.

We look more closely at some of the characteristics of masculinity in crisis, and open up a way of looking at the right-wing political movements that goes beyond the confrontation in the streets; we see how racism and fascism grow out of the changes that are happening in people's lives, and raise the question, as the women's and gay movements have done, of how to fight these phenomena on the ideological and cultural level.

Women's liberation—and men

For almost 20 years now, the women's movement has been in open struggle against women's oppression in our society. An important part of the struggle has been the need to continuously define and theorize the nature of that oppression, the different dimensions of patriarchal power, its historical roots and relation to particular periods in the development of capitalist and non-capitalist society. At the same time, women have begun to find a new kind of unity, to explore new, non-hierarchical ways of organizing and to demand the redefinition of what is seen as 'political' to include whole areas of people's lives that had previously been seen as 'merely personal' and irrelevant; at least, until 'after the revolution'. At the same time they have demanded a different way of looking at the society as a whole, ceasing to see a factory as the determining heartland of all social oppressions, but looking at the 'factory-ization' of all areas of life—home, school, community and workplace.

For men in close contact with the women's movement—and now we in this collective are beginning to describe our own histories—this process has been both incredibly threatening to our previous conceptions of ourselves, and at the same time immensely exciting in the possibilities for our own change, it began to open up. Men's groups and the men's movement have emerged out of the recognition that our power in society as men not only oppresses women but also imprisons us in a deadening masculinity which cripples all our relationships—with each other, with women and with ourselves. In our men's groups we have begun to fracture those barriers of privacy, of competitiveness and control that were part of our upbringing. We have learnt to admit our need for one another as men; we have begun to re-examine our gayness; we have gained a confidence in our inner lives and in ourselves.

In doing so, we have begun to transform our relationships with the women we are close to. It's hard to generalize about the changes: for some it means being less demanding; for others being able to admit dependence. We have usually taken on more housework and childcare, and so learnt both about the drudgery and the pleasures we had often denied ourselves. It means being less controlling; for some it means finding the confidence to get into a relationship. For others it means being able to end it.

Consciousness-raising groups and occasionally therapy have so far been the main expressions of the men's movement because it has been in our close relationships that the need and pressure to change and to look for support has been most keenly felt. In addition, men have been active around organizing crèches for the women's movement and in campaigns around day care and abortion—a reflection of the changes happening in our domestic lives.

For those of us who are socialists, however, men's politics has always meant more than our immediate relationships. Sexual oppression, like class and racial oppression, is built into our relationships at all levels. The way our working situations are organized, our education and our relationships to political institutions and the media are all part of our lives. To change ourselves involves changing them, too. So part of our involvement with men's politics has been a continuing desire to make connections between socialism and our more immediate changes.

Men's history—

It has been important for us to see that masculinity and male power are historical creatures. Men are no more synonymous with their gender conditioning than women are, rather we exist in contradictory and uneasy relation to it. There is no simple equation between 'patriarchal power' and men. In very complicated ways sexual, class and racial oppression cut across each other producing subtle layers of relative power and powerlessness. The stereotypical model of oppressive maleness or even male-gender conditioning fits very few individual men. From this perspective we can begin to understand the ways men, individually and collectively, live in struggle against their conditioning —class, racial *and* sexual.

As individuals men have the private and isolated struggle of growing up in the face of the authority around them—usually in the shape of other men like fathers, teachers, policemen and judges. Men respond in quite different ways, of course. All are marked for life by the process of being squashed into some semblance of the narrow world of manliness. We resist in our individual ways. For some men it means becoming a failure in the eyes of parents and teachers and often themselves, for some it means coming out as gay, for some resistance is far more violent, for others giving way in one area of life to protect or compensate for another, and for yet others just playing the game, giving in and hiding any inner life utterly. Whatever the response the scars are there, as are the contradictions and the half-hidden kernels of potential change.

Hidden, too, is the history of men's more collective and public struggle around sexual politics. Central to any such account must be the history of gay men, gay culture and gay struggle—both for personal freedom and for the transformation of society. Over the centuries gay men have faced the deeply contradictory position of being men in a male-dominated society and at the same time defying the assumption of 'natural' heterosexuality upon which so much patriarchal power is based. Again responses to this contradiction have varied but since the late nineteenth century at least a gay consciousness has persistently challenged notions of masculinity and sexuality which are relevant to all men. In this collective our own histories have been heterosexual on the whole. So has the history of the men's movement. We feel it important to acknowledge our debt to the gay movement over recent years and voice our hopes towards the development of relationships between the two movements. For the journal we see the raising and discussion of the whole issue of heterosexuality and gayness as crucial and hope gay men will regard it as open for participation and contribution.

—and socialist history

At the same time we begin to see within the history of working-class struggle dimensions that have largely been hidden by the rather narrow, economistic perspectives of many male historians and socialists. Working-class struggle has always involved more than the economic dimension. Among the hand-loom weavers of the early nineteenth century and the unemployed of the 1930s, for example, the issues at stake were as much to do with notions of manhood, pride and personal dignity, the connections of masculinity to skill and work ethic— issues fascinating and contradictory in themselves. Contained within the history of trade union action are struggles against hierarchy and competition and *for* collectivity, *for* one another; they have been struggles against the alienation of labour, and for more time and money to enjoy ourselves, to enjoy our relationships and our children, to be supportive in the home. We are not saying this is the whole side of the story; we are saying that there is a hidden history of personal life within working-class men's struggles—one that can be reinterpreted and rediscovered with our new understanding, and can lend us support in our own attempts to redefine ourselves.

We recognize within the socialist tradition strands of cultural, personal and sexual politics to which we feel a natural affinity and whose reclamation we see as crucial. The tensions within 'left' group-ings during the English Revolution ring all too familiar in the con-temporary ear, while in the nineteenth century the same kinds of tensions between personal change and institutional change, between utopian vision and material pragmatism, between hierarchy and anti-authoritarianism were part of the Owenite and Chartist movements which alongside Jacobinism, radical non-conformity and trade-union growth formed a diverse pre-Marxist socialist tradition in Britain.

In the late nineteenth and early twentieth century socialism main-tained and developed this diversity of tradition, within which men as well as women were involved in questioning the sexual division of labour—in practice as well as theory. Men like Morris, Ellis and Carpenter represent a strong presence within the Socialist League and later the branches of the ILP of a notion of socialism being a living process, a changing of self and personal relations not just society as a set of external structures. Similarly among anarchists and syndical-ists of the early twentieth century there was a tradition of life-style politics, of free sexual union and inner change.

The growth of Marxism since the late nineteenth century, its devel-opment through Leninism and Trotskyism in the twentieth century, has on the whole been antithetical to these earlier strands. Clearly Leninism has risen to a position of hegemonic power within the left for specific reasons since the 1920s and it will be interesting to look more closely at that ascendancy and its contradictions. We disagree about how positively or negatively we see the history of Leninism and the permanence of its contribution to the contemporary left. We are also divided in the extent to which we attribute the legacy of economism and scientism and the dismissal of personal questions to Leninism as well as to the effect of Stalin on Marxism. Since the late 1960s a new wave of non-Leninist revolutionary energy, represented most crucially by the women's movement, has revitalized the tradition of utopianism and sense of total politics.

For the members of this collective, these currents do not have to—indeed, must not—remain separate, and one of the things we would like to do in this journal is to find ways of bringing them together, out of our own experience and history as men. In doing this, we are trying to deal with a split that for many of us has been a part of our own history—a split between our lives as political activists, some of us in left groups and some not—and our 'personal' lives and problems, as expressed in our men's groups. Much work has already been done in this area, and it is clear that we are going to find no magical solution to a division that runs so deep in our experiences and in history; there will be articles that remain 'objective' and analytical in style, and others that read much more like subjective accounts; we have yet to find a style of writing that integrates the two. Yet that unity of the 'personal and the political' remains our aim; the unity, ultimately, of creative individuality and collective strength that is the essence of socialism.

Having said this, it must be clear that we are by and large unhappy with the existing organized left in this country, for its 'demotion' of sexual politics, or separation of sexual politics into special categories. We are critical of the economism of most left groups, which seem to fail to touch huge areas of people's lives that we consider to be important, and to forget the deepest questions of what the revolution is about and what it is for—the kind of life that we are trying to build for ourselves; the kind of social relations that we want to start developing.

Men in left groups, including ourselves in our time, have traditionally seen themselves as responsible to the world: as generators of 'total' theories of class politics, reflecting their own importance within the movement; they have seen themselves as having the overview *within* which other movements—e.g. women—could locate themselves. This assumption of superior understanding particularly among middle-class men is tied to a conception of politics as a duty, as an obligation to the less privileged, in which the need for a social revolution is grasped from the outside, but little attempt is made to locate their own needs within it. We are not against theories. But we feel that there is an urgent need for men to stop standing outside and above a historical process, but to locate ourselves as men and as individuals *within* it, and to make our generalizations and, indeed, our revolution, from a clear sense of who we are and where we come from.

The content of male politics on the left is inseparable from much of its style: authoritarianism, commandism, leadership fetishism—often undermining the genuine need for comradeship, for support, for learning and for mutual strength that brings people into political groups in the first place. Political work is often experienced as being more alienating than the bourgeois work we are trying to get away from. There are too many times we leave meetings let down, bored, blasted by rhetoric or arrogant assumptions of the mantle of correct politics, intellectually put down, 'responsible' for the women who didn't speak, and disgusted with ourselves for our own passivity in the face of the machine. The left is often not a place to feel good in.

Again, there are no easy answers. We recognize that it is sometimes easier to criticize than to develop new and different ways of struggling that reflect better the society we wish to make. Yet make those changes we must, and in doing so we open up possibilities of support for one another and of a strength in revolutionary politics that would previously have been hard to imagine. We know that we are not alone in considering these problems, that there are many men within and outside the organized left who share our convictions. We need to compare experiences, and to begin to discuss the role that an autonomous men's movement might or might not play in bringing these changes about. Despite its workerism, the left often fails to make contact with the way most people experience the world and its problems—it doesn't reach people's hearts! We'd like to feel we can help that happen.

The men's movement in this country has been largely hidden, largely silent about itself, though there are many men who have been deeply influenced and moved by women's struggles. We have been isolated, both locally and nationally, and uncertain about how and whether to speak out for ourselves. It has been hard to feel the validity of our autonomous struggle *as men*, when women's oppression is so clear, and so much a part of everyday reality.

Within the men's movement at the moment, there is a huge area of debate, a huge range of perspectives: about who we are, about how we can change, about the nature of patriarchy, and capitalism, about what kind of relationships we can have with the women's and gay movements, about how we go about getting the kind of society we want. We want to reflect some of that debate in this publication, and to open it out to a wider audience. As an editorial collective, we expect to have the final say about what goes into the journal. But we want others in the men's movement to send letters, reviews, articles, discussions, interviews, poems, stories, pictures and graphics, too.

We want the journal to express not only our own views but also some of the general discussions that go on in the men's movement as it grows and develops. Perhaps first and most important we want to make public some of the issues we have been dealing with in our men's groups, in a way that helps us understand our own changes, and that lends support to men who are more isolated: problems of jealousy and possessiveness; difficulties in relating to our kids; depression; isolation; feeling put down in our jobs; being left; dealing with unemployment; working in mixed groups; how to work in trade unions or political groups; living collectively; sexual fear; questions of our own health . . . it is incredible still how little there is for us to read about 'being a man', about our own experience, as it's actually lived. Our lives are as mythologized in the mass media as women's, and our true voice remains silent.

Yet it is no service to women or to ourselves to avoid the issues of who we are, how, as men, we fit into the society, what contributions we can make in the struggle against sexism, and in doing so, what we gain for ourselves. If there is any one sentence that can sum up our purpose in bringing out this magazine, then perhaps this is it.

We in this collective do not agree with men who say that the men's movement as such has no right to exist, except perhaps in a service role in relation to the women's movement. We see this attitude partly as another aspect of the guilt and self-denial we have been brought up with since birth. It also reflects contempt for other men. And in its extreme form it becomes another form of being dependent on women, allowing *them* to do all the work in making the changes that we need. Men can put feminism up on a pedestal just as they do to women in general. Feminism is idealized, which serves to distance and put it on one side rather than having to bring it into our lives through the changes it stimulates.

We also do not agree with the notion that the men's movement can eradicate sexism by sheer moral pressure and force of will. We do not think that the problem is one of psychology alone, nor do we believe that we can change overnight by forcing ourselves to adopt some kind of 'correct' behaviour. While this moral sense about equal relationships, against possessiveness, jealousy and authoritarianism has been important for us, in its extreme form it always seems to be self-defeating. Our learned behaviour runs very deep in us, from the way we hold our bodies to the details of the way we construct our lives. Part of our struggle is to know and to recognize these patterns in our bodies and in our daily interactions and to understand how these defences grew out of our life histories. There has been a lot of idealism and negative moralism in some of our attempts to create new ways of being men. These have often led to incredible pain and eventual disillusionment and abandonment of the struggle. We are not devils, nor are we saints.

We included in the first issue an article about NSU—the first, we hope, of a number that will relate to questions of men's health. Traditionally, as men, we are taught to use our bodies much as if they were machines directed by our heads. Only as we learn to respect our own bodies will we stop abusing the bodies of women. So much of our attitude to our bodies, our bravado in the face of danger, the way we drive ourselves in the face of tiredness does more service to our employers than to ourselves. The struggle—*our* struggle—for control of our health and our bodies is inseparable from our struggles in and against our work.

We can think of a hundred other articles we'd like to see: We'd like to do some interviews with men from different backgrounds and class about different aspects of their lives. We'd like to compare our experiences and problems of men learning to do 'women's work', single-parent fathers, for example, and look at their legal and financial situation in relation to the state. We'd like to look again at our own history as men—recent and more distant—through articles or reviews of historic material, to see if we can find a deeper sympathy with ourselves through our collective past, as well as looking at lessons for now. We'd like to look at some dimensions of ourselves that are usually 'out of bounds' for men on the left, but which the women's movement have been rediscovering; questions of our spirituality, our creativity, our power in positive rather than negative senses. We want to raise—carefully—the possibilities of active engagement, rather than passive support, in women's struggles with which we identify—for example, questions of day care provisions, contraception and abortion, housing, health and equal pay. And finally we want to look at ways in which men are changing themselves, and changing the society we live in. We want to draw strength from what one another are doing, both here and internationally. [. . .]

8 White Hero Black Beast: Racism, Sexism and the Mask of Masculinity

Paul Hoch

BRIEF INTRODUCTION

The continual celebration of a certain consciousness of manhood, of masculinity, of what it means to be male, has been rudely interrupted in the past fifteen years by the rise of movements against male chauvinism. The charge of chauvinism (or racism), reasonably enough, attempts to identify the 'oppressor' and separate him from the oppressed. But this is only the first step. To eliminate oppression, one has to destroy its social roots, and to do this one has to have at least some idea of the precise processes, interests, fears, repressions and institutional structures which create chauvinists (or racists). Without this, the implication might all too readily persist that the male is naturally a chauvinist (or the white a racist), and such a supposition if left unchallenged could actually fortify the oppression by uniting all males (or whites) on its side and providing them with an apparently biological basis for their behaviour. Indeed the assertion of inherent behavioural tendencies above and beyond the social institutions in which they occur is more commonly associated with those—usually considered conservatives—who believe men to be inherently bestial and in need of strict control. For liberationists to allow such notions into their own theories—even by omission—would be to fight the oppressor while conceding in advance the most important part of his theory of human nature. Even more, such a misstatement of the problem could be not only needlessly divisive, but actually counterproductive, for, accepted literally, it encourages a struggle against chauvinistic ideas (and their temporary embodiments) rather than against the concrete social and historical institutions which have produced them. At best this would perhaps do only for upper middle class women (or blacks), concerned not so much to overthrow these oppressive institutions as to seize a greater piece of the action. For others, it would be to misdirect their struggle into an attack on the immediate (and temporary) instruments of oppression, while leaving its causes intact.

Of course, even on the level of ideas, behind the particular manifest-ations of male (or racial) chauvinism lie particular social and histor-ical conceptions of what is meant by maleness (or race) and how they are to be measured—for example, in terms of a hierarchy of 'masculin-ity' (or racial dominance). There is indeed a close interrelation between the predominant Western conception of manhood and that of racial (and species) domination. The notion, originally from myth and fable, is that the summit of masculinity—the 'white hero'—achieves his manhood, first and foremost, by winning victory over the 'dark beast' (or over the barbarian beasts of other—in some sense, 'darker'—races, nations and social castes). So important is this particular understand-ing of manhood (and its collective embodiment, nationhood) that for many years the English gold sovereign carried the stirring imprint of what may be called the nation's founding myth—St George triumph-ing over the dragon. Very similar was the central Athenian myth of Theseus triumphing over the Minotaur, the celebration of Rome's victories over the barbarians, or—in our own time—the triumphs of cowboy over indian, hero over villain, civilisation over anarchy, West over East.

On the other hand, rather than analysing conceptions of masculin-ity alongside those of sexual (or racial) domination, sociologists have generally explained them in terms of the male's social and sexual roles, an approach most closely associated with the structural-functionalist paradigm of the Parsonian school. To see masculinity as a socially institutionalised role is in many ways superior to seeing it as merely a set of ideas, or behaviours, or biologically based orientations, because it attempts to relate it to a particular pattern of 'socialisation' (in which one learns what it is to be male) and to its functions within a particular institutional structure. On the other hand, though role and function have been related to structure, the question would still remain: what creates the structure? (and in whose interests?). More-over, since such models deal with roles and functions within a particu-lar social structure taken as a given (and usually as static), they have difficulty explaining how roles, functions, or structure have developed or how they could possibly be transcended. Such models therefore produce their fundamental hidden assumption of an unchanging structure by validating for all time the very roles and institutions they are supposedly assessing. In addition, the concept of sex role has usually been distorted further by being applied indiscriminately to all members of a particular sex, without regard for their separate places within the occupational and social limits on the amount of competitveness in their masculine ideal. For all of these reasons, the concept of sex role must be expanded to include both a historical and a social class dimension of the kind we attempt to provide here. [. . .]

Along with its social class dimensions, a concept such as masculinity—perhaps even more obviously than the related conceptions of nationhood, race and political ideology—has important psychological dimensions. An individual's ideas of masculinity—as well as his idea of *his* masculinity—would involve far more than his own (or his social class's) economic interest or ideology; it would involve—in ways by no means even fully a part of his consciousness—his whole psychology, including those aspects of his character that have arisen as a defence against all he has had to repress. Such a character structure would, in turn, be closely conditioned by his family history and, more generally, by the form and functioning of the family structures appropriate to his particular social class during any given historical period. Such family structures are a bridge between social classes and their predominant individual psychologies. The analysis of a concept such as masculinity which has both social and psychological dimensions requires, therefore, the tools of both socio-historical and psychological analysis (as well as considerable knowledge of the changing family structures of the particular social classes concerned). Thus the present work is almost inevitably situated in the context of the current debate about the extent to which such apparently different, and often mutually hostile, approaches as the historical materialism of Marx and the psychological materialism of Freud can be validly combined. Indeed the present project, for better or worse, provides a model for the combined insights of these two by no means clearly complementary approaches. On the other hand, the assumption that the main traditions of these two approaches *can be made* complementary requires detailed justification, and this question is taken up in the Epilogue.

To the extent that the polarisation into practitioners of 'masculine' and 'femine' sex roles has manifested itself on the political left as a split between predominantly politically oriented and male (or at least male-led) *socialists* and predominantly personalistically oriented female *feminists*, the attempt to understand and transcend these roles is of considerable importance in healing the split. It is also crucial if one is going to bridge the related gaps between the 'political' and the 'personal', 'outer' and 'inner', 'public' and 'private', 'political economy' and 'psychology', 'reason' (understood as masculine) with 'emotion' (understood as feminine), 'science' and 'art', 'technology' and 'nature'. It is in this more general sense that the problem has its most crucial ramifications. For it is becoming clearer every year that unless we can somehow reconcile the masculine emphasis on domination that permeates our science and technology with the demands of nature (including our own natures), we will at best rapidly degenerate into a cancer and birth defect ridden species unable to exist within nature.

PART I THE CULT OF MASCULINITY—WHAT MANHOOD IS AND ISN'T

If Rome was an empire maintained by diverting its plebeian population with brutal gladiator matches and circuses, our own civilisation employs the gladiators of professional sports, elections, TV cop shows, film battles between cowboys and indians, and mass entertainment and consumption industries fuelled by the belief that status may be achieved through the ever larger consumption of those products and spectacles declared to be most 'masculine' and 'feminine'. The media's constant re-enactment of the rites of masculine passage—whether in work, war, sex, sport, or social one-upmanship—has become the main staple of entertainment, the main scenario for erotic fantasy, the dominant social metaphor for understanding international politics (a struggle for collective manhood between our heroes and the enemy), the performance of our political leaders (daily and incessantly evaluated in terms of their 'strength' and manly 'credibility'), the accumulation of property or sexual partners (tests of individual prowess), or even the all-consuming emphasis that men place on saving 'face' lest we—or our country—be considered 'impotent'. Closely linked to the related devotionals of muscular nationalism, racial chauvinism and sexual status through consumerism, the quest for individual (or collective) manhood has eclipsed Christianity as an ontology for directing our activity and orienting it toward a coherent, ultimate goal.

In recent decades the number and variety of pressures on men to 'prove themselves' as men have become particularly great and particularly inconsistent. On the one hand, our whole social apparatus for buying and selling incessantly trumpets the commodities it claims are the *sine qua non* of the masculinity required for the 'playboy' life of leisure and conspicuous sexual consumption. On the other hand, our production system still insists that men orient to the more traditional masculinity of work, family, discipline and control. Without doubt, our evolving understandings of masculinity seem to flow out of our systems of production and consumption, but only in a fairly uneven, and almost self-contradictory way which increasingly gives rise to much individual turmoil. [. . .]

....

CHAPTER 3 MASCULINITY AS INTERRACIAL COMPETITION FOR WOMEN?

....

The male as hero and beast

The conquest of manhood by the victory of the white godlike hero over the bestial villain in a life or death struggle for possession of what Robert Graves has called 'The White Goddess' is, according to him, at the heart of almost all Western myth, poetry and literature. 'All true poetry', he writes in *The White Goddess*, 'celebrates some incident or other of this ancient story; and the three main characters are so much a part of our racial legacy that they also assert themselves in dreams and paranoid visions.' H. Rider Haggard, the author of the novel *She*, and the psychoanalyst Carl Gustav Jung, likewise found the hero's quest for the eternal feminine white goddess to be at the centre of our most secret desires. The archetypal figure of the threatening super-sensual dark villain or black beast, though less clear cut, is also as old as the class societies of Western civilisation, perhaps as old as the Western family itself. Graves calls him the hero's 'twin, his second self, his weird'. He appears first in such figures as the Egyptian god of darkness and evil, Set, arch-rival of the god of light, Osiris; for the white goddess, Isis (a theme recently alluded to in the popular science fiction film *Star Wars*). He appears again and again in Greek mythology as the hero's protagonist, often being depicted as a sex crazed half-man-half-beast satyr or centaur—their archetypal myths being the fabled victories of manly Hercules over the licentious centaurs, Theseus over the Minotaur, and Perseus over the dark sea monster that menaced the fair Princess Andromeda. The early Danes considered the summit of manly achievement to be the triumph of their white hero, Beowulf, over the dark monster, Grendel; and their Anglo-Saxon descendents celebrated the famous victory of St George over the dragon. The theme was further developed in more celestial form, in the epic struggle of an all-but-chaste God and a super-sensual Devil that dominated medieval Christian theology. In the era of the witch hunts the Devil was often depicted as a lascivious black male with cloven hoofs, a tail, and a huge penis capable of super-masculine exertion—an archetypal leering 'black beast from below'. Thus, in a white civilisation which considers many forms of sexuality to be immoral— and consigns them to the dark dungeons of the unconscious—the 'devil', dark villain or black beast becomes the receptacle of all the tabooed desires, therby embodying all the forbidden possibilities for ultimate sexual fulfilment and becoming the very apotheosis of masculine potency. [. . .]

[. . .] Almost by definition, the villain is threatening and immoral— a representative of the *dark, bestial* forces of lust and perdition, an embodiment of the *lower* and *sexual*, as against the higher and spiritual ties of the hero's conscience. The very polarisation of villain from hero implies one between sexual and spiritual; between 'lower' and 'higher' moralities, as well as the corresponding elements of the psyche and of society. (Even the word *villain* stems from the earlier *villein* which in medieval times was used to describe the lowest class of society.) The conflict between hero and beast becomes a struggle between two understandings of manhood: human versus animal, white versus black, spiritual versus carnal, soul versus flesh, higher versus lower, noble versus base. These all correspond to the basic moral dichotomy that was assumed in order to provide legitimacy for the first hierarchical societies: the superior morality and manhood of 'civilised' and 'noble' upper class white heroes (who monopolise the functions of the soul and the mind) in contrast with 'barbaric' and 'base' lower class villains (consigned to the merely animal realms of the carnal and the body). Similar dichotomies of heroes versus villains, good versus evil and light versus dark were invoked to justify the struggle of Christian against infidel at the time of the Crusades; and, later, of colonisers against natives, cowboys against indians, Texans against Mexicans, and Yanks against communists in Vietnam. A similar clash between the white heroes of the West and the dark, inscrutable villains of the East has long been the scarcely hidden background of such popular culture favourites as the evil *Dr Fu Manchu, Terry and the*

Pirates and almost every one of the novels of Ian Fleming, (where the villains are invariably foreign and non-Aryan i.e. the oriental *Dr No*; the black 'Mr Big' of *Live and Let Die*; the Jews, Jewish prototypes, or those who might merely 'have some Jewish blood' in them like Sol Horowitz of *The Spy Who Loved Me*, Herr Ziffer of *Casino Royale*, and of course Goldfinger, not to mention the international conspiracy elder, Blofeld).

The first attempt to identify the conquest of the 'beast' with the control of desires buried deep *within* the Western psyche was made not by Freud but by Plato. He noted in Book IX of his *Republic* that a 'lawless, wild Beast' lurks 'in all of us, even in good men', and 'peers out in sleep', when the 'reasoning and human and ruling power' is off guard. [. . .] The quest for manhood represented by the battle between hero and beast is, thus, exactly paralleled by a similar struggle between the 'moral' and 'immoral' parts of thc civilised psyche, the 'heroic' forces of light (the 'ruling powers' of conscience) against the 'bestial' forces of darkness (which inhabit the depths of the Freudian unconscious). Thus the almost stereotypical victories of white heros over dark villains that fill up almost all our popular fiction, film and TV, seem to reinforce the control of the 'higher' over the 'lower' parts of the psyche, and of the corresponding social forces in society, the control of rulers over ruled. The need for the ruling powers of white Christian civilisation to defend against the dark, untamed and revolutionary plebeian *brute* dominated the writings of political conservatives from Ancient Rome to Edmund Burke, culminating more recently in the hysterical fears of 'socialist barbarism' expressed by people like Winston Churchill, Margaret Thatcher and Ronald Reagan. Indeed the very concept of *civilisation*[1] was defined in terms of the achievement—by men of a particular class and race—of a level of culture, civility and order which was most sharply defined by contrast with its opposite—*barbarism*—the inherently disorderly and sexually rapacious level of villains, brutes and beasts. The breakdown of law and order, it was repeatedly argued, would result in an upsurge of lust, raping, brutality and villainy of all kinds—man would sink down to the level of a beast. The call for upper caste white heroes to prove their manhood by exerting 'civilisation' over the 'dark brutes' of all the subordinate classes and castes was thus a key rationale for the maintenance of a class stratified society at home, and for the conquest and control of the 'darker' peoples of Africa, Asia and the Americas. It thereby became one of the firmest supports for class elitism, colonialism, slavery and all succeeding doctrines of social and racial supremacy. Such a demand implicitly linked the fight for a particular kind of hierarchical order in society, with a struggle to maintain a similarly hierarchical order within the psyche. The achievement of manhood by the conquest of hero over beast became the allegory for the struggle of civilisation against barbarism, white Europe against the dark continent of Africa, West against East—and of the civilised consciousness over the dark, bestial sexual forces in its unconscious.

Defence of the white goddess

The notion of interracial conquest as an ultimate test of heroic masculinity was quite visible in late nineteenth century assertions that the struggle between white Europe and dark Africa represented only an inevitable competition between the races, male survival of the 'fittest'. In such a struggle the most shattering (though rarely admitted) assertion of virility often lay in taking control of the other group's females—most obviously in the institution of slavery—and at all costs excluding them from access to one's own. Defence of manhood demanded, above all, the defence of the white goddesses of civilisation against the dark, sex-crazed barbarians at the gates, and such fears provided the most explosive fuel for interracial hatreds, lynching and war. [. . .] The black as super-stud. On the loose. After our women. [. . .]

Blacks as beasts?

[. . .] Indeed the upper classes of European and American societies have always considered their white goddesses to be in perpetual danger from the super-masculine lusts of lower class barbarians and villains of all kinds, both at home and abroad. In this sense, the defence of Christian virtue (from this viewpoint considered female) against atheistic communist barbarism, international terrorism or anarchy (sometimes depicted as a jungle of drooling, ape-like males) is a projection of the white goddess–black beast theme on to the international stage. Indeed if we examine the history of Western class stratified societies we notice a complete continuity in the alleged *sexual threat* posed by barbarians and pagans outside the Roman Empire (and the disorderly rabble and rebellious slaves within); heathens and infidels outside medieval Christendom (and villeins, peasant rebels and heretics within—not to mention those lustful devils, satyrs, incubi and the like); fifteenth and sixteenth century Anabaptists; seventeenth century Levellers and Ranters; eighteenth century Jacobins; nineteenth century socialists and twentieth century communists. ([. . .] former American Secretary of State Dean Rusk has declared that he saw the fight against communists in Vietnam as the modern version of the stand of the Venetian Knights against the 'hordes of Mohammedans'.[2]) Likewise, there was assumed to be a definite sexual threat from sturdy beggars, tramps, vagabonds, servants, rogues, immigrants—in short, from 'outsider', 'foreign', 'rebellious' and 'lower' social orders and castes of all kinds. The implication was that all those unfitted by birth or colour or political ideology to be part of the dominant group were clearly inferior within the moral terms then available, That is to say, they were deemed less pure, less clean, less white, less 'manly' in the 'white heroic' sense of the term.

What seems to be at stake in all this is the attribution of certain dark and unclean, even animalistic, practices—especially sexual practices (in the Middle Ages the most popular variant was sodomy)—to rebellious, outsider or subordinate groups, thus justifying (according to the prevailing sexual ethic) their repression. In a psychological sense we could say that in societies where sex has been regarded as suspect, a sexual outsider (or scapegoat) caste was needed on to which the men of the more established groups could *project* their own forbidden sexual desires, and through which they could legitimate their own superior social position. To be sure, to the extent that the men of a particular immigrant group began to advance up the social class structure, their use as this kind of sexual scapegoat could, and did, decline. On the other hand, *someone* had to serve as the source of the repressed desires, and the men of the lower castes were (and are) the obvious targets. These men therefore took on the characteristics of those dark elements of the civilised unconscious which the more respectable considered to be in need of careful control, regulation or—if they got out of 'their place'—of outright repression. Oddly enough, such men thereby became models, of both super-masculine potency and absolute debasement.

[*Sections on 'The Beast as Embodiment of Repressed Sexuality', 'The Super-Masculine Villain in Pornography', and 'Beauty and the Beast' were dropped.*]

CHAPTER 4 MASCULINITY AS A DEFENCE AGAINST IMPOTENCE?

Sexuality as trial and performance

Absolutely the worst thing a man can be is impotent. Indeed to be in this condition is regarded—even by oneself—as being something less than a man. [. . .]

Indeed the fear of being labelled impotent has been a factor, not only whipping men along to 'prove' themselves in the bedroom, but continuously to 'demonstrate' their manliness in every area of life. For many men it is as if the present form of society has become a sort of obstacle course, an endless series of existential tests in which the contestants must prove their potency by beating back all rivals, getting up and over all hurdles, keeping absolutely cool, not losing face, showing no signs of weakness. The very language with which we describe social life often betrays this fear of not making it, losing it, failing. Thus we talk about *getting up* for the day's endeavours, making a conquest, the need to have balls. 'It's what's up front that counts' declares one cigarette commercial. 'If you haven't got it there, you haven't got it.' You must keep at it, stick to it, keep plugging, hang on in there. There are numerous celebrations for the man of super bedroom potency. He is called stud, stallion, bull, beef, cock, sword, blade, stickman, a walking phallus. Yet even these apparently complimentary terms have for the most part either an animalistic or a mechanistic connotation— almost as if we believed that the sexual penetration of bodies was an indulgence best left to animals and machine parts. On the other hand, there is not even a word available in our language to describe an impotent man—the whole subject is so feared that a noun that might acknowledge the malefactor is literally repressed. The closest we can come to it is to call him a dud, failure, beat, nurd, a nothing. Of course *dud* means literally 'a bomb which failed to go off'. Thus, here as elsewhere, the notion of sexuality as a kind of warfare is incorporated into the very language used to describe it. There are two key questions. Warfare against whom? And in defence of what?

The simple answer—and the one given by Norman Mailer—is warfare in defence of one's manhood, which is being attacked by the competition of all other men and, especially, the dreaded insinuations of certain women (particularly one's unsatisfied lovers). These are

especially damaging—almost damning—within the context of expectations of a bedroom masculinity in which the male is defined as the
only active performer, the hard working *producer* of the passive female
consumer's satisfaction, and the one who takes the praise or blame for
the entire performance. It is no accident that the active woman is
always accused of being out to 'castrate' men, 'cut them down to size',
subvert their 'power'. Common to almost all patriarchal cultures is,
likewise, the notion of the castrating *vagina dentata*, the female genital
with teeth that threatens total emasculation. Within the context of
assumptions in which they are expressed, there can indeed be some
justification for these male fears. As long as patriarchal cultures insist
on imposing on their men a competition for masculinity based in
large part on a one sided sexual performance, any given contender
can be treacherously undermined by a slip of his potency, or even by
a rebellious female's insinuation that such was the case. As long as
women are relatively powerless in other areas of such societies, there
will certainly be some who will use this way of redressing the balance.
(Of course most women are terrified of occasions of male impotence,
see them as a slight of their own femininity and are quite prepared to
fake orgasm as a way of avoiding any offence to the sensitive male ego.)
The tensions of this situation go a long way towards explaining why
the men of today almost always exhibit at least a subconscious hatred
of women who, by the final verdict of *their* orgasms, have the power to
confirm or deny what men understand to be their most important test
of manhood. This fear and hatred of women [. . .] often lead to the
male fantasy of rape, both as a way of getting back at women, and
because debasement of the woman to a mere body seeks to exclude her
from the final decision about one's manhood—and thus seems to
offer an alternative to the performance anxieties associated with
impotence.

The pressure to perform is also seen in the anxious attention given
to the performing 'apparatus' and the difficulties of 'getting it into
gear'. Under the influence of a consumer society whose motto is 'bigger is better', the men of today have been encouraged to agonise about
whether their's 'measures up'. Anxiety on this subject is still such that,
until recently, the organs were more or less banned from public view.
Even at the outer limits of pornography a male erection is still taboo.
In contrast to the padded bras that are supposed to push the female
breast into public prominence, the penis remains, for the most part,
carefully and discreetly hidden. The anxieties about it are, nevertheless,
sharply visible in page after page of advertisements in porn mags for

expensive ointments, lotions, salves, powders, weights, pulleys and so forth which will 'make it grow'. At least that is the claim. (Similar paraphernalia is available for the 'underdeveloped' female breast.) Since many of these 'treatments' are extremely painful, as well as completely useless—and often dangerous—the fact that their promoters still have a market is eloquent testimony to the atmosphere of terror that surrounds the whole subject. It indicates as nothing else how far the concerns with status and power have penetrated into our most private functions.

Many men even speak of their penis as if it were not a part of the body, but a distinct personality apart. Often, 'it' is even given a name (Peter). The fact that Peter, but not me, does the copulating, of course, removes me from any responsibility. He, not me, is the animalistic one, the savage, the avenger. He represents mankind in its most carnal aspect—the beast below. The split that Christian and Platonic philosophy makes between man's 'higher' *spiritual* and 'lower' *carnal* functions, between mind and body, is thus reproduced in a further split between the 'higher' and 'lower' parts of the body, between the psyche and the penis. The psyche just thinks, the penis acts. But is it really so simple? What about when something goes wrong?

The dread of woman

[. . .] A common technique by which most men in our society manage to 'get through' the sex act, avoid impotence, and keep the feminine 'other' within the unconscious under control, seems to be creating in their minds the fantasy of dominating or debasing some woman (not necessarily the one being made love to), and thus through debasement forcing the forbidden mother into the background (or pushing her back down into the unconscious). This is a peculiar process that seems to duplicate in fantasy the process by which the repressing part of the psyche 'dominates' the repressed elements within the unconscious. But in dominating this feminine 'other' we are only reproducing (and reinforcing) our own domination—the domination of the repressed aspects of our own sexuality. In this sense a failure to dominate the partner (or carry through the *fantasy* of domination) often reduces potency and carries with it the risk of impotence. [. . .] Thus, the male of our society seems to differentiate quite radically between the woman-as-body (who is dominated and *fucked*) and the woman-as-pure-spirit (who is idealized and brought home to mother), the playmate and the wife, the whore and the virgin, lust and love, 'making love' and 'being in love', body and mind. [. . .] In this way, the masculine role in successful sexual intercourse becomes one—whether in fact or fantasy—of conceiving of one's partner as the sort of mere body or object ('cunt') with whom it is permissible to *fuck*. Failure to do so runs the risk of identifying her with the forbidden mother and thus bringing into consciousness all those neurotic anxieties that produce impotence. The fantasy of rape and domination becomes an alternative to the actual possibility of impotence; the two are extremely close to one another, and may be considered as two sides of the same coin of split sexuality and sexual repression. The *repressing* masculinity and aggression-directed-outwards of the rape fantasy is merely the *repressed* masculinity and aggression-directed-inwards caused by the sexual repression suffered in childhood.

[*A section on 'The Rape Fantasy Explained' was dropped.*]

Fucking as conquest . . . of the woman within

Another commonly employed alternative to even the suspicion of impotence is the exaggerated pose of *machismo* among the various virility cults. Any irreverent female can be silenced—if not in actuality, then at least in fantasy—by the 'threat of a good fuck'. (This, of course, only holds within the context of a socially imposed sexual repression which makes fucking *threatening*.) [. . .] The equation of the 'existential tests' of a bedroom masculinity with existence itself has a certain tautological truth to it *only* within the ideological conception which equates existence with 'manhood'—and, in particular, with sexual potency and power. Nevertheless, to fail at erection is *not*, actually, to cease to exist in material space. Nor is it to physically lose one's manhood in the sense of being castrated (although, within the context of the prevailing social pressures, it can well lead in individual cases to a *psychic* castration of chronic impotence). In what sense, then, can it be regarded conceivably as a loss of identity, even self? Apparently, within the prevailing ideology of selfhood, the self—particularly the male self—is defined by its masculine 'presence' and 'force': its opposition to, and competition with, every similar individual male self for domination over nature, other men, and particularly over women. So, if a given contender fails to preserve his reputation, he will 'lose face' ('credibility'), thus exposing his 'territory' (or women) to 'invasion', after which—since he will *have* nothing—he will *be* 'a nothing'. (Note especially: *being* is defined as *having*, particularly having control over women.) But the woman who has mainly to be controlled is none other than the feminine other within the unconscious, for her eruption (revolution) which could actually threaten the existence of the male's mutilated conscious self. The internal battle to keep 'her' under control is then *displaced* outwards and transformed into an orientation towards domination and control generally, particularly towards a domination over nature conceived of as a woman i.e. 'mother nature'. (Conversely, the extreme importance given to the mother, and the repression of feminine elements into a feminised unconscious, represents an *internalisation* by the psyche of the requirements of a particular *historically-based* political economy and family structure.) The mechanism by which this displacement occurs is, of course, the well-known one in which the conscious self mistakes its interface with the unconscious for its interface with the external world. In this sense, the men of Western societies only *seem* to be in struggle with each other to dominate and possess the world. In the deepest recesses of their psyches, what they are really striving to control are the powerful repressed forces within their own unconscious—their own repressed sexuality. This is also the reason why the threatening 'outsides' against whom men do battle almost always have a threatening sexual aspect. By a further mechanism of displacement and denial, the orientation toward domination, especially sexual domination, is then projected on to the outsiders: thus, it is not 'me' who is trying to dominate 'her' (ultimately, the 'feminine other' in the unconscious); it is 'they' who are trying to dominate 'me' and 'mine'. Therefore 'we' (the collectivity of repressing *me's* like myself) must band together to oppose 'them'. By defending the nation, the nation's way of life, the system of law and order (especially against 'revolution'), we defend our own repression.

The root of the problem, at least on the family level, is the exclusive role our society assigns to the mother in the care and emotional nurturing of her children. The possessiveness with which this all-important mother figure is regarded then lays the basis for the emphasis on *possession* that dominates our society, and also for the importance—even idolization—that the men of our society often give to their quests for a suitable wife-mother, but also to the unconscious dread in which this figure (and the respected, sexually judgemental, lovers who are her successors) are often held. To the extent that desire for her is repressed, her qualities will be unconsciously projected outward, to one degree or another, on to other women. Therefore, the most fulfilling sexual object—in the sense of being able to produce a fusion of tenderness and sexual desire—is a woman who is sufficiently like the ideal of mother to be loved, yet not so close as to bring to mind the neurotic anxieties that surround her and which might lead to impotence. Indeed, ironically, the more the woman is loved, the more she is to be feared. This opposition between love and anxiety— characterised by strong guilt at the sexual 'debasement' of the woman one loves—undoubtedly causes a significant loss from full potency (i.e. from a full release of sexual tension during intercourse). [. . .]

The usefulness of such cravings to a society based on ever greater excesses or production and consumption seems clear. Being sexually unsatisfied and—under these conditions—unsatisfiable such men have little defence against their sexual manipulation by advertisers who tell them that various consumer products will make them more 'masculine' (and hence more sexually desirable to the partners they are so desperately in search of). Likewise, the sexual fulfillment promised at the end of the rainbow is used as the ultimate carrot to keep men in competition in war and in production. This partial impotence syndrome has thus enabled societies with our form of family structure to divert a greater and greater amount of what would otherwise be libidinal energy into acquisitive competition for masculinity in work, warfare and consumption.

In the final analysis, manly potency is threatened not by the woman who seems to be man's immediate judge and opponent but by those social institutions, like the sexually repressive nuclear family, that limit the male child's access to other adults and other children, forcing him into conflict with his father for the love of the only remaining love object (his mother). More generally, it is threatened by all those restrictive social institutions that limit the male's exercise of potency and creativity in his work, leisure and everyday life, especially all those institutions of capitalist production and consumption that require the stimulus of diverted sexual energies to enforce their authority and promote this form of economy.

Notes

1. R. Williams, *Keywords* (London: Fontana, 1976), p. 48.
2. *The Guardian Weekly*, 12 March 1978, p. 9.

Shop Floor Culture, Masculinity and the Wage Form

Paul Willis*

The noise on our line is what drives you almost mad. You can never really get used to it, and I have been there ten years (and in another factory ten years before that). It would drive you mad, if you let it. Imagine nine men beating hammers and mallets on steel. If there were some sort of rhythm to it, it wouldn't be so bad.

Bryan Slater, a line worker[1]

Excruciating noise is probably the most unpleasant sensual concomitant of industrial work. Its invocation serves to remind, even those who pride themselves on their penetration of the consumer-egalitarian-liberal mythology, that not only are commodities produced under specific and determinate social conditions, but also that they are produced under specific and determinate *experiential* conditions. What is the human meaning and actual experience that lies behind our easy use of cars, cosmetics, clothes and buildings? What degree of frenzy, activity, boredom and suffering has been objectified into the thousand articles on glamorous display in the department store? Is the meaning and pleasure of these things as they are consumed any more important than the meaning of the drudge of their production? It is often forgotten that the main reality for most of the people, for most of the time, is work and the sound of work—the grind of production, not the purr of consumption, is the commonest mark of our industrial culture. [. . .]

There is then no question, for me, of counterposing the 'cultural' with the 'productive' or the 'real' as if the former had no actual constitutive role in the basic social relations which govern the form of our society. I am arguing against a *trivialization* of the notion of culture, of working-class culture and especially of its central domain: cultural relations/struggles/forms at the point of production. Culture is not

---

* Reprinted with permission of Paul Willis.

simply a *response* to imposition which blinds or blunts a 'proper' understanding, nor is it merely a compensation, an adjustment to defeat—these are essentially mechanized, reactive, models. Cultural forms occupy precisely those same spaces and human potentialities which are fought over by capital to continue valorization and capital accumulation. There are different logics possible in the direct experience of production than are posed in the capital relation itself, for itself. Merely because capital would like to treat workers as robots does not mean they are robots. The direct experiences of production are worked through and over in the praxis of different cultural discourses. To be sure, these discourses do not arise purely on the basis of production, and many of their important contents and inner relationships arise from or in articulation with external forces and institutions: the family, state, labour organizations, etc. It is also clear that in this society, for the moment, the material consequences of these cultural forms are for continued production in the capitalist mode. But none of this should blind us to the complexities, struggles and tensions on the shop floor even if they do not always call their name in a way that we can recognize. There are forms of praxis arising from definite human agency at the site of production which, in the very same moment, provide the conditions for capitalist relations, and also partially penetrate and variably challenge those relationships.

It is also specifically working-class cultural forces from the place of production that help to mould the whole of the class culture. Production is not simply the engine house of the social totality producing, somehow, its 'effects' elsewhere on the social plane. Production, and its relations, is social and cultural to its very roots, to its very surface. It is the privileged site and generator of working-class culture both because of its massive presence and also because the struggle there *fixes*, organizes in a particular combination, those discourses and external influences which play over the place of work—helping to develop them in a particular way, clinching certain features, even when appearing manifestly outside of production. Work is where the demands of capital must be met but from the resources not simply of potential *abstract* labour but from concrete, cultural forms of labour power. Whatever 'free' play there is in cultural forms articulates always around this most central point of reference. Non-work supplies many of the categories and meanings for work but it can only be understood in relation to work and is finally shaped by it. The following data, unless noted to the contrary, was collected in a town which is part of a large Midland's conurbation in the course of an SSRC-supported research project of 'The transition from school to work' between 1973 and 1975.[2] This article refers to male cultures of work.

The first thing to say about the working-class culture of the workplace is that it exists in hard conditions set by others. It is also worth remembering that for all the talk of 'massive' wage settlements in the face of union 'blackmail' since the war, the income of wage earners, as a proportion of GNP, has not changed in the last fifty years.

The system of capitalism still means essentially, despite its contemporary 'human face', that labour is bought, detached from the individual, and directed towards the production of commodities for the profit of others. Labour is dispossessed from its owners. This labour is directed, emphatically, not for the satisfaction of its providers, but for the profit of its new owners. If this requires work in inhuman and meaningless circumstances, then, there is nothing in the logic of capitalism to prevent this. Writing in a completely different context, and addressing a completely different problem, G.C. Matthews,[3] claims that fully 79 percent of the ESN (educationally sub-normal) could be placed in *normal* employment, since such employment requires only a mental and emotional age of twelve. Now while one may welcome this news on behalf of the ESN, what are its implications for the other 95 percent—the regular incumbents of these jobs? It must be that they are doing work which twelve-year-olds could do.

The main effect of this dispossession is most obvious in the case of boring, repetitive, mindless jobs—a numbing sense of boredom and meaninglessness: sheer unhappiness, if you like. This is most dramatically shown up by the many working-class accounts of how *time* drags at work. Time and the task to be done become utterly divorced. A job is undertaken not out of interest, but merely because one's *bought* labour is directed there. Without an intrinsic interest in the job, then, the full focus of the detached consciousness is thrown on to the passing of time. This focus *itself*, to say nothing of the actual drudgery of the job, slows time down to a painful existential drag. [. . .]

Although distinctions must be made for region and occupation, the absolutely central thing about the working-class culture of the shop floor is, however, that, despite the dispossession, despite the bad conditions, despite the external directions, despite the subjective ravages, people do look for meaning, they do impose frameworks, they do seek enjoyment in activity, they do exercise their abilities. They repossess, symbolically and really, aspects of their experience and capacities. They do, paradoxically, thread through the dead experience of work a living culture which isn't simply a reflex of defeat. This culture is not the human remains of a mechanical depredation, but a positive transformation of experience and a celebration of shared values in symbols, artefacts and objects. It allows people to recognize and even to develop themselves. For this working-class culture of work is not simply a foam padding, a rubber layer between humans and unpleasantness. It is an appropriation in its own right, an exercise of skill, a motion, an activity applied towards an end. It has this specifically human characteristic, even in conditions of hardship and oppression.

What are the elements of this culture? In the first place there is the sheer mental and physical bravery of surviving in hostile conditions, and doing difficult work on intractable materials. It is easy to romanticize this element, of course, and in one way it is simply charting the degree of brutality a heavy work situation can inflict. But in another way it is the first and specifically human response—the holding of an apparently endless and threatening set of demands by sheer strength and brute skill. Already in this there is a stature and self-respect, a human stake on the table against the relentless pressure of work to be done. This is the vital precondition of more developed cultural forms and accomplishes the basic and primitive humanization of a situation: it marks a kind of limit of dispossession. It halts the rout of human meaning and takes a kind of control so that more specifically creative acts can follow. This primitivist base of work experience is also the material for a crude pride and, as will be developed much more fully later, for the mythology of *masculine* reputation—to be strong and to be known for it. Here is a retired steelman describing the furnaces in a steel-making area of the west of Scotland as they were before World War II:

They were the cold, metal, hand-charging sort and they catered for strong men, only very strong men. About one steel worker in every ten could stand up to them successfully, which was one reason why the furnacemen were looked up to in the world of heavy industry. That they got the biggest pay packets was another reason. They also had the biggest thirsts and that too was a prideful possession in that part of the world. {. . .} a legend grew up about the steel smelters. {. . .} The whole district and for miles beyond it was a hotbed of steel works, iron puddling works and coal mines. It was a place given over to the worship of strength and durability. Indeed it needed strength to look at it, and durability to live in it.[4]

In a much less articulate way, but for that perhaps more convincing, [*another*] extract shows the same elemental self-esteem in the doing of a hard job well. It also shows that in some respects the hard environment can become the most natural environment. There is also the grudging recognition of the profound charge this kind of acclimatization can make on a normal social life, *even at the same time* that it is one of the major ways in which the hostile work environment is made habitable. [. . .]

It may be objected that the pattern of industrial work has changed: there are no rough jobs today. Besides, it can certainly be argued that there is nothing heroic about the elemental qualities of strength and pride. They are not only made anachronistic by today's technology, but are insulting, oppressive and right at the poisonous heart of male chauvinism and archaic machismo.

Be that as it may be, two things are clear. Rough, unpleasant, demanding jobs *do* still exist in considerable numbers. A whole range of jobs from building work, to furnace work to deep-sea fishing still involve a primitive confrontation with exacting physical tasks. Secondly, the basic attitudes and values developed in such jobs are still very important in the general working-class culture, and particularly the culture of the shop floor; this importance is vastly out of proportion to the number of people actually involved in such heavy work. Even in so-called light industries, or in highly mechanized factories with perhaps mixed sex work-forces, where the awkwardness of the physical task has long since been reduced, the metaphoric figures of strength and bravery *worked through* masculinity and reputation still move beneath the more varied, visible forms of work-place culture.

Let us go on from this general minimum proposition to look at some of the more specific and developed human patterns of the workplace. One of the marks of the lived and contemporary culture of the shop floor is a development of this half-mythical primitive confrontation with *the task*. It is a familiarity and experiential sense of control of technology, or at least a sharing of its power. At the most positive and extreme this can be not merely a meeting of demands, but a strange kind of celebration. Here is a description from a toolmaker of his first day at work.[5] It inverts the usual middle-class account of the dark satanic mill:

On every piece of open ground lay metal shapes; some mere bars and sheets straight from the steelworks: others gigantic welded constructs covered in a deep brown rust . . . Then I entered the great main workshops. Each chamber, or aisle as they were called, was about 150 feet across and anything between 500 and 700 hundred yards long. Several of these great vulcan halls lay parallel to each other {. . .} Over-head rolled the girded cranes capable of carrying weights of more than two hundred tons {. . .} one passed over my head. {. . .}

My startled attitude to the crane's passage amused the men at work {. . .} a series of catcalls followed my passage down the aisle. Mostly the shouts were good-natured advice to get out of the plant while I had the youth to do so. Such advice never even penetrated my outer consciousness, for how could anyone abhor this great masculine domain with its endless overtones of power and violence?

Of course this is a special case of a skilled, elitist view of work. Changes in the labour process are no doubt squeezing out the space for such views.[6] But we should not underestimate the surviving degree to which mechanical, sensuous and concrete *familiarity* with the tools of production (despite the dispossession of labour) mediates the demands of the labour process, allowing, for instance, the possibility of an easy and confident mobility which at least brings alleviating changes in the *form* of particular work experience if not in its deep structures.

Even, or perhaps especially, among the formally 'un/semi/skilled' there is a process of obtaining skills as if by osmosis from the technical environment. There is a profound air of competence in the culture of the shop floor, a competence which always exists prior to the particular situation. It is not always based on strict ability, but mixed in with cheek and confidence; it is enough to pull a worker through any number of jobs and problems. [*One*] man [*who talked*] about his industrial career [. . .] gives [. . .] a glimpse of the real paths beaten between different jobs and occupations: the paths, incidentally, which make it sensible to speak of the working class not only as an abstract group of those who share similar interest, but as at least something of a self-experienced organic whole with real and used inner connections. [. . .]

In one sense this can be seen as a way of regaining *some* control over one's labour power and its disposition. This leads us to another important element in shop-floor culture: the massive attempt to gain informal control of the work process. Limitation of output or 'systematic soldiering' and 'gold bricking' have been observed from the particular perspective of management from Taylor onwards, but there is evidence now of a more concerted—though still informal—attempt to gain control. In many plants the men, themselves, to all intents and purposes actually control at least manning and the speed of production. Of course the downward limit for this possibility is set by the production of the costs of subsistence of the worker. If control is exerted on production it is indeed a control of minima as well as of maxima. Nevertheless the exertion towards *control* should not be minimized. Here is a man on track production of car engines:

Actually the foreman, the gaffer, don't run the place, the men run the place. See, I mean you get one of the chaps says, 'Allright, you'm on so and so today.' You can't argue with him. The gaffer don't give you the job, the men on the track give you the job, they swop each other about, tek it in turns. Ah, but I mean the job's done. If the gaffer had gi'd you the job you would . . . They tried to do it one morning, gi'd a chap a job you know, but he'd been on it, you know, I think he'd been on all week, and they just downed tools. {. . .} There's four hard jobs on the track and there's dozens that's, . . . you know, a child of five could do it, quite honestly, but everybody has their turn. That's organized by the men.

This tendency rests on the social force most basically of the informal group. It is the zone where strategies for wresting control of symbolic and real space from official authority are generated and disseminated. It is the massive presence of this informal organization which most decisively marks off shop-floor culture from middle-class cultures of work.

Amongst workers it is also the basis for extensive bartering, 'arranging foreigners' and 'fiddling'. 'Winning' materials is widespread on the shop floor and is endorsed by implicit informal criteria. Ostracism is the punishment for not maintaining the integrity of this world against the persistent intrusions of the formal. [. . .]

Another clear aspect of shop-floor culture is the distinctive form of language use and a highly developed form of intimidatory humour. Many verbal exchanges on the shop floor are not serious or about work activities. They are jokes, or 'piss-takes', or 'kiddings' or 'windups'. There is a real skill in being able to use this language with fluency: to identify the points on which you are being 'kidded' and to have appropriate responses ready in order to avoid further baiting.

This badinage is necessarily difficult to record on tape or to represent, but the highly distinctive ambience it gives to shop-floor exchanges is widely recognized by those involved, and to some extent recreated in their accounts of it. [. . .]

Associated with [a] concrete and expressive verbal humour is a well-developed physical humour: essentially the practical joke. These jokes are vigorous, sharp, sometimes cruel, and often hinge around prime tenets of the culture such as disruption of production or subversion of the boss's authority and status. [. . .]

Many of the jokes circle around the concept of authority itself and around its informal complement, 'grassing'. [One] man:

He [Johnny] says, 'Get a couple of pieces of bread pudding Tony [a new worker] we'll have them with our tea this afternoon see.' The woman gi'd him some in a bag he says, 'Now put them in your pocket, you won't have to pay for them when you go past, you know, the till' {. . .} Tony put 'em in his pocket didn't he and walked past with his dinner {. . .} When we come back out the canteen, Johnny was telling everbody that he'd [i.e. Tony] pinched two pieces of bread pudding {. . .} he told Fred, one of the foremen see, 'cos Fred knows, I mean . . . Johnny says, I've got to tell you Fred,' he says, 'Tony pinched two pieces of bread pudding' I mean serious, the way they look you know {. . .} He called Johnny for everything, young Tony did. Fred said, 'I want to see you in my office in twenty minutes', straightfaced you know, serious. Oh, I mean, Johnny, he nearly cried. {. . .} We said, 'It's serious like, you're in trouble, you'll get the sack', you know and all this. {. . .} they never laugh. He says, 'What do you think's gonna happen?' 'Well, what can happen, you'll probably get your cards.' {. . .} 'Oh what am I gonna do, bleeding Smith up there, he's really done me, I'll do him.' I says, 'Blimey, Tony', I says, 'it ain't right, if other people can't get away with it, why should you 'a' to get away with it.' 'Ooh.' Anyway Fred knocked the window and he says, 'Tell Johnny I want him.' He says, 'You've got the sack now, Johnny', you know. 'Hope I haven't', he says, 'I dunno what I'm gonna do.' {. . .} After they cum out, laughing, I said, 'What did he say to you, Johnny?' He says, 'He asked me if I pinched two pieces of bread pudding, so I couldn't deny it, I said I had. He says, "All I want to know is why you didn't bring me two pieces an' all."'

Another important element of this culture is the massive feeling on the shop floor, and in the working class generally, that practice is more important than theory. As a big handwritten sign, borrowed from the back of a matchbox and put up by one of the workers, announces on one shop floor: 'An ounce of keenness is worth a whole library of certificates'. The shop floor abounds with apocryphal stories about the idiocy of purely theoretical knowledge. Practical ability always comes first and is a *condition* of other kinds of knowledge. Whereas in middle-class culture knowledge and qualifications are seen as a way of shifting upwards the whole mode of practical alternatives open to an individual, in working-class eyes theory is riveted to particular productive practices. If it cannot earn its keep there, it is to be rejected. [. . .]

This can be seen as a clear and usually unremarked class function of knowledge. The working-class view would be the rational one, were it not located in class society, i.e. that theory is only useful in so far as it really does help to do things, to accomplish practical tasks and change nature. Theory is asked to be in a close dialectic with the material world. For the middle class, more aware of its position in a class society, however, theory is seen partly in its social guise of qualifications as the power to move up on the social scale. In this sense theory is well worth having even if it is never applied to nature. It serves its purpose in society as a ticket to travel. Paradoxically, the working class distrust and rejection of theory comes partly from a kind of recognition, even in the moment that it oppresses, of the hollowness of theory in its social guise.

The wage and the Thursday afternoon wage packet are an essential element of shop-floor culture. Weekly wages, not yearly salaries, mark the giving of labour. The quantity of the wage packet is the quantitive passage of time. Its diminution is loss of measured time, its increase 'overtime'. Such an orientation makes it that much easier to overlook the real, continuous, sensuous and variable quality of labour power and to miss the sense in which its full giving over time opens up enormous human energies which are actually unmeasurable. What amounts to a fetishism of the wage packet—nurtured with tight-gummed compact brown envelope—breaks up the weeks, quantifies effort, and presents to consciousness the massive effort and potential of human labour power as a simple concrete weekly equivalent to the crisp 'fair' wage. In the elemental weekly exchange, it seems, labour power must be spent in order to obtain every week the cash necessary to live. The loss of the wage packet is the loss of a week. That is why this loss is so feared and mythologized on the shop floor. This loss posits concretely the atomization of labour power and its quantitative equivalence with the wage. More effectively than a monthly cheque paid unseen into a bank account, the weekly wage prevents a realization of the disjunction between the variability of long-term vital effort and a fixed wage return.

Of course, part of the case here is that shop-floor relations operate at a *cultural* level in a number of ways to resist intensification and to exert *some* control on production. There is, so to speak, a *partial* recognition of the special nature of labour power as a commodity 'like no other', of its essentially *variable* nature. There are 'cultural instincts' to limit its use and further exploitation. These processes should be understood, though, not as finally and formally successful, but as in permanent tension with counteracting ideological tendencies. Perhaps they are most held in check by the classic version of the wage form considered here. Experiential forms of the awareness of time, for instance, can centre decisively around the wage packet and what it offers. Though even here a resistance is registered, at least negatively and individually in the strange time warp around the inherently meaningless weekly work cycle and its illusory wage form. The young lad in a car components factory:

You know, at work, say stapling sort of thing, you come 'Cor blimey, what am I doing here?' sort of thing you know. I just imagine me in say ten years time, I'll still be doing the same thing I expect, and I just don't you know . . . It'd send me mad I think, just keep doing it, a lifetime, I want something better out of life. {. . .} The nice part of the week is Friday dinner time when I get me wages . . . they bring it on a tray, the wages. It's funny though, all week I'm thinking, 'Roll on Friday, and we can go down town Saturday' and you look forward to it. When you get to town Saturday, you think, 'What was I looking forward to?' But I still look forward to it every week, just the same.

Perhaps the most prosaic but actually startling element of shop-floor culture is the articulation of manual labour power—as it is concretely practised—with assertive male gender definitions. There is an infusion of assertive masculine style and meaning into the primitive, mythologized elements of confrontation with 'the task'. It is also a masculine *expressivity* which often delivers or makes possible some of the *concrete* revelatory or oppositional cultural practices we have considered: resistance to authority; control through the group; humour and language; distrust of theory. There are profound implications here for the *internal* (to production) disorganization of a proper recognition of the nature and capitalist use of labour power and for *external* gender definitions and forms of family life. The conjunction of elements of manual labour power with certain kinds of masculine gender definitions in the culture of the shop floor is one of the truly essential features of the social organization of the shop floor. Yet it is usually un- or mis-recognized.[7] The sexist attitudes of the male shop floor, the inevitable nubile pin-up over well-worked machinery, heavy sexual references and jokes in language are simply accepted as the *natural* form of shop floor life. One of our central tasks must be to critically understand this relationship.

Manual labour is suffused with masculine qualities and given certain sensual overtones. The toughness and awkwardness of physical work and effort—for itself and in the division of labour, and for its strictly capitalist logic quite without intrinsic heroism or grandeur—takes on masculine lights and depths and assumes a significance beyond itself. Whatever the specific problems of the difficult task, they are always essentially masculine problems, requiring masculine capacities to deal with them. We may say that where the principle of general abstract labour has emptied work of significance from the inside, a transformed patriarchy has filled it with significance from the outside. Discontent with work is turned away from a political discontent and confused in its logic by a huge detour into the symbolic sexual realm.

The brutality of the working situation is partially reinterpreted into a heroic exercise of manly confrontation with 'the task'. Difficult, uncomfortable or dangerous conditions are seen, not for themselves, but for their appropriateness to a masculine readiness and hardness. They are understood more through the toughness required to survive them, than through the nature of the imposition that asks them to be faced in the first place.

Though it is difficult to obtain stature in work itself, both what work provides and the very sacrifice and strength required to do it provides the materials for an elemental self-esteem. This self-esteem derives from the achievement of a purpose which not all—particularly women —are held capable of achieving. The wage packet is the provider of freedom and independence: the particular prize of masculinity in work. This is the complement of, and what makes it possible, the fetishism of the wage packet. A trade is judged not for itself, nor even for its general financial return, but for its ability to provide the central, domestic, role for its incumbent. Clearly money is part of this—but as a measure, not the essence: 'You can raise a family off polishing.' The male wage packet is held to be central, not simply because of its size, but because it is won in a masculine mode in confrontation with the 'real' world which is too tough for the woman. Thus the man in the domestic household is held to be the bread-winner, 'the worker', while the wife works for the extras. Very often, of course, the material importance of her wage may be much greater than this suggests, and certainly her domestic labour is the lynchpin of the whole household economy. The wage packet as a kind of symbol of machismo dictates the domestic culture and economy and tyrannizes both men and women.

In the machismo of manual work the will to finish a job, the will to really work, is posited as a masculine logic, and not as the logic of exploitation. 'It's a man's want to be finished when he starts a job.' The very teleology of the process of work upon nature, and the material power involved in that, becomes, through the conflation of masculinity and manual work, a property of masculinity and not of production. Masculinity is power in its own right, and if its immediate expression is in the completion of work for another, then what of it? It has to be expressed somewhere because it is a quality of being. That is the destiny that a certain kind of self-esteem and dignity seems natur- ally to bring. Where the intransigence and hardness of a task might bring weakness, or collective opposition or questioning, an override of masculinity—a transferred teleology of production—can cut in to push back fatigue and rational assessment of purpose.

And if the nature of masculinity in work becomes a style of teleology, completion and production, femininity is associated with a fixed state. Its labour power is considered as an ontological state of being, not a teleological process of becoming. Housework is not completion. It is rather maintenance of status. Cooking, washing and cleaning reproduce what was there before. Female domestic work is simply subsumed under *being* 'mum' or 'housewife'. Mum will always do it, and should always be expected to do it. It is part of the definition of what she *is*, as the wage packet and the productive world of work is of what dad is.

Though this is speculation only, I pose the following concluding remarks just to explore the breaking open of the constructedness of cultural forms. The public and visible struggle of the labour movement too often renders invisible the ocean of what it moves through: shop floor culture. This is not to minimize the historic importance of the trade unions but it might be suggested that the type of masculine expression and identity we have considered influence *the form* of trade union struggle in the most profound ways. It has certainly been remarked that the acceptance of the wage form—and of the struggle delimited by that—has profoundly influenced British trade unionism. Can we add that both conscious and unconscious masculine structures have confirmed this and also helped to develop a characteristic trade union consciousness? And on both accounts we should not ignore the reverse shaping force of trade unions on cultural forms—or at least the significance of their *failure* to formally develop nascent forms not only of opposition but of repossession in shop-floor culture.

Certainly the union official or shop steward uses particular shop-floor cultural forms to mobilize 'the lads'—the spectacle or bluff, or strong and combative language which are suffused with masculine feelings. This establishes a real expression of anger and opposition that may be very effective in the short term, and is certainly a force to be reckoned with. This is, however, a *selective* working up and use of cultural forms, one that ominously corresponds with certain profound features of the wage form. It may be that longer-term objectives— which are at least partially expressed in other cultural forms—simply cannot be conceptualized in this way and are, to a certain extent, made inoperative by default at the face-to-face and grass-roots level. The masculine style of confrontation demands an appropriate and honourable resolution: visible and immediate concessions. If this is its price, however, it can be bought off in the most 'concrete' of all forms:

'hard cash'. But the visibility of the concessions won in this way—the *larger*, masculine, fetishized, brown wage packet—may actually conceal longer-term defeats over the less visible issues of control and ownership. It is possible to satisfy violent and possibly even frightening demands by short-term, visible and dramatic concessions without changing any of those basic arrangements which the violence might appear to threaten.

It may be the unholy interlocked grip of masculinity and the wage form which holds in check the other possibilities of shop-floor culture and settles, for the moment, the nature of its influence on other social regions.

Notes

1. R. Fraser (ed.), *Work* (Penguin, 1969), p. 63.
2. Now written up as a book which includes an ethnography of working-class forms of counter-school culture and their intrinsic connection with cultural forms of the work-place, plus a theoretical analysis of this reproduction. P. E. Willis, *Learning to Labour* (Saxon House, 1977).
3. G. C. Matthews, 'Post-school adaptation of educationally sub-normal boys.' (Unpublished MEd thesis, University of Manchester, 1963).
4. R. Fraser (ed.) *Work 2* (Penguin, 1969), pp. 56–7. In the transcriptions, time passing is indicated by . . . and material edited out is denoted by {. . .}.
5. Ibid., pp. 22–3.
6. See, for instance, the deskilling thesis outlined in H. Braverman, *Labor and Monopoly Capital* (Monthly Review Press, 1974).
7. For a further explanation of these connections see Willis, *Learning to Labour.*

10 Black Masculinity: The Black Male's Role in American Society

Robert Staples*

[*This chapter concludes Robert Staples's 1982 study of the black man in America. Staples's book is divided into five parts: 'Black Men and the Social System', 'Crime and Violence', 'Sex and Sexuality', 'Male/Female Relationships', and 'Masculinity and Sexism'. The other chapter in Part V, and the one that immediately precedes the one reprinted here, takes a close look at 'Black Manhood in the 1970s'. Additional chapters focus on such issues as race and masculinity in general, black male adolescence, the myth of black sexual superiority, homosexuality, the changing roles and relationships between black men and black women. I decided to include the last chapter in the book as it focuses most explicitly on the relationship between black masculinity and feminism. The significance of Staples's analysis can be appreciated fully, of course, only with an understanding of the arguments he pursues in the chapters leading up to his conclusion.*]

CHAPTER TEN BLACK MACHO VS. BLACK FEMINISM

The modern women's movement is barely ten years old. In that decade it was largely populated by middle class white women who focused on symbolic and class-bound issues, such as protesting against the use of women as sex objects in magazines and attempting to put more women into corporate boardrooms and other male domains. By and large, black women were not present, in large numbers, in the mainstream women's movement, a conspicuous absence since many white women took them as models of strong, independent women, though black women such as Aileen Hernandez, Flo Kennedy, et al., were leading spokeswomen for women's issues. It was said that black

---

* Reprinted with permission of Robert Staples and The Black Scholars Press.

women were already liberated, that white women were as racist as white men and that the middle class issues on which the movement focused were irrelevant to the largely working class black population.

Moreover, until recently the black male has been spared as a target of feminists. After all, he was certainly in no position to be a sexist, whether he wanted to be or not. White feminists generally left him alone in their assault on men. Many were careful to refer to white male domination as their main gripe. In the last few years, however, a few of them adopted a more strident approach. Black males can now be attacked, not as the banker denying white women credit, but as the sadistic rapist lurking in the alley to terrorize and sodomize them. Although mostly black women were raped, white women were screaming rape.[1] This almost seemed a throwback to the fifties and before when the worst crime possible was the violation of a white woman's body. To rape black women was tolerable; to sexually assault a white woman was an abomination and a sign of not knowing one's place. This is the gist of the matter as revealed in the works of Susan Brownmiller[2] and Diana Russell.[3]

In this era of racist retrenchment it would not be appropriate for white women to come down too hard on black men. After all, white women had meticulously set themselves apart from white men only a few years ago when they were labeled 'minorities' and placed into the affirmative action pool with Afro-Americans, Asians, Latinos and Native Americans. Some have called this a cynical manipulation of the symbols of minority status. At best it served to defuse the movement of other minorities and to decrease their chances of upward mobility. Since white feminists could not marshall an all-out attack on black males, and well-known black female activists such as Joyce Ladner and Angela Davis would not, a few black feminists took up the pen as a sword, among them Ntozake Shange[4] and Michele Wallace.[5]

It is strange that this attack on black men should occur when black women threaten to overtake them, in terms of education, occupation and income by the next century. True, lower class black women are not faring well, but lower class black men are in even worse condition. Perhaps one factor in the rise of feminism among middle class black women is the lack of suitable male partners: There are 118 college educated black women to every 100 similar black males; the interracial marriage rate increased by one third in the seventies and 54 percent of all adult black women never marry, or are separated, widowed or divorced.[6]

Black male sexism

What obscures the issue at hand here is the lack of a reasonable and articulate male point of view. Those things that bother black men— feelings of inferiority, fear of vulnerability—are not often talked about. What is articulated comes out sounding like insensitive male chauvinism: accusing black women of being domineering, sexually hung up and the like. Little wonder that workshops on black relationships sometimes degenerate into shouting matches.

On the other hand, black women have begun to link their grievances to the feminist cause. Some feminists, for example, seem to be angriest at black men who date and marry white women, and at the poverty of black women. Whether one is for or against miscegenation, and I am indifferent, it would appear to be a matter of personal choice. Certainly, it seems a strange choice of subject to link to the feminist cause. As far as the poverty of black women is concerned, there is little that black men have to do with that and even less that they can do to improve the condition. Of course, most people would agree that men should help to support, even raise, children that they sire—within the extent of their ability to do so. Again, that is a matter between the father and mother, or the courts as a last resort. It does not seem to be a strong issue among white feminists.

Some black feminists have charged that black men deny women meaningful positions in civil rights organizations. It would be more objective to place the issue in a historical context. During the sixties there was a general consensus—among men and women—that black men would hold the leadership positions in the movement. The reasoning behind this philosophy was that black women had held up their men for too long and it was time for the men to take charge. That some black men used the movement to their exclusive advantage cannot be denied. Again, the rationale was based on the 'trickle-down' theory: that by enabling black men to advance, the entire black family would be uplifted, and the majority of the black men in the movement pursued a more decent and humane existence for all black people.

If we choose to view gender roles and behavior, that was traditional and normative ten years ago, as sexist today, then all black men stand guilty of retroactive male chauvinism. The fact that male behavior was normative behavior until recently redefined as sexism poses some theoretical problems for feminists. Unlike other minorities who suffered physically at the hands of their oppressors, women were generally a protected group who were revered by men and children alike.

Obviously they were limited in their intellectual and creative expression, but society operated on a *quid pro quo* basis. Many men never liked the idea of having to work to support a family either. Yet, society never held out any other option for them nor any exemption from fighting America's wars or doing its dirty work. Black women, of course, did not share in the privileges of white women and neither did black men partake of the dominant power of white men. The issue here is that what is often defined as sexist behavior is nothing more than men acting in ways in which they have been socialized to act. That they continue to act this way, in the face of warnings from feminists, signals that life-long socialization is not easily reversed; many women cater to and prefer traditional male behavior and no group gives up its privileges without a prolonged struggle.

Still, the problem of defining what is sexist behavior among black men is a complicated one. On the institutional level, most black men do not have the power to force women into subordinate roles. Most of the institutions in which black people are located are controlled by whites. The most significant exception, the black church, has a male leadership and a largely female constituency. However, it is difficult to make a case for black male sexism in the church, simply because most black men are not in the church. That only leaves one other black-controlled institution in which sexism can manifest itself: the family and there is considerable disagreement over how much power black men have in the family, since they are almost as absent from the family as they are from the church. As stated earlier, the majority of black families are headed by women.

In this fluid period, women will not find it easy to carve out independent careers and lifestyles *and* to maintain stable relationships with men. In one study of the characteristics of divorced and married women, the divorced women turned out to be significantly more aggressive and independent than the women who remained married.[7] Women, to a large extent, are victimized by the fact that the very same characteristics they need to obtain career mobility (assertiveness, strong achievement drive) are the ones which make it difficult to attract and hold a man. Thus, they are often placed in the position of a forced choice between career and marriage. And, men often place them in this position by their insistence on women playing supportive, not competitive, roles.

This practice may be defined as sexism. It is, also, a matter of personal choice that cannot be denied men. They have the right to choose women who meet their perceived needs, even if their exercise of that right limits the life options of women. In much the same way, women have the right to refuse to enter into a marriage or relationship of any kind that will not permit them freedom of expression. Some black men and women live in a union based on a quasi-equalitarian model. However, there can rarely be a completely equalitarian relationship between any two human beings. So, this is not really the issue. The issue is what, and who, determines the various kinds of inequalities that will exist in a male/female relationship?

One source of black male/female inequality lies in the shortage of black men, thus limiting the choices and alternatives of black women as well as exposing them to the abuse of black men keenly aware of that fact. However, before we decry the abuse of black women and the advantages black men achieve from this situation, it would behoove us to closely examine just how great an advantage it is. First, why is there a black male shortage since at birth the ratio of men to women is about equal? The answer lies in the higher morbidity and mortality rate of black men in the marriageable years. In the 15–30 age bracket black men have a mortality rate that is twice that of black women. Even sadder is the fact that homicide and suicide are two of the top three causes of death among them.[8] However, even the remaining black men suffer from serious problems. Almost a half million of them are behind bars; an estimated one-third of the black men in the inner city have a drug problem; and 25–50 percent of them are without steady employment.[9]

The black feminist thesis is that the last 50 years have seen a growing distrust, even hatred, between black men and women. They acknowledge that it is perpetuated by white racism but claim that black ignorance of the sexual politics of their experience in this country has played its part. However, it is a questionable conclusion that the addicted, imprisoned and unemployed black male is the main culprit in this scenario. In agreement with Pauline Stone, I acknowledge that 'within Afro-American culture maleness creates privileges—that is, certain freedoms and rights are attached to being male.'[10] However, she correctly attributes this to the societal strategy of manipulating blacks through the maintenance of sexual inequalities in the home and workplace. In both cases the main beneficiaries of the division that ensues are white male capitalists.

The divisive effect of sexism is a double-edged sword. As psychiatrist Alvin Poussaint notes: 'At the college level, particularly in black colleges, black females outnumber the males and (outdo them) in terms of achievement. That's going to tell you something about who's going to be achieving and moving into different spots. The white male and the white female feel much more threatened by the black male than by the black female, which may set up a condition for easier access.'[11] There is every reason to believe that, by the turn of the 21st century, black women will exceed black men in terms of occupation and income. They already have more education. As for black men, their future is revealed in the statistic that of 23 million Americans who are functional illiterates, the highest proportions are among black males.[12]

Other feminists are critical of black women who choose to pursue an independent course but have children. Obviously, what is left is for the black woman to go it alone, without children or men as excess baggage, while she writes her own history. I just finished a study of middle class black singles, most of whom were women.[13] Many of them had become *de facto* practitioners of the feminist theory: they were alone, upwardly mobile, without man or child. The older they were, the less satisfactory was this condition. And, the reason why is simple enough. The male or female cannot stand alone and develop a sense of identity. It only makes sense, satisfies the soul, when it relates to some other role. To be ontological, humans are not meant to live out their lives alone with no higher purpose than self-satisfaction.

Sexism and black feminism

Sexism is an essential element in U.S. capitalist society and it is a force that corrupts and limits all the relationships that black men and women have with themselves and with each other. It is a very positive development that the criticism of sexism among black people has emerged. But it is only a beginning, and the dialectics have yet to be developed. Care must be taken not to blame the victims for actions which must be largely placed on the machinations of racism and capitalism. Black feminists must avoid actions which aid and abet these forces rather than contribute to the dialogue needed to iron out the differences between black men and women.

While many blacks are not opposed to feminism as a social movement nor black women as full, equal partners in all aspects of black life, we must be cognizant of the implications of feminism for an oppressed community. Female equality is more than a function of political and economic relationships. It involves personal relationships as well. Therefore, it reaches to the very core of human relationships, intruding into the most intimate aspects of our lives. Many of the inequalities that feminists perceive in male/female relationships cannot be corrected exclusively by governmental action, nor even by economic changes. They must be remedied through a combination of efforts, including the re-education of men and women and changes in sex-role socialization. It will not be resolved through acrimonious plays and books that place most of the blame for the conditions of black women at the feet of black men.

Because current black feminist analysis is often based on problems in interpersonal relationships, it, in many cases, is subjective. Personal relationships are never perfect, regardless of the political awareness of the persons involved. There are always difficulties, problems, and struggles. We must distinguish between such inevitable problems, and those that come directly from sexist abuse. Much of the popular feminist literature blurs the distinction between the inevitable difficulties that arise from human interaction, and those that stem directly from sexist motives. Moreover, some women give as much as they get. There are men, believe it or not, who have been abused or betrayed by women. Yet, they have no movement, no ideology, to articulate their role as oppressed beings; they are only the victims of their own culpability.

Much of contemporary black feminism is motivated by problems in interpersonal relationships, not political or economic domination by black males. That was the point in citing the statistics on single black women, interracial marriages and the imbalance in the sex ratio. While not all of black feminism stems from such factors, it is clear that much of it does. Even Michele Wallace admits to this in her statement that: 'Some black women have come together because they can't find husbands. Some are angry with their boyfriends. The lesbians are looking for a public forum for their sexual preference. Others notice that if one follows in the footsteps of the white feminists, a lucrative position or promotion may come up before long.'[14] While such motivations should not be used to discredit the legitimate grievances of black women, it does lend a complexity to the situation that does not confront other social problems.

What, in particular, diminishes the credibility of black feminism is the lack of balance between pure feminist ideology and the reality of the black community. The political and economic subordination of black women is a function of racism and capitalism, forces to which all blacks are subjected. It is primarily in the sphere of personal relations that changes in male behavior can occur and there is neither consensus nor consistency among black women about what those changes should be. Without a concise definition of black male sexism, each heterosexual dyad must work out its own definition of the resolution for sexual inequality. First, we must recognize that male sexism is a world view, not a conspiracy. It is a world view that places a woman's needs as always subordinate to the male's perquisites. This self-centered philosophy is a result of socialization processes that are many centuries old, often carried out by women, and internalized by virtually all people on this planet.

Women who have had their consciousness raised rightly expect the American creed of democracy to be extended to them. As long as male dominance was accepted as a God-given right, the exercise of male privilege created little subjective discomfort. Once women realize the constraints placed on their autonomy, their potential, it becomes more painful to those subjected to it. Yet, so much of white sexism has never had the same magnitude in the black community. Black women were in the labor market, received an education, participated in the decision making process and studies consistently show black men to have a less sexist attitude toward women's role than their white counterparts.[15] The remnants of sexist attitudes should be dealt with through education, communication and conciliation. Men should be sensitized to the need to participate equally in housework and child rearing, should cease the physical abuse of women, should accept the assertive black woman as an asset to his goals, and those of the community.

Meanwhile, we must be alert to the actual advancements black women are making and the effects of these advancements in an oppressed community. Witness, for example, the statistics which show that the ratio of white female to white male earnings decreased slightly between 1963 and 1974 (59 to 56 percent). During that same period of time, black women increased their income to the ratio of black male income, from 57 to 74 percent.[16] And, college educated black women have a higher median income than college educated white women.[17] In 1977 the black woman had 79 percent of the median annual income of black men. College educated black women, the majority of the black feminists, earn 90 percent of the annual median income of college educated black men.

There is nothing negative about this trend. In the main, black women are more educated, and often more competent. As long as their income is used in the service of the black community, and blacks remain united, there is little reason to fear their economic superiority over black males. The central point, moreover, is that given this trend it seems unnecessary to mount vicious public attacks on black men. We cannot avoid taking note of the fact that the black woman's ascendancy in the labor force is, in part, white society's attempt to keep the black male in check. And, there is growing evidence that the black woman's progress, too, is being slowed by the tendency of white employers to favor white women for slots usually assigned to minorities.

Power or poverty: the black matriarchy revisited

One of the most familiar academic terms to black Americans is matriarchy. Originally, this concept was used to describe an entire society ruled by women. In the past thirty-five years it has been used to depict what many regard as a typical pattern of female dominance in the black family. This belief that black women rule the roost was strengthened by a study popularly known as the 'Moynihan Report' which reached the conclusion that the 'deterioration' of the black family was in large part due to the unnatural dominance of black women in a society where male control is the normal rule.[18]

Some years ago I wrote an article entitled 'The Myth of the Black Matriarchy' in which I asserted that this labeling of black women was a cruel hoax.[19] Two factors were given in Moynihan's document as examples of black matriarchy. One was the large number of female-headed households in the black community; the other was the disproportionate number of decisions black women made regarding important matters of family concern. My response to the former charge is that while there are a much larger number of female-headed households among blacks than whites, the majority of black families are headed by a male and female adult. Moreover, there is little currency to the argument of female dominance if heading a household is the primary characteristic. After all, whom does she have to dominate? And the problems of being the major breadwinner and a female overwhelmingly outweigh the advantages.

In response to the assumption that because black women have greater participation in family decision-making they dominate black men, who have been reduced to irresponsible, and spineless caricatures, there is little evidence that this situation exists. In fact, as has been observed, black women are much more likely to feel powerless in their dealings with black males. Although they put up a visible and valiant fight against black male domination, they usually wind up losing many more battles than they win. Why, for example, would we speak of female dominance, when there are numerous situations where a black woman gives birth to a child out of wedlock and is saddled with the problems of raising the child while the father accepts no responsibility. It is also common knowledge among blacks that the male children often have greater value to the parents and are reared to expect certain advantages over women. And, the reality of the situation is that, as with white males, the system of male supremacy works to their benefit.

One of the reasons for black male dominance is simply the shortage of them. There are a number of factors responsible for the decrease in the supply of eligible black males. Among them are (1) the very large number of black men in prisons and the military, (2) a much higher rate of interracial dating and marriage among black men, (3) the high mortality rate of black men between the ages of 15–30, (4) more black men have become gay than black women, and (5) the increasing tendency of black males to remain unmarried.[20]

These factors also explain, in part, why there are so many more black female-headed households than in the white community. The Census Bureau reports that in 1978, 45 percent of all such families existed among blacks compared to only 13 percent for whites.[21] Because of the shortage of black males there is just no opportunity for all black women to form a monogamous family. Some estimates are that there is a shortfall of almost two million black males available for marriage. Added to the reasons already given, the higher rate of separation and divorce and out-of-wedlock births contribute to the large number of black female-headed households.

One should not assume any lack of desire to remain married or have legitimate children on the part of blacks from the above fact, rather their divorce rate is high because they are disproportionately concentrated in the low-income group where the marital break-up rate is highest. As for out-of-wedlock births, wide racial disparities in those rates continue to exist. Among the major reasons for this is the greater access of whites to contraceptive services. And, estimates that almost half of American marriages involve a pregnant bride indicate that we can make few valid statements about illegitimate births based on official records.[22]

It is this same group of black women who have been so adversely affected by the inflationary rise in consumer products and services. First, many of them receive their basic income from welfare and jobs that are not unionized. Thus, they have few ways of bringing their income in line with price increases. Secondly, blacks and particularly the poor, have been more seriously affected by the increased cost of certain items. A National Urban League study reveals that cost increases of such items as food, fuel and utilities had a greater impact on low-income black consumers since they pay a larger share of their income for them than do middle-income consumers.[23]

Another unfortunate result of the matriarchy myth is the negative image it projects onto black males, the majority of whom are living with and carrying out their family responsibilities. Even among the very low-income groups, the major breadwinner is most often the male. Perhaps it is time to put to rest these old and inaccurate stereotypes of black women and black men.

The real task before us remains an alleviation of the persistent forces of poverty and racial discrimination in employment opportunities. Until something effective is done to combat those problems, they, along with the aid of raging inflation, can only create more female-headed households. And, that means poverty—not power—for the women in them.

Class, culture and sexism

Much of the discussion of black feminism is a preoccupation of the middle class. Its concerns are not usually the concerns of poor and working class blacks. Lower class black women are burdened with low-income and the major responsibility for rearing children. And the men have been consigned to society's dumping grounds and have retreated to drug and alcohol abuse, suicide and unsuccessful careers of crime.

Arguing the relative weight of their oppression is a mere cavil. The issue of feminism reflects a crisis of the black bourgeoisie. James Baldwin, in commenting on Michele Wallace's book, noted; 'I hazard that it (sexual tension) is one of the symptoms of black middle-classdom. I doubt very much that the women I grew up with, my sister, my mother, I doubt very much that is their complaint . . . the inevitable tension, fury, always erupts against the one closest to you. But they understood that. That had nothing to do with our manhood as such. The anti-male thing which is now beginning seems to me to be one of the offshoots of the American dream as ingested by blacks.'[24]

Certainly, it is a far cry from the black folk traditions of the South, where men and women, stormy relationships and all, worked and loved together, in the face of the constant, unrelenting pressures of racism. What appears to be happening, among the black bourgeoisie as they ascend the socio/economic scale is the internalization of white values. Among these values will be sexism, materialism and individualism.

Thus, as the black male reaches middle class status he seeks the traditional passive, subordinate female model as a wife and avoids the self-actualizing assertive black woman. We have always had strong, independent black women in our midst. They are the mothers, the sisters, the daughters of the race. That is how blacks survived the travail of slavery and modern day racism. To reject them is the ultimate exercise in self-negation. The relaxation of the racial caste lines have led to our diversion from the larger struggle against racism and capitalism to secondary issues of sex role privileges, skin color and class divisions.

Some say the abolition of capitalism will not eliminate sexism. However, a rational economic system designed to meet social needs, not elicit profits for a small elite, will create the conditions where the need for sexist attitudes and practices will diminish. Otherwise, we will forever remain captives to the divide and conquer strategy of the ruling classes. While women should continue to fight sexism, it is folly to believe they can achieve full equality for over half of this country's population, with no changes in the political and economic order. Female separatism does not seem like a viable possibility and a struggle waged along gender lines in an oppressed community, contains the potential for defusing all larger struggles.

Either black women must accept the necessity of waging a tripartite struggle against sexism, racism and capitalism or continue to blame black men for all the problems they face. Although black men must accept some responsibility for their actions, much of what is happening is beyond their control. Black men are not such privileged creatures as many women seem to think, for there is a high price to be paid for being male in this society. Unwittingly, many black men do not realize the high price that they pay for their sexism. And, the highest price we may all pay, man and woman and child, is the destruction of our community. To avoid that fate, compassion and compromise are required on the part of all of us. We can neither achieve that objective by unfair and acrimonious charges of sexism against anyone who is male nor by persisting in unbridled male chauvinism. What we need is a universalistic ethos which will bind us as one, while simultaneously protecting our integrity as special and different entities. We stand at a point of crisis and this time it is the danger within which we must defeat.

Summary

Ultimately the issue in America is not that of sexism or racism; it is monopoly capitalism and its impact on human potential. In terms of the Maoist concept of major and minor contradictions in a society, sexism and the problems black women face are derivatives of a larger contradiction between capital and labor. Sexism, as in racism, benefits the capitalist order by maintaining differentials in privileges and rewards within the working class. Some feminists, unfortunately, do not place the issue of black male sexism in any kind of theoretical framework, thus losing sight of the structural context in which sexism manifests itself. Indeed, the most glaring flaw in their ideology is the acceptance of the status quo in the degree to which capitalism is exonerated for the problems between black men and women. To completely ignore capitalism's systemic features, and its role in black oppression, is to adopt the normative approach of neoconservative social analysis and bias that is no different from that of whites.

If feminists placed their work in a perspective that was more global, rather than visceral and racially nationalistic, we might understand why black men exhibit these symptoms of sexism. Feminists speak, for example, of the growing distrust and hatred between black men and women in the last fifty years. Yet, they do not tell us why this distrust and hatred exists. Could it be that the urban industrial transition from the rural peasant culture sowed the seeds for the alienation of black men from their cultural moorings? In the south, black women were respected and men *helped* to provide for their families. As they came to the urban North, materialistic values gained ascendancy. The symbols of manhood, sexual conquest, dominance of women, etc., became important to black men because they lacked the real symbols—political and economic power.

A most fatal flaw of the feminist thesis is the misreading of the life experience of blacks and a tendency to read into it the problems of the larger society. Because white women are opposed to the sexist behavior of white men in the form of their complete domination of them, some middle class black women assume the analogous counterpart that can be found in black culture. But, the structural underpinnings for sexism are not the same in black society. The problem of some black feminists is, that being middle class, they were raised away from the realities of the black experience and tend to see it all as pathological in the same way that whites do. Many of these problems of interpersonal relations between black men and women are resolved in very creative and adaptive ways. The feminists put down working class black culture without really understanding it. The internal machinations of the capitalist order are sufficient reason to keep most black men and women together, if only in a symbiotic relationship.

The feminist polemic for all its flaws, has revealed some very truthful and painful issues, with which we have to deal. But, the politics of confrontation can be counter productive when practiced in a society of unequals. When all is said and done, it is not a matter of being male or female. It is, instead, a matter of people understanding that they are products of their culture and cannot free themselves from it for greater individual freedom unless they first understand the constraints that culture imposes. Thus, perspectives, one's own as they are derived from or freed from culture, largely determine what kinds of experiences men and women have with each other. Stated differently, we are a product of our cumulative experiences and the interpretations we give those experiences. Hence, experience, culture and perspective are essentially one, unless we consciously separate them, and most people do not. Feminists are correct when they say we must make our own history or remain victims of it. However, I think we should do it together.

Notes

1. Nathan Hare, 'Revolution without a Revolution: The Psychology of Sex and Race,' *The Black Scholar* (April 1978), 2–7.
2. Susan Brownmiller, *Against Our Will* (New York: Simon and Schuster, 1975).
3. Diana Russell, *The Politics of Rape* (New York: Stein and Day, 1975).
4. Ntozake Shange, *For Colored Girls Who Have Considered Suicide When The Rainbow is Enuf: A Choreopoem* (New York: Macmillan, 1977).
5. Michele Wallace, *Black Macho and the Myth of the Superwoman* (New York: Dial Press, 1979).
6. U.S. Bureau of the Census, *Perspectives on American Husbands and Wives*, Series p-23, No. 77, U.S. Government Printing Office, Washington, D.C. 1979.
7. Jack Horn, 'Personality and Divorce,' *Psychology Today*, 9 (October, 1976) p. 138.
8. James B. Stewart and Joseph W. Scott, 'The Industrial Decimation of Black American Males,' *Western Journal of Black Studies*, 2 (Summer 1978) 82–92.
9. Ibid.
10. Pauline Terrelonge Stone, *Feminist Consciousness and Black Women in A Feminist Perspective*, 2nd Edition, Jo Freeman, Ed., (Palo Alto, California, Mayfield, 1979), pp. 575–88.
11. Alvin Poussaint, quoted in *Jet*, January 4, 1979, p. 32.
12. Robert Staples, 'To Be Young, Black and Oppressed,' *The Black Scholar*, (December, 1975) 2–9.
13. Robert Staples, *The World of Black Singles: Changing Patterns of Male/Female Relationships* (Westport, Connecticut: Greenwood Press, 1981).
14. Wallace, op. cit., p. 176.
15. Leland Axelson, Jr., 'The Working Wife: Differences in Perspective Among Negro and White Males,' *Journal of Marriage and the Family* (August 1970)

pp. 457–64; Ann Steinman and David I. Fox, 'Attitudes Toward Women's Family Role Among Black and White Undergraduates,' *The Family Coordinator* (October 1970) pp. 363–7.

16. Diane K. Lewis, 'A Response to Inequality: Black Women, Racism and Sexism,' *Signs: A Journal of Women in Culture and Society*, (Winter, 1977):339–61.

17. Cynthia F. Epstein, 'Positive Effects of the Multiple Negative: Explaining the Success of Black Professional Women,' *Changing Women in a Changing Society*, J. Huber, ed., (Chicago: University of Chicago Press, 1973).

18. Daniel P. Moynihan, 'The Negro Family: The Case for National Action,' Washington, D.C.: U.S. Government Printing Office, 1965.

19. Cf. Robert Staples, 'The Myth of the Black Matriarchy,' *The Black Scholar*, (January 1970), pp. 8–16.

20. Robert L. Hampton, 'Institutional Decimation, Marital Exchange and Disruption in Black Families,' *Western Journal of Black Studies*, 4 (Summer 1980): 132–9.

21. U.S. Bureau of the Census, *Divorce, Child Custody and Child Support*, Washington, D.C.: U.S. Government Printing Office, 1979.

22. Suzanne Bianchi and Reynolds Farley, 'Racial Differences in Family Living Arrangements and Economic Well-Being: An Analysis of Recent Trends,' *Journal of Marriage and the Family*, 41 (August, 1979):537–52.

23. The National Urban League, 'Inflation and the Black Consumer,' Washington, D.C.: National Urban League Research Department, 1974.

24. Hollie I. West, 'Black America's Cassandra of the 60s Is Foretelling Doom in Race Relations in the 80s.' *The Washington Post*, April 8, 1979, p. 71.

Holy Virility: The Social Construction of Masculinity

Emmanuel Reynaud*

....

1. INTRODUCTION

....

Old ideas die hard; in spite of our increasingly precise understanding of the mechanisms of oppression, the division of humanity into men and women is still generally presented as natural. The fact that throughout history 'nature' has always been invoked to justify the power of one group over another has not, for most people, cast any doubt over the validity of the division of humankind into sexes. People who assert that the mother's presence is essential to a child's development during the first eighteen months, or that childbearing is woman's greatest fulfillment, are disguising what is cultural by claiming that it is natural. The same attitude is found in people who argue that it was natural for black people to be slaves on the cotton plantations as the pigmentation of their skin protected them from the sun's rays. When physical characteristics like black people's skin pigmentation or women's aptitude for pregnancy are used as arguments to subject the former to cultivating cotton and the latter to rearing children, then it is no longer a question of nature but, quite simply, of oppression. Cotton-picking or childcare are not prescribed by biology, they are imposed by a social relation of power in which one group exploits another and tries to camouflage its exploitation with naturalist or biologising explanations. [. . .]

To [. . .] list [. . .] examples of societies where there is little dimorphism or where the male and female attributes and roles are inversed would not make it any more convincing. It is not necessary to gather proof of the contradictory character of the supposedly natural sexual differences, to remind ourselves of the too frequently forgotten fact concerning man and woman, which is that humans do not exist in a

* Reprinted with permission of Emmanuel Reynaud.

natural state, outside social relationships, but that they are precisely a product of those relationships.

The division into sexes

[. . .] Whatever the biological differences between males and females may be, they should not mask the fact that the division into men and women is purely social. From the minute a child is born, it is assigned to a sex category, according to its possessing a penis or a vulva. A person's entire identity develops on the basis of this sexual differentiation and through identification within that category; to such an extent that what has been imposed eventually seems natural. The category is so well assimilated that to question it would be to run the risk of being confronted with a vacuum—'If I am not a man, what am I? Who am I?' And so when it is a question of 'male' and 'female' roles, we are not dealing with a role played here and there in such and such a situation, but with a real shell which the person has completely adopted, and which has been gradually built up during an existence governed by the differences between the sexes.

This division of human beings into two groups depending on their anatomy has been radically questioned by the feminist movement. Following Simone de Beauvoir's 'One is not born, but rather becomes, a woman',[1] the radical feminists have been determined to destroy the notion of the sex difference and attack the naturalist ideology, according to which, for instance, women are freely placed at men's disposal, not because they are appropriated by men, but because passivity, washing up and tenderness are specifically 'feminine' characteristics. They have shown that the concepts of 'woman' and 'man' are the justification and the result of a relationship of oppression, and only when these concepts have been eliminated will it be possible for each person to develop her or his potential as an individual.

Men's reactions to this clarification have not varied much. Even today they oscillate mainly between varied attempts by the majority to salvage their threatened power, and feelings of guilt among a minority for belonging to the oppressive sex; but those who agree to question the idea of being a 'man' are few and far between. Obviously a person who wields power and a person who endures it do not share the same perceptions of reality. For a woman, being confined within a sex category is all the more sharply felt to be a form of mutilation for it corresponds directly with her oppression: 'to kill the myth of the "woman", including its most seductive aspects',[2] for women, means to get rid of an ideological structure which denies their identity as individuals and justifies their exploitation. For men, on the contrary, their category symbolises their power; and everything which defines them as 'masculine' is valorising, even to the extent that men do not generally see themselves as a separate group, but rather as a reference for the species—are not humans as a rule referred to as 'man'?

Why should a man question the category 'man'? The question could be rephrased. Why should a man want to give up all the material, psychological and emotional advantages that he enjoys as a result of the division into sexes? Why would an oppressor give up his dominant position of his own free will?

Of course, recently, since the appearance of the women's liberation movement, this position has become less stable: male prerogatives are not as solid as they were before. Christine Delphy[3] describes it as the change in perspective 'which separates the "I'm not a feminist but . . ."' of the pre-seventies and the "I'm not a chauvinist but . . ." of the eighties.' In homes, factories and offices affected by feminist ideas—and there are more and more of them—men actually have to stall and justify obtaining what was previously their 'natural' due. The arguments are multifarious: from the 'You're not mistaken but I'm too old to change now' to 'I would iron my shirts but I was never taught to iron' or 'Honestly! Why do you always belittle yourself? Isn't it wonderful to be a good cook; isn't it as important as building nuclear power stations?' The tone varies but a man sometimes has to use his imagination if he wants to continue being waited on hand and foot. What was formerly taken for granted—shopping, cooking, housework, production and rearing of children, conjugal rights, love, admiration, tenderness, etc.—give rise more and more frequently to conflicts and compromises.

Whatever the discomfort this new state of affairs causes men would doubtless be of little importance if men–women relationships could be reduced to the sum of individual relationships. But one of the achievements of the feminist movement is to have shown that the antagonism between the sexes, far from being limited to conflicts between isolated individuals, is part of a well-defined social structure—patriarchy. Thus the categories 'man' and 'woman' are not simply entities that could be tinkered with in order to solve the problem of oppression; they are the product and the instrument of patriarchal power. And if the question of why a man should question his category does not have an obvious answer, we can ask another question first: what does being a 'man' within patriarchy mean?

The origins of patriarchy

Patriarchy generally succeeds in deceiving people; even though our daily lives are governed by it, many people only see it in distant lands or remote periods of history. The forms through which it is articulated today, private or state capitalism, can disguise its own mechanisms of oppression and exploitation. But whatever the particular modes of production it secretes, patriarchy is characterised first and foremost by the division of humans into sexes, which is expressed by the appropriation of women and the struggle for power among men. [. . .]

Although we cannot satisfy our curiosity about the origin of patriarchy, we can still study the ideological description of it with some hopes of understanding its modern forms. It is not feasible here to study all the myths of the different patriarchal cultures; I shall confine myself to the one that concerns us most directly: Judeo-Christian civilisation. The genesis and basis of its ideology have the advantage of being easily accessible, thanks to the opening pages of the Old Testament. Naturally we do not find any explanation of the hierarchical division of human beings into sexes, because the ABC of any patriarchal ideology is precisely to present that division as being of biological, natural or divine essence. On the other hand, we can get a clear picture of patriarchal logic which, from the division of the sexes, develops into the appropriation of women and the struggle for power among men. The distinctive feature of the Old Testament account of the Creation is that it divides into two separate narratives that offer contradictory versions of the recreation of human beings. They do not always appear as such because of the mechanisms of patriarchal thinking and deceptive language, where to be human and to be a man are considered one and the same thing; but nevertheless they are divergent. [. . .]

After this [*second*] long account of the life of 'man', the allusion to returning to dust completes his identification with the human being who was created from that same dust, but who was not yet a 'man' because he still had all his 'ribs'. This final sleight of hand endeavours to make us forget that the creation of 'man' was that of a mutilated human being, missing a part of itself, called 'woman', and whose sexuality is limited to an external phallus/snake. In spite of this final attempt to conceal the reality of the myth, it is nevertheless apparent that it is through his own mutilation that man establishes his domination over woman.

Mutilation as foundation

This division of the human being into 'man' and 'woman' by the unequal mutilation of the individual depending on the anatomy of the sexual organs is the basis on which the entire Judeo-Christian ideology is built. The Bible itself, once the sex categories have been defined through the myth of original sin, hardly does more than illustrate how they work. [. . .]

Judeo-Christian ideology has become more sophisticated since its beginnings in the Old Testament. Through its various transformations, it has served as a foundation for the most powerful form of patriarchy, which now threatens to destroy the world in its struggle for hegemony. Judeo-Christian patriarchy is so highly developed that it finds itself confronting the antagonism born from the very origin of patriarchal organisation: the division of humans into sexes, or, in other words, the division of society into sex classes.

The bourgeoisie broke the old religious order that upheld the power of the feudal lords, and developed their own power by developing the productive forces. This process set in motion forces that threaten the basis of Judeo-Christian patriarchy—all the contradictions that spring from the appropriation of the woman class, and the power struggle within the man class are coming to a head. As the economic crisis worsens and the risk of nuclear war increases, the last twenty years have brought, for the first time it seems, earnest attempts to answer the fundamental question that the reign of patriarchy raises for humanity: how can power be eliminated?

By the end of the sixties, it was clear, for some people, that 'The problem of the proletariat is no longer to take power, but to put an end to it once and for all.'[4] And a few years later the feminist movement forcefully reminded us that power 'is at the tip of the phallus'. It is not difficult to make the connection between the two: it is to be found in every one of us, biologically male and socially 'men'. It is of crucial importance that we grasp the situation, especially as there is not much time left to untangle history.

Whatever the truth about the origins of patriarchy, since it has been established, human history has been that of a fundamental division which has created and conditioned all the others: the social distinction between men and women. Today, now that it is so highly developed that we have been brought face to face with the question of its origin, it is not a matter of reinforcing the sex division, but of abolishing it: of unmasking images which disguise power relations. Reappraising an underestimated 'femininity' and reassessing a wrongly evaluated 'virility' will not make any difference to oppression: our lives are not governed by values which each one of us can modify as we please to escape the oppressive reality; they are ruled by ideologies, institutions and modes of production which patriarchy secretes all over the globe.

When it comes to abolishing patriarchy the problem for men is not for them to create a 'new man', but, on the contrary, to destroy that 'man' from whom, as males, we have *all* been created, and who, in one way or another, we have *all* reproduced. It is to that process of destruction that I hope to contribute by describing men's attitudes to their body, their penis, sexuality and relationships with women and other men.

As for the question which worries some men—knowing what a male who is not a 'man' could be: each man can discover that for himself in a variety of pleasures available when one is relieved of the burden of fitting into a category. It would, however, be an act of deception to divorce this issue from the fact that as men within patriarchy we are, whether we want it or not, the embodiment of power.

2. MAN AND HIS BODY

In his race for power, man is able to separate mind and body: he sees the mind as transcending the human condition, and he turns his body into the place of natural alienation. He does not generally acknowledge that his body takes any part in thought, 'an activity of the brain as walking is an activity of the legs',[1] he most frequently perceives it as a faculty distinct from the body. He sees his body as a mere support for the mind, a support which can be cumbersome given the material contingencies it depends on: 'For the body causes us a thousand problems through the need for us to feed it; what is more it is subject to illness, and we are hindered in our search for reality. It fills us with loves, desires, fears, all kinds of fancies, innumerable stupidities to the extent that it makes it totally impossible for us to think' (Plato).

The separation of mind and body is illustrated by the primacy of the mind and the sacrifice of the body. It is the base on which philosophers have 'interpreted the world' and, in the last analysis, it is on this premise that they have attempted to 'change' it; but, on a more general level, the way man relates to his body revolves round this dichotomy. In fact, whatever his approach, from the training of the sportsman who seeks to endure suffering, to the sophisticated techniques of the monk who forces himself to withdraw from his flesh, the ultimate aim is invariably the same: to dominate the body in the hope of being free of it. Religion is doubtless the most extreme expression of this attitude; all man's dreams and aspirations are united in the desire to create a disembodied entity, a pure mind, a god. Christianity even brings off a *tour de force* in personifying its god, and then doing away with his body in full view of everybody. This blood-soaked body, nailed to the cross, is moreover such an apt symbol of the body sacrificed by man in his race for power that it is the image on which present day Judeo-Christian patriarchy has been built.

The disappearing body

Man reproduces the body/mind separation that he creates in himself in his relationships with women. Just as he tends to picture himself as pure mind, so he sees woman as unrestrained flesh, a body over which the head has no control. He likes to consider himself a cultural being, almost completely free of natural contingencies, while he represents woman as a sort of natural being still subject to the obscure forces of nature. On this basis he defines as 'masculine', not only the few characteristics associated with the male sex, but all the human traits in which he acknowledges an ability to combat natural alienation. In the same way, he calls 'feminine' all those characteristics which submit to that alienation. Thus he makes woman into the symbol of his own dependence, and in addition, the further he dissociates himself from her, the more he feels he is his own master; he creates two definitions, femininity and virility, which exacerbate the anatomical differences, increase women's dependence and concentrate everything that seems to represent human strength in himself.

Man seeks to rid himself of the 'rib' that he parts with symbolically: while he cultivates all that he defines as 'virile', he does his best to reject what he calls 'feminine'. He wants to be strength, rationality and transcendence, whereas woman is weakness, irrationality and immanence. At one fell swoop he imposes 'femininity' on woman and is determined for his part, to be virile, and to differentiate himself clearly from her. He searches out and prizes the slightest details that distinguish males from females; so, body-hair, beard and penis become images of strength and symbols of power.

As for penis and testicles, they are the very criteria on which belonging to the man class depends. They assume paramount importance.

Body-hair and beard denote virility and its first appearance. In adolescence man rushes to buy a razor; until he has ravaged his face with its blade, he is not really a man. As soon as a light down appears he starts to shave, especially as it is well known that the more hairs are cut, the faster and thicker they grow. To be beardless is no trifle—it evokes the innocence of childhood, or even worse, femininity. Of uncertain virility, a man without a beard is therefore not to be trusted. [. . .]

However, man is not only preoccupied with being hairy, he also takes an interest in his muscles and his brain; he sees the strength of the human being in them and sees them as typically masculine organs. Unlike the penis, and, to a lesser degree, body-hair and beard, they are present in both the male and female. Man must therefore, in order to make them into criteria of differentiation, favour them in the male, and do his best to discount them in the female. Whilst he sees himself as strong and rational, woman should be fragile and irrational; and whereas he considers himself capable of thinking and transforming the world, he likes to imagine that she is hardly capable of coping.

And when, in spite of everything, a woman comes out with an indisputably pertinent statement, it is not because of the activity of her brain, but because of her renowned 'feminine intuition': women are not supposed to know how to think logically. [. . .]

This attitude has a twofold advantage for man: it deepens the rift between the sexes, enhancing his own physical and mental abilities to face the world, whilst it restricts those of the woman. This way he establishes his power so firmly that he ends up presenting it as 'natural'. Indeed, why shouldn't he dominate since he is the strongest and the most intelligent?

Whereas woman is supposed to be flesh with neither brain nor muscle, man interprets the body/mind dichotomy by seeing himself as a head that commands his muscles. He makes his body the instrument of his power by setting greater store on his cerebral and muscular activities; and he attaches more or less importance to the one or the other depending on his hierarchical position within the man class. Whereas the mind always controls the body, body and mind do not always belong to the same man. [. . .]

So strong is his desire to be rid of his body that man sometimes succeeds in doing so, but he does not become the pure mind he likes to imagine: instead he ends up an invalid or a corpse. War and sport, of course, provide him ample opportunities to surpass himself—to fill the hospitals with the remains of his exploits, to enrich the earth with the bones of his glory. But he also finds scope in the most mundane activities: straddling his motorbike, for example, he enjoys risking a serious accident at every bend, or, downing five shots in a row, he can show that he, a man, is not afraid of alcohol, even if his liver, his arteries and his stomach cannot take any more. What does it matter what the means and the end are, as long as the mutilated body shows signs of the heroic struggle man has waged against his fears and his own flesh? [. . .]

Manly aesthetics

[. . .] Man identifies woman with nature and treats her accordingly: he tames and cultivates her. Just as he turns forests into fields and gardens, so he makes women into housewives and models. As woman is supposed to hold the key to all the dark and disturbing mysteries of the body, man seeks to give her a reassuring and seductive image. She represents the fear and disgust he feels for the flesh; by moulding her according to his own interests, he is trying to give her a reassuring form. And so when a woman takes off her pinafore she must be 'beautiful'; it is out of the question for her to be natural—she is supposed to be natural enough as it is. She must wear make up, be deodorised, perfumed, shave her legs and armpits, put on stockings, high-heels, show her legs, emphasise her breasts, pull in her stomach, paint her nails, dye her hair, tame her hairstyle, pierce her ears, reduce her appetite and, without making a single clumsy gesture, or uttering one word too many, she must seem happy, dainty and original.

By imposing femininity on women, man not only establishes his power and creates objects which are pleasant to behold, he also aims to produce, out of the restrictions and discomfort that women suffer, the inverted image of his own freedom and independence [. . .]: the more man restricts the freedom and well-being of a woman through her body, the more he feels he is in control of his own body and certain of his pleasures. [. . .]

[*A section on 'Desiring to Be a Woman' was dropped.*]

....

4. MAN AND SEXUALITY

....

Man does not allow his sexuality to develop fully, he stifles it by confining it to his penis. He projects it onto woman by making her into a sexual creature. The role attributed to Eve in the Bible illustrates this as does the Ancient Greek myth of Pandora who is held responsible for all the evils on earth after opening her 'box'. But one of the best illustrations of his attitude is the way man compares male and female pleasure and marvels at the potential for orgasm with which he credits woman. [. . .]

[. . .] man does not see the richness of his own sexuality and decrees that sex is woman. Obviously this does not imply that a woman may enjoy her supposed extraordinary sexuality in her own way, but, on the contrary, the pleasure that a man keeps for himself is precisely that of power, in particular, power over woman's pleasure. Man feels sexual pleasure as a threat to his power; he controls and channels it as best he can for fear of being submerged by pleasure. He is at sixes and sevens: he sees its domination as a way of dominating nature; but whereas sexuality is essentially letting go, communication and delight, he represents it as self-control, struggle and a means of asserting his power.

The music of power

His general attitude is shown in the language he uses: he fucks and she gets fucked; he portrays heterosexual relationships based on this theme through images which are as graphic as they are varied. [. . .]

[. . .] There is no shortage of metaphors, and they all originate from man's obsession with dominating sexuality through woman and dominating woman through sexuality. Man imagines his fulfilment not really in the pleasure he could experience, but rather in the obstacles he overcomes; sometimes he even goes as far as to create difficulties in order to assert himself. Knowing that the outcome is never certain goads him on in his struggle. Just as he may be wounded by the animal, engulfed by the sea, spurned by the mountain, so may he be refused or bewitched by woman. And so, although he is tempted by his dreams of conquest and adventure, man is often happy to sit back and admire the success of those who have realised them successfully. [. . .] He purely and simply ignores woman's pleasure and reduces his own to mere ejaculation. Man can easily relieve his sexual needs thanks to three institutions deeply rooted in patriarchy: marriage, prostitution, and rape. [. . .]

[. . .] Man is constantly trying to regain the beauty and sensuality which he lacks, by appropriating a woman to whom he attributes those qualities that he refuses to recognise in himself. [. . .]

Man is alienated from his own sexuality; he only experiences pleasure through his penis and his head. His body is no more than an intermediary between the two, and he does not always know quite what to do with it. He occasionally feels frustrated by this lifeless flesh, but rather than discovering his sensuality by considering himself as a whole—where penis, body and mind make up a single indissociable entity—he tries instead to compensate mentally for what he refuses physically. He does not allow himself to be led by feelings that rise in him: he controls and channels them to prevent them from spreading and causing him to lose control of himself and the situation. He represses them so much that when he can no longer hold them in he often becomes violent. His pleasure can then take a murderous form.

Trapped between his fear of letting himself go and his use of the penis as a means of appropriation, man does not see that sexuality could be something other than a struggle for power or a means of comparison. His general attitude has little to do with love or pleasure, but much more with hatred, disgust and jealousy. And its nature is well illustrated in one of the most democratically shared sentiments among men: the fear of homosexuality.

Fearful homosexuality

[. . .] If [*the fear of homosexuality*] often breaks through in these ways, [*it*] does not stop there. If it were only a matter of getting over a simple aversion, it would probably not be as frequent or intense as it is: in fact it is more deeply rooted. For homosexuality itself is not just a relation between individuals of the same biological sex, it is also sexuality outside the traditional relation of man–woman appropriation.

Homosexuality directly threatens man's power, as it excludes him when it is between women, and when it is between men it represents the risk for him of being sexually appropriated. He is not inordinately put out by lesbianism, he often creates a reassuring image of it which pervades his fantasies—'It's so beautiful to see two women together!'—and when he is tired of being a voyeur, or it does not satisfy him, he knows he can always retrieve his power through insult, derision or rape. On the other hand, the possibility of being used as a sexual object by a man usually causes him great anxiety.

It is not masculine homosexuality in itself that frightens man, but a certain type of homosexuality. In its so-called 'active' form, it does not necessarily make him feel ill at ease: it does not go against his usual values—he may even find it more exciting to dominate a man rather than a woman. [. . .]

Whereas man can consider homosexuality in its 'active' form as a means of asserting his power, in its 'passive' form it is, on the contrary, a symbol of humiliation. As is often the case, words speak for themselves: man does not 'get fucked', he 'fucks'.

He wants to maintain control over himself, and the image he has of 'passive' homosexuality symbolises the loss of his powers. To 'get stuffed' is to be had, to no longer be a man, to be passive in the face of circumstances and his own pleasure, not to dominate the situation but to submit to it. The very use of the terms 'active' and 'passive' to define homosexuality (and sexual behaviour in general) reveals how sexuality is seen as a struggle; for, outside the context of a power struggle, activities such as 'penetrate' or 'be penetrated' are both as passive or active as each other, and pleasure itself is neither active nor passive, it simply flowers when given a chance.

Man's fear of homosexuality is the expression of his fear of sexuality and his wish to dominate through sex. He does not consider his penis as an organ associated with pleasure, but as an instrument of power and appropriation. And so often he is afraid that the weapon will be used against him. When confronted with a woman's vulva he generally feels a certain sense of security, as he sees himself as the only one who is armed: in reality he is more afraid of the possibility of defensive reaction from the vulva. Legends of toothed vaginas abound on all continents, and in certain societies it is frequent for the husband to be afraid of 'deflowering' his bride himself; but whatever his fears may be, man generally succeeds in getting round them, and it is rare for them to prevent him from appropriating a woman. [. . .]

When he is in the presence of homosexuals, the man who is not one himself, generally feels uncomfortable: he is worried and confused when he comes into contact with a world in which roles do not appear to be socially rigid, and seem likely to develop according to an individual balance of power. His reactions vary depending on appearances: in the face of a 'feminine'—looking homosexual, he may feel threatened by the image of a man who is not a real man, and this aversion to the representation of what he himself could be sometimes manifests itself in a need to beat up a 'poof' or a desire to screw him, to 'let him have it'. On the other hand, with a homosexual who looks 'virile' he may have a vague fear of ending up in his arms against his will: he is afraid of being picked up or even raped, for, in this respect, man knows he is not in the habit of letting the object of his desire have any say in the matter. He experiences, on a small scale and for a short period of time, what a woman permanently lives through; but he has the security of belonging to the man class and the reassurance of knowing that the situation will not last, that it is only a hiatus in a sex life which he experiences as the assertion of his power. [. . .]

If it were not for the social division of human beings into sexes, the terms heterosexuality and homosexuality would lose their meanings; each person would be able to freely experience richer and more varied relationships than those confined within the difference between the sexes. At present, not only do they both have a meaning, but, in addition, sexuality itself, locked inside the categories 'man' and 'woman', generally does not have much to do with voluptuousness. When man pronounces such words as pleasure, love and fulfillment, he should really be saying revulsion, hatred and violence. Hanging on to the notion that his penis is an instrument of power and to his perception of the sex act as a relationship of appropriation, he struggles to find fulfilment but usually does nothing more than flounder: he only experiences emotional intensity through either inflicting or undergoing violence, and, in most cases, he experiences a frigidity which is all the more serious because he does not even know that he is frigid.

Notes

1. Introduction

1. Simone de Beauvoir: *The Second Sex*, Harmondsworth, Penguin, 1972.
2. Monique Wittig: *Questions Féministes*, no. 8, May 1980.
3. Christine Delphy: *Questions Féministes*, no. 7, February 1980.
4. Raoul Vaneigem: *Traité de Savoir-Vivre*.

2. Man and His Body

1. Joseph Dietzgen: *The Nature of Human Brainwork*, Chicago, Kew & Co, 1906.

Part II. 1985–The Present

12 Toward a New Sociology of Masculinity

Tim Carrigan, Bob Connell, and John Lee*

[*In the forty pages that precede the excerpt included here, the authors provide a close, thoughtful, and provocative analysis of 'the upheaval in sexual politics of the last twenty years [that] has mainly been discussed as a change in the social position of women'. Examining the impact of the Women's Liberation Movement, the Men's Liberation Movement, and Gay Liberation politics, the authors call into question the conventional understanding of what it is to be a man' by interrogating the assumptions and assertions of these varied perspectives.*

They begin with a survey of the 'prehistory of this debate' with early attempts at a sociology of gender, the emergence of the 'sex role' framework, and research on masculinity before the advent of Women's Liberation. From there the essay focuses on 'the Male Role' literature of the 1970s (what they call, in part, 'the Books-About-Men genre'), the Men's Liberation movement and its opponents. The authors work to redefine men's roles based partly on the application of psychoanalysis to help understand 'the deep-seated resistance to change in masculinity'. Later in the essay, a review of Gay Liberation's insights into an understanding of masculinity are reviewed, and it is from that important section of the essay that this one emerges.]

....

OUTLINE OF A SOCIAL ANALYSIS OF MASCULINITY

....

Men in the framework of gender relations

The starting point for any understanding of masculinity that is not simply biologistic or subjective must be men's involvement in the

* Reprinted wth kind permission of Bob Connell and Kluwer Academic Publishers from *Theory and Society* 14, no. 5 (September 1985).

151

social relations that constitute the gender order. In a classic article Rubin has defined the domain of the argument as 'the sex/gender system,' a patterning of social relations connected with reproduction and gender division that is found in all societies, though in varying shapes.[1] This system is historical, in the fullest sense; its elements and relationships are constructed in history and are all subject to historical change.[2] It is also internally differentiated, as Mitchell argued more than a decade ago.[3] Two aspects of its organization have been the foci of research in the past decade: the division of labor and the structure of power. (The latter is what Millett originally called 'sexual politics,'[4] and is the more precise referent of the concept 'patriarchy.') To these we must add the structure of cathexis, the social organization of sexuality and attraction—which as the history of homosexuality demonstrates is fully as social as the structures of work and power.

The central fact about this structure in the contemporary capitalist world (like most other social orders, though not all) is the subordination of women. This fact is massively documented, and has enormous ramifications—physical, mental, interpersonal, cultural—whose effects on the lives of women have been the major concerns of feminism. One of the central facts about masculinity, then, is that men in general are advantaged through the subordination of women.

To say 'men in general' is already to point to an important complication in power relations. The global subordination of women is consistent with many particular situations in which women hold power over men, or are at least equal. Close-up research on families shows a good many households where wives hold authority in practice.[5] The fact of mothers' authority over young sons has been noted in most discussions of the psychodynamics of masculinity. The intersections of gender relations with class and race relations yield many other situations where rich white heterosexual women, for instance, are employers of working-class men, patrons of homosexual men, or politically dominant over black men.

To cite such examples and claim that women are therefore not subordinated in general would be crass. The point is, rather, that contradictions between local situations and the global relationships are endemic. They are likely to be a fruitful source of turmoil and change in the structure as a whole.

The overall relation between men and women, further, is not a confrontation between homogeneous, undifferentiated blocs. Our argument has perhaps established this sufficiently by now; even some role theorists, notably Hacker,[6] recognized a range of masculinities. We would suggest, in fact, that the fissuring of the categories of 'men' and 'women' is one of the central facts about patriarchal power and the way it works. In the case of men, the crucial division is between hegemonic masculinity and various subordinated masculinities.

Even this, however, is too simple a phrasing, as it suggests a masculinity differentiated only by power relations. If the general remarks about the gender system made above are correct, it follows that masculinities are constructed not just by power relations, but by their interplay with a division of labor and with patterns of emotional attachment. For example, as Bray has clearly shown, the character of men's homosexuality, and of its regulation by the state, is very different in the mercantile city from what it was in the pre-capitalist countryside.[7]

The differentiation of masculinities is psychological—it bears on the kind of people that men are and become—but it is not only psychological. In an equally important sense it is institutional, an aspect of collective practice. In a notable recent study of British printing workers, Cynthia Cockburn has shown how a definition of compositors' work as hypermasculine has been sustained despite enormous changes in technology.[8] The key was a highly organized practice that drove women out of the trade, marginalized related labor processes in which they remained, and sustained a strongly-marked masculine 'culture' in the workplace. What was going on here, as many details of her study show, was the collective definition of a hegemonic masculinity that not only manned the barricades against women but at the same time marginalized or subordinated other men in the industry (e.g. young men, unskilled workers, and those unable or unwilling to join the rituals). Though the details vary, there is every reason to think such processes are very general. Accordingly we see social definitions of masculinity as being embedded in the dynamics of institutions—the working of the state, of corporations, of unions, of families —quite as much as in the personality of individuals.

Forms of masculinity and their interrelationships

In some historical circumstances, a subordinated masculinity can be produced collectively as a well-defined social group and a stable social identity, with some well-recognized traits at the personal level. A now familiar case in point is the 'making of the modern homosexual' (to use Plummer's phrase[9]) in the late nineteenth and early twentieth centuries. One aspect of the collective process here was a change in forms of policing that criminalized homosexuality as such, creating a criminal sexual 'type.' And one aspect of the psychological process was the creation of 'camp' personal style, both internalizing and sardonically transforming the new medical and clinical definition of the homosexual as a type of person.

In other circumstances, a subordinated masculinity may be a transient identity. The printing apprentices in Cockburn's study provide one example of this. Another is provided by the New Guinea culture studied by Herdt where younger men gain their masculinity through ritualized homosexuality under the guardianship of older men.[10] In other cases again, the collective and individual processes do not correspond. There may be stable enough personalities and configurations of motive produced, which for various reasons do not receive a clear social definition. A historic case of this is the vague social identity of English homosexuality before the advent of 'Molly' at the end of the seventeenth century. Closer to home, another example would seem to be the various forms of effeminate heterosexual masculinity being produced today. There are attempts to give such masculinities an identity: for instance by commercial exploitation of hippie styles of dress; and by conservative transvestite organizations such as the Beaumont Society (UK) or the Seahorse Club (Australia). But for the most part there is no very clear social definition of heterosexual effeminacy. It is popularly assimilated to a gay identity when it is noticed at all—an equation its publicists furiously but unavailingly protest.

The ability to impose a particular definition on other kinds of masculinity is part of what we mean by 'hegemony.' Hegemonic masculinity is far more complex than the accounts of essences in the masculinity books would suggest. It is not a 'syndrome' of the kind produced when sexologists like Money reify human behavior into a 'condition,'[11] or when clinicians reify homosexuality into a pathology. It is, rather, a question of how particular groups of men inhabit positions of power and wealth, and how they legitimate and reproduce the social relationships that generate their dominance.

An immediate consequence of this is that the culturally exalted form of masculinity, the hegemonic model so to speak, may only correspond to the actual characters of a small number of men. On this point at least the 'men's liberation' literature had a sound insight. There is a distance, and a tension, between collective ideal and actual lives. Most men do not really act like the screen image of John Wayne or Humphrey Bogart; and when they try to, it is likely to be thought comic (as in the Woody Allen movie *Play It Again, Sam*) or horrific (as in shoot-outs and 'sieges'). Yet very large numbers of men are complicit in sustaining the hegemonic model. There are various reasons: gratification through fantasy, compensation through displaced aggression (e.g. poofter-bashing by police and working-class youths), etc. But the overwhelmingly important reason is that most men benefit from the subordination of women, and hegemonic masculinity is centrally connected with the institutionalization of men's dominance over women. It would hardly be an exaggeration to say that hegemonic masculinity is hegemonic so far as it embodies a successful strategy in relation to women.

This strategy is necessarily modified in different class situations, a point that can be documented in the research already mentioned on relationships inside families. A contemporary ruling-class family is organized around the corporate or professional career of the husband. In a typical case the well-groomed wife is subordinated not by being under the husband's thumb—he isn't in the house most of the time—but by her task of making sure his home life runs on wheels to support his self-confidence, his career advancement, and their collective income. In working-class homes, to start with, there is no 'career'; the self-esteem of men is eroded rather than inflated in the workplace. For a husband to be dominant in the home is likely to require an assertion of authority without a technical basis; hence a reliance on traditional ideology (religion or ethnic culture) or on force. The working man who gets drunk and belts his wife when she doesn't hold her tongue, and belts his son to make a man of him, is by no means a figure of fiction.[12]

To think of this as 'working-class authoritarianism' and see the ruling-class family as more liberal would be to mistake the nature of power. Both are forms of patriarchy, and the husbands in both cases are enacting a hegemonic masculinity. But the situations in which they do so are very different, their responses are not exactly the same, and their impact on wives and children is likely to vary a good deal.

The most important feature of this masculinity, alongside its connection with dominance, is that it is heterosexual. Though most literature on the family and masculinity takes this entirely for granted, it should not be. Psychoanalytic evidence goes far to show that conventional adult heterosexuality is constructed, in the individual life, as one among a number of possible paths through the emotional forest of childhood and adolescence. It is now clear that this is also true at the collective level, that the pattern of exclusive adult heterosexuality is a historically-constructed one. Its dominance is by no means universal. For this to become the hegemonic form of masculine sexuality required a historic redefinition of sexuality itself, in which undifferentiated 'lust' was turned into specific types of 'perversion'—the process that is documented, from the under side, by the historians of homosexuality already mentioned. A passion for beautiful boys was compatible with hegemonic masculinity in renaissance Europe, emphatically not so, at the end of the nineteenth century. In this historical shift, men's sexual desire was to be focused more closely on women—a fact with complex consequences for them—while groups of men who were visibly not following the hegemonic pattern were more specifically labelled and attacked. So powerful was this shift that even men of the ruling classes found wealth and reputation no protection. It is interesting to contrast the experiences of the Chevalier d'Eon, who managed an active career in diplomacy while dressed as a woman (in a later era he would have been labelled a 'transvestite'), with that of Oscar Wilde a hundred years later.

'Hegemony,' then, always refers to a historical situation, a set of circumstances in which power is won and held. The construction of hegemony is not a matter of pushing and pulling between ready-formed groupings, but is partly a matter of the *formation* of those groupings. To understand the different kinds of masculinity demands, above all, an examination of the practices in which hegemony is constituted and contested—in short, the political techniques of the patriarchal social order.

This is a large enterprise, and we can only note a few points about it here. First, hegemony means persuasion, and one of its important sites is likely to be the commercial mass media. An examination of advertising, for instance, shows a number of ways in which images of masculinity are constructed and put to work: amplifying the sense of virility, creating anxiety and giving reassurance about being a father, playing games with stereotypes (men washing dishes), and so on.[13] Studying versions of masculinity in Australian mass media, Glen Lewis points to an important qualification to the usual conception of media influence.[14] Commercial television in fact gives a lot of airplay to 'soft' men, in particular slots such as hosts of daytime quiz shows. What comes across is by no means unrelieved machismo; the inference is that television companies think their audiences would not like that. Second, hegemony closely involves the division of labor, the social definition of tasks as either 'men's work' or 'women's work,' and the definition of some kinds of work as more masculine than others. Here is an important source of tension between the gender order and the class order, as heavy manual labor is generally felt to be more masculine than white-collar and professional work (though perhaps not management).[15] Third, the negotiation and enforcement of hegemony involves the state. The criminalization of male homosexuality as such was a key move in the construction of the modern form of hegemonic masculinity. Attempts to reassert it after the struggles of the last twenty years, for instance by fundamentalist right-wing groups in the United States, are very much addressed to the state—attempting to get homosexual people dismissed as public school teachers, for instance, or erode court protection for civil liberties. Much more subtly, the existence of a skein of welfare rules, tax concessions, and so on which advantage people living in conventional conjugal households and disadvantage others,[16] creates economic incentives to conform to the hegemonic pattern.

To argue that masculinity and femininity are produced historically is entirely at odds with the view that sees them as settled by biology, and thus as being pre-social categories. It is also at odds with the now most common view of Pender, which sees it as a social elaboration, amplification, or perhaps exaggeration of the biological fact of sex—where biology says 'what' and society says 'how.' Certainly, the biological facts of maleness and femaleness are central to the matter; human reproduction is a major part of what defines the 'sex/gender system.' But all kinds of questions can be raised about the nature of the *relation* between biology and the social. The facts of anatomical and physiological variation should caution us against assuming that biology presents society with clear-cut categories of people. More generally, it should not be assumed that the relation is one of *continuity*.

We would suggest that the evidence about masculinity, and gender relations at large, makes more sense if we recognize that the social practice of gender arises—to borrow some terminology from Sartre—in *contradiction* to the biological statute.[17] It is precisely the property of human sociality that it transcends biological determination. To transcend is not to ignore, the bodily dimension remains a presence within the social practice. Not as a 'base,' but as an *object of practice*. Masculinity invests the body. Reproduction is a question of strategies. Social relations continuously take account of the body and biological process and interact with them. 'Interact' should be given its full weight. For our knowledge of the biological dimension of sexual difference is itself predicated on the social categories, as the startling research of Kessler and McKenna makes clear.[18]

In the field of this interaction, sexuality and desire are constituted, being both bodily pain and pleasure, and social injunction and prohibition. Where Freud saw the history of this interaction only as a strengthening prohibition by an undifferentiated 'society,' and Marcuse as the by-product of class exploitation,[19] we must now see the construction of the unconscious as the field of play of a number of historically developing power relations and gender practices. Their interactions constitute masculinities and femininities as particular patterns of cathexis.

Freud's work with his male patients produced the first systematic evidence of one key feature of this patterning. The repressions and attachments are not necessarily homogeneous. The psychoanalytic exploration of masculinity means diving through layers of emotion that may be flagrantly contradictory. For instance in the 'Wolf Man' case history,[20] the classic of the genre, Freud found a promiscuous heterosexuality, a homosexual and passive attachment to the father, and an identification with women, all psychologically present though subject to different levels of repression. Without case study evidence, many recent authors have speculated about the degree of repression that goes into the construction of dominant forms of masculinity: the sublimated homosexuality in the cult of sport, repressed identification with the mother, and so on. Homosexual masculinity as a pattern of cathexis is no less complex, as we see for instance in Genet. If texts like *Our Lady of the Flowers* are, as Sartre claims, masturbatory fantasies,[21] they are an extraordinary guide to a range and pattern of cathexes—from the hard young criminal to Divine herself—that show, among other things, Genet's homosexuality is far from a mere 'inversion' of heterosexual object-choice.

In this perspective the unconscious emerges as a field of politics. Not just in the sense that a conscious political practice can address it, or that practices that do address it must have a politics, as argued (against Freud) by the Red Collective in Britain.[22] More generally, the organization of desire is the domain of relations of power. When writers of the Books About Men ejaculate about 'the wisdom of the penis' (H. Goldberg, who thinks the masculine ideal is a rock-hard erection), or when they dilate on its existential significance ('a firm erection on a delicate fellow was the adventurous juncture of ego and courage'—Mailer), they have grasped an important point, though they have not quite got to the root of it. What is at issue here is power over women. This is seen by authors such as Lippert, in an excellent paper exploring the connections of the male-supremacist sexuality of American automobile workers with the conditions of factory work. Bednarik's suggestion about the origins of popular sadism in the commercialization of sex and the degradation of working life is a more complex case of how the lines of force might work.[23]

The psychodynamics of masculinity, then, are not to be seen as a separate issue from the social relations that invest and construct masculinity. An effective analysis will work at both levels; and an effective political practice must attempt to do so too.

Transformations

An 'effective political practice' implies something that can be worked on and transformed. The question of transformation, its possibilities, sources, and strategies, should be central to the analysis of masculinity.

It has had a very ambiguous status in the literature so far. The 'male role' literature has spoken a lot about changes in the role, but has had no very clear account of how they come about. Indeed this literature generally implies, without arguing the point very explicitly, that once a man has been socialized to his role that is more or less the end of it. On the other side, the gay movement, in its contest with psychiatrists who wished to 'cure' homosexuality, has had its own reasons for claiming that homosexual masculinity, once formed, is settled.

The strength of sexual desire as a motive is one reason why a pattern of cathexis may remain stable for most of a lifetime. Such stability can be found even in the most implausible patterns of cathexis, as the literature of sexual fetishism has abundantly shown, ever since Krafft-Ebing introduced his middle-European hair, handkerchief, corset and shoe enthusiasts back in the 1880s.[24] Yet the strength of desire can also be a mighty engine of change, when caught up in contradiction. And as the last two sections have suggested, contradiction is in fact endemic in the processes that construct masculinity.

The psychodynamics of change in masculinity is a question that so far has attracted little attention. There is one exception: the highly publicized, indeed sensationalized, case of male-to-female 'transsexuals.' Even this case has not brought the question quite into focus, because the transsexuals are mostly saying they are really women and their bodies should be adjusted to match, while their opponents say their bodies show they are really men and their psyches should be adjusted to match. Both look on masculinity and femininity as pure essences, though of different kinds. Roberta Perkins's fascinating study shows the true situation is much more complex and fraught.[25] The conviction of being really a woman may grow, rather than being present from the start. It may not be complete; ambiguity and uncertainty are

159

common. Those who push on must negotiate their way out of the social position of being a man and into that of being a woman, a process liable to corrode family relationships, lose jobs, and attract police attention. (The social supports of conventional masculine identities are very much in evidence.) Sexual ambiguity is exciting to many people, and one way of surviving—if one's physique allows it—is to become a transsexual prostitute or show girl. But this tends to create a new gender category—one becomes known as 'a transsexual'—rather than making a smooth transition into femininity. There is, in short, a complex interplay between motive and social circumstance; masculinity cannot be abandoned all at once, nor without pain.

Although very few are involved in a process as dramatic and traumatic as that, a good many men feel themselves to be involved in some kind of change having to do with gender, with sexual identity, with what it is to be a man. The 'androgyny' literature of the late 1970s spoke to this in one way, the literature about the importance of fathering in another.[26] We have already seen some reasons to doubt that the changes discussed were as decisive as the 'men's movement' proclaimed. But it seems clear enough that there have been recent changes in the constitution of masculinity in advanced capitalist countries, of at least two kinds: a deepening of tensions around relationships with women, and the crisis of a form of heterosexual masculinity that is increasingly felt to be obsolete.

The psychodynamics of these processes remain obscure; we still lack the close-up research that would illuminate them. What is happening on the larger scale is somewhat clearer. Masculinities are constituted, we argued above, within a structure of gender relations that has a historical dynamic as a whole. This is not to say it is a neatly-defined and closely-integrated system—the false assumption made by Parsons, Chodorow, and a good many others.[27] This would take for granted what is currently being fought for. The dominion of men over women, and the supremacy of particular groups of men over others, is sought by constantly re-constituting gender relations as a system within which that dominance is generated. Hegemonic masculinity might be seen as what would function automatically if the strategy were entirely successful. But it never does function automatically. The project is contradictory, the conditions for its realization are constantly changing, and, most importantly, there is resistance from the groups being subordinated. The violence in gender relations is not part of the essence of masculinity (as Fasteau, Nichols, and Reynaud, as well as many radical feminists, present it)[28] so much as a measure of the bitterness of this struggle.

The emergence of Women's Liberation at the end of the 1960s was, as feminists are now inclined to see it, the heightening of a resistance that is much older and has taken many other forms in the past. It did nevertheless represent two new and important things. First, the transformation of resistance into a liberation project addressed to the whole gender order. Second, a breakdown of masculine authority; if not in the society as a whole, at least in a substantial group, the younger professional intelligentsia of western cities. Though it has not widened its base as fast as activists expected, the new feminism has also not gone under to the reaction that gained momentum in the late 1970s. Like Gay Liberation it is here to stay; and at least in limited milieux the two movements have achieved some changes in power relations that are unlikely to be reversed.

This dynamic of sexual politics has met up with a change in class relations that also has implications for masculinity. In a very interesting paper, Winter and Robert suggest that some of the familiar economic and cultural changes in contemporary capitalism—the growth of large bureaucratized corporations, the integration of business and government, the shift to technocratic modes of decision making and control—have implications for the character of 'male dominance.'[29] We think they over-generalize, but at least they have pointed to an important conflict within and about hegemonic masculinity. Forms of masculinity well adapted to face-to-face class conflict and the management of personal capital are not so well suited to the politics of organizations, to professionalism, to the management of strategic compromises and consensus.

One dimension of the recent politics of capitalism, then, is a struggle about the modernization of hegemonic masculinity. This has by no means gone all one way. The recent ascendancy of the hard-liners in the American ruling class has involved the systematic reassertion of old-fashioned models of masculinity (not to mention femininity—*vide* Nancy Reagan).

The politics of 'men's liberation' and the search for androgyny have to be understood in this field of forces. They are, explicitly, a response to the new feminism—accepting feminism in a watered-down version, hoping that men could gain something from its advent. This required an evasion of the issue of power, and the limits were clearly marked by the refusal of any engagement with gay liberation. Yet there was an urgency about what the 'men's movement' publicists were saying in the early 1970s, which drew its force partly from the drive for the modernization of hegemonic masculinity already going on in other

161

forms.[30] The goal (to simplify a little) was to produce forms of masculinity able to adapt to new conditions, but sufficiently similar to the old ones to maintain the family, heterosexuality, capitalist work relations, and American national power (most of which are taken for granted in the Books About Men). The shift in the later 1970s that produced 'Free Men' campaigning for fathers' rights, and the ponderings of conservative ideologues like Stearns on how to revive intelligent paternalism, is clearly connected with the antimodernist movement in the American ruling class. This offered strategies for repairing men's authority in the face of the damage done by feminism, much as the Reagan foreign policy proposed to restore American hegemony internationally, and monetarism proposed a drastic disciplining of the working class. The political appeal of the whole package—mainly to men, given the 'gender gap'—is notable.

The triumph of these ideas is not inevitable. They are strategies, responding to dilemmas of practice, and they have their problems too. Other responses, other strategies, are also possible; among them much more radical ones. The ferment that was started by the new left, and that produced the counter-culture, the new feminism, gay liberation, and many attempts at communal households and collective childcare, has also produced a good deal of quiet experimentation with masculinity and attempts to work out in practice un-oppressive forms of heterosexuality. This is confined at present to a limited milieu, and has not had anything like the shape or public impact of the politics of liberation among gay men.

The moment of opportunity, as it appeared in the early 1970s, is past. There is no easy path to a major reconstruction of masculinity. Yet the initiative in sexual politics is not entirely in the hands of reaction, and the underlying tensions that produced the initiatives of ten years ago have not vanished. There are potentials for a more liberating politics, here and now. Not in the form of grand schemes of change, but at least in the form of coalitions among feminists, gay men, and progressive heterosexual men that have real chances of making gains on specific issues.

Notes

1. G. Rubin. 'The Traffic in Women: Notes on the "Political Economy" of Sex,' in R. Reiter, ed., *Toward An Anthropology of Women* (New York: Monthly Review Press, 1975), 157–210.
2. R. W. Connell. 'Theorising Gender,' *Sociology* 19 (May 1985): 260–72.

3. J. Mitchell, *Woman's Estate* (Harmondsworth: Penguin, 1971).
4. K. Millett, *Sexual Politics* (New York: Doubleday, 1970).
5. Dowsett, et al., 'Gender Relations in Secondary Schooling,' *Sociology of Education* 58 (January 1985): 34–48.
6. H. M. Hacker, 'The New Burdens of Masculinity,' *Marriage and Family Living* 19 (August 1957).
7. A. Bray, *Homosexuality in Renaissance England* (London: Gay Men's Press, 1982).
8. C. Cockburn, *Brothers: Male Dominance and Technological Change* (London: Pluto Press, 1983).
9. K. Plummer, ed., *The Making of the Modern Homosexual* (London: Hutchinson, 1981).
10. G. H. Herdt, *Guardians of the Flutes* (New York: McGraw-Hill, 1981).
11. J. Money, 'Sexual Dimorphism and Homosexual Gender Identity,' *Psychological Bulletin* 74 (1970): 425–40.
12. See, for example, Dowsett, *et al.*, 'Gender Relations in Secondary Schooling'; V. Johnson, *The Last Resort* (Ringwood: Penguin, 1981).
13. R. Atwan, D. McQuade, and J. W. Wright, *Edsels, Luckies and Frigidaires* (New York: Delta, 1979).
14. G. Lewis, *Real Men Like Violence* (Syndey: Kangaroo Press, 1983).
15. A. Tolson, *The Limits of Masculinity* (London: Tavistock, 1977).
16. C. V. Baldock and B. Cass, eds., *Women, Social Welfare and the State* (Sydney: Allen and Unwin, 1983).
17. R. W. Connell, 'Class, Patriarchy and Sartre's Theory of Practice,' *Theory and Society* 11 (1982): 305–20.
18. S. J. Kessler and W. McKenna, *Gender: An Ethnomethodological Approach* (New York: Wiley, 1978).
19. S. Freud, 'Civilization and Its Discontents,' *Standard Edition of the Complete Psychological Works*, Vol. 21 (London: Hogarth, 1930); H. Marcuse, *Eros and Civilization* (London: Sphere Books, 1955).
20. S. Freud, 'From the History of an Infantile Neurosis,' *Standard Edition of the Complete Psychological Works*, Vol. 17 (London: Hogarth, 1918).
21. J. P. Sartre, *Saint Genet* (London: W. H. Allen, 1964).
22. Red Collective, *The Politics of Sexuality in Capitalism* (London: Red Collective/PDC, 1978).
23. H. Goldberg, *The Hazards of Being Male* (New York: Nash, 1976); N. Mailer, *The Prisoner of Sex* (London: Weidenfeld and Nicholson, 1971); J. Lippert, 'Sexuality as Consumption,' in J. Snodgrass, ed., *For Men Against Sexism* (Albion: Times Change Press, 1977), 207–13; K. Bednarik, *The Male in Crisis* (New York: Knopf, 1970).
24. R. von Krafft-Ebing, *Psychopathia Sexualis* (New York: Paperback Library, 1965 [1886]).
25. R. Perkins, *The Drag Queen Scene* (Sydney: Allen and Unwin, 1983).
26. S. L. Bem, 'The Measurement of Psychological Androgyny,' *Journal of Consulting and Clinical Psychology* 42 (1974): 155–62: G. Russell, *The Changing Role of Fathers?* (St. Lucia: University of Queensland Press, 1983).
27. T. Parsons and M. F. Bales, *Family, Socialization and Interaction Process* (London: Routledge and Kegan Paul, 1953); N. Chodorow, *The Reproduction of Mothering* (Berkeley: University of California Press, 1978).

28. M. Fasteau, *The Male Machine* (New York: McGraw Hill, 1974); J. Nichols, *Men's Liberation* (New York: Penguin, 1975); E. Reynaud, *Holy Virility* (London: Pluto Press, 1983); A. Dworkin, *Pornography: Men Possessing Women* (London: The Women's Press, 1981).
29. M. F. Winter and E. R. Robert, 'Male Dominance, Late Capitalism and the Growth of Instrumental Reason,' *Berkeley Journal of Sociology* 24/25 (1980): 249–80.
30. B. Ehrenreich, *The Hearts of Men: American Dreams and the Flight From Commitment* (London: Pluto Press, 1983).

Men Loving Men: The Challenge of Gay Liberation

Gary Kinsman*

The limits of 'acceptable' masculinity are in part defined by comments like 'What are you, a fag?'[1] As boys and men we have heard such expressions and the words 'queer,' 'faggot,' and 'sissy' all our lives. These words encourage certain types of male behavior and serve to define, regulate, and limit our lives, whether we consider ourselves straight or gay. Depending on who is speaking and who is listening, they incite fear or hatred.

Even among many heterosexual men who have been influenced by feminism, the taboo against loving the same sex remains unchallenged. Lines like 'I may be anti-sexist, but I am certainly not gay' can still be heard. These men may be questioning some aspects of male privilege, but in attempting to remake masculinity they have not questioned the institution of heterosexuality.[2] As a result their challenge to male privilege is partial and inadequate.

Gay men have often found much support in the 'men's movement' or in groups of men against sexism. At the same time we have also seen our concerns as gay men marginalized and pushed aside and have often felt like outsiders. Joe Interrante expresses some of the reservations of gay men about the 'men's movement' and its literature:

As a gay man . . . I had suspicions about the heterocentrist bias of this work. It told me that my gayness existed 'in addition to' my masculinity, whereas I found that it colored my entire experience of manhood. I distrusted a literature which claimed that gay men were just like heterosexual men except for what they did in bed.[3]

The literature of the men's movement has tended to produce an image of men that is white, middle-class, and heterosexual. As Ned Lyttelton

* Reprinted with permission of Gary Kinsman and Oxford University Press, from *Beyond Patriarchy: Essays by Men on Pleasure, Power and Change*, edited by Michael Kaufman (1984).

has pointed out, 'an analysis of masculinity that does not deal with the contradictions of power imbalances that exist between men themselves will be limited and biased, and its limits and biases will be concealed under the blanket of shared male privilege.'[4] A series of masculinities becomes subsumed under one form of masculinity that becomes 'masculinity.' As a result, socially organized power relations among and between men based on sexuality, race, class, or age have been neglected. These power relations are major dividing lines between men that have to be addressed if progressive organizing among men is to encompass the needs and experiences of all men. The men's movement has reached a turning point.[5] It has to choose whether it is simply a movement for men's rights—defending men's rights to be human too—or whether it will deepen the challenge to an interlocked web of oppression: sexism, heterosexism, racism, and class exploitation. We have to choose between a vision of a world in which men are more sensitive and human but are still 'real' men at the top of the social order, and a radically new vision that entails the transformation of masculinity and sexuality and the challenging of other forms of domination.

In developing this radical vision—radical in the sense of getting to the roots of the problem—the politics of gay liberation and the politics of lesbian feminism are important. So too are the experiences of those of us who have been made into outsiders, people labeled 'faggot,' 'queer,' or 'dyke' who have reclaimed these stigmatized labels as ways of naming experiences of the world and as weapons of resistance to heterosexual hegemony. The struggle against the institutionalized social norm of heterosexuality opens up the door to other kinds of social and personal change.

GAY LIBERATION VERSUS HETEROSEXUAL PRIVILEGE

In our society heterosexuality as an institutionalized norm has become an important means of social regulation, enforced by laws, police practices, family and social policies, schools, and the mass media. In its historical development heterosexuality is tied up with the institution of masculinity, which gives social and cultural meaning to biological male anatomy, associating it with masculinity, aggressiveness, and an 'active' sexuality. 'Real' men are intrinsically heterosexual; gay men, therefore, are not real men.

While gay men share with straight men the privilege of being in a dominant position in relation to women, we are at the same time in a subordinate position in the institution of heterosexuality. As a result, gay men's lives and experiences are not the same as those of heterosexual men. For instance, while we share with straight men the economic benefits of being men in a patriarchal society, we do not participate as regularly in the everyday interpersonal subordination of women in the realms of sexuality and violence. Although, like other men, we have more social opportunities, we are not accepted as open gays in corporate boardrooms or in many jobs, sports, and professions. We can still be labeled 'national security risks' and sick, deviant, or abnormal. Consequently, gay men experience a rupture between the presumably universal categories of heterosexual experience and their own particular experience of the world, a rupture that denies many of our experiences; for gay men exist in social situations that allow us to see aspects of life, desire, sexuality, and love that cannot be seen by heterosexual men.[6]

Gay men have had to question the institution of masculinity—which associates masculinity with heterosexuality—in our daily lives. We have experimented with and developed new ways of organizing our sexual lives and our love and support relations, of receiving and giving pleasure. Heterosexual men interested in seriously transforming the fabric of their lives have to stop seeing gay liberation as simply a separate issue for some men that has nothing to say to them. They should begin to ask what the experience of gay men can bring into view for them. As we break the silence and move beyond liberal tolerance toward gays and lesbians, we can begin to see how 'queer baiting' and the social taboo against pleasure, sex, and love between men serves to keep all men in line, defining what proper masculinity is for us. Gay liberation suggests that heterosexuality is not the only natural form of sexuality but has instead been socially and culturally made the 'normal' sexual practice and identity. As the Kinsey Institute studies suggested, the actual flux of human desire cannot be easily captured in rigid sexual categories. Many men who define themselves as straight have had sexual experiences with other men.[7] This has demonstrated the contradictions that can exist between our actual experiences and desires and the rigid social categories that are used to divide normal from deviant and that imply that any participation in homosexual activity automatically defines one as a homosexual.

Breaking the silence surrounding homosexuality requires challenging heterosexism and heterosexual privilege. Lesbian-feminist

Charlotte Bunch once explained to heterosexual women that the best way to find out what heterosexual privilege is all about is to go about for a few days as an open lesbian:

What makes heterosexuality work is heterosexual privilege—and if you don't have a sense of what privilege is, I suggest that you go home and announce to everybody that you know—a roommate, your family, the people you work with—everywhere that you go—that you're a queer. Try being a queer for a week.[8]

This statement could also be applied to the situation of straight men, and any heterosexual man can easily imagine the discomfort, ridicule, and fear he might experience, how his 'coming out' would disrupt 'normal' relations at work and with his family. Such experiences are the substance of gay oppression that make our lives different from those of straight men. Gay men in this heterosexist society are labeled with many terms of abuse. Young boys hurl the labels 'queer,' 'fag,' or 'cocksucker' at each other before they know what the words mean. As we grow up we are denied images of men loving men and any models for our lives outside heterosexuality. In the United States, the age of consent varies from state to state, usually from sixteen to eighteen, although in some states all homosexual acts remain technically illegal. Under Canadian and British law males under twenty-one are denied the right to have sexual relations with other boys and men. Many members of the medical and psychiatric professions still practice psychological and social terrorism against us by trying to adjust us to fit the norm. We are excluded as open lesbians and gay men from most activities and institutions. When the mass media does cover us they use stereotypes or other means to show us to be sick, immoral, indecent, as some sort of social problem or social menace, or they trivialize us as silly and frivolous.[9] The police continue to raid our bookstores and seize our magazines. In 1983–6, the media fostered fear and hatred against gay men by associating all gay men with AIDS. Such media stories shift and mold public opinion against us. On city streets we are often violently attacked by gangs of 'queerbashers.' Most countries deny lesbians and gay men the basic civil and human rights, leaving us open to arbitrary firings and evictions.

A variety of sexual laws are used to regulate and control gay men's sexual and community lives. Police in many cities have a policy of systematically entrapping and harassing gays. In recent years hundreds of men across North America have been arrested and often entrapped by the police in washrooms and parks. These campaigns—especially in small towns and cities—and the associated media attention have torn apart the lives of these men, many of whom define themselves as heterosexual and are married with families. In fact, the society in which we have all grown up is so profoundly heterosexist that even many gays have internalized the social hatred against us in forms of 'self-oppression.'[10] This fear keeps many of us isolated and silent, hiding our sexuality. One of the first steps in combating this self-oppression is to reject this denial of our love and sexuality by affirming our existence and pride publicly. Assertions that 'gay is good' and affirmations of gay pride are the beginnings of our resistance to heterosexual hegemony on the individual and social levels.

THE HISTORY OF SEXUALITY

In addressing the matter of gay and lesbian oppression, we have to ask where this oppression has come from. How did heterosexuality come to be the dominant social relation? How did homosexuality come to be seen as a perverse outcast form of sexuality? If we can answer those questions, we can begin to see how we could break down the institution of heterosexuality and its control over our lives.

As a result of numerous cross-cultural and historical studies that have demonstrated that there is no natural or normal sexuality, we can no longer see sex as simply natural or biologically given. Our biological, erotic, and sexual capabilities are only the precondition for the organization of the social and cultural forms of meaning and activity that compose human sexuality. Our biological capabilities are transformed and mediated culturally, producing sexuality as a social need and relation. As Gayle Rubin explained, each social system has its own 'sex/gender system,' which

is the set of arrangements by which a society transforms biological sexuality into products of human activity, and in which these transformed sexual needs are satisfied.[11]

Recent historical studies have challenged the assumed natural categories of heterosexuality and homosexuality themselves.[12] Gay, lesbian, and feminist historians have expanded our understanding of sexual meaning and identity, contesting the dominant ways in which sexuality has been discussed and viewed in our society.[13] The dominant perspective for looking at sexuality is what has been called the 'repression hypothesis,' which assumes that there is a natural sexuality that is repressed to maintain social and moral order. Many leftists argue that sexuality is repressed by the ruling class—to maintain class society because of capitalism's need for the family and a docile work force. This interpretation was popularized in the writings and activities of Wilhelm Reich,[14] who called for the end of sexual repression through the liberation of natural sexuality, which was for him completely heterosexual. Variations of this repression theory, and its corresponding call for the liberation of natural sexuality, have inspired sexual liberationist politics, including much of the gay liberation movement, which sees homosexuality as a natural sexuality that simply needs to be released from social repression.

The experience by women of the male sexual (i.e., heterosexual) revolution of the sixties and seventies has led much of the feminist movement to a more complex understanding of sexuality than simple theories of sexual repression. Feminism has exposed the contradictions in a sexual revolution that increased women's ability to seek sexual satisfaction but only within male-dominated heterosexual relations. Feminism has also begun to explore how sexuality and social power are bound together and how sexuality has been socially organized in male-dominated forms in this society.[15] This view of sex opens up new possibilities for sexual politics—our sexual lives are no longer seen as divorced from human and social activity but as the results of human praxis (the unity of thought and activity). Sexual relations are therefore changeable and are themselves the site of personal and social struggles. We can then begin to question the natural appearance of such sexual categories as heterosexual and homosexual and to make visible the human activity that is involved in the making of sexuality. This opens up a struggle, not for the liberation of some inherent sexuality that just has to be freed from the bonds of capitalism or repressive laws, but for a much broader challenge to the ways our sexual lives are defined, regulated, and controlled. It opens up questions about the very making and remaking of sex, desire, and pleasure.

Enter the homosexual

The historical emergence of the 'homosexual' required a number of social preconditions, which can be summarized as three interrelated social processes: first, the rise of capitalist social relations, which created the necessary social spaces for the emergence of homosexual cultures;[16] second, the regime of sexuality that categorized and labeled homosexuality and sexual 'deviations'; and third, the activities, cultural production, and resistance to the oppression of men in these same-sex desire-based cultures,

The rise of capitalism in Europe between the fifteenth and nineteenth centuries separated the rural household economy from the new industrial economy and undermined the interdependent different-sex household economy. The working class was made, and made itself, in the context of this industrialization, urbanization, and commercialization. This separation of 'work' from the household and the development of wage labor meant that it became possible for more men in the cities to live outside the family, earning a wage and living as boarders. Later they would be able to eat at restaurants or taverns and rent their own accommodation. This created the opportunities for some men to start organizing what would become, through a process of development and struggle, the beginnings of a homosexual culture, from the eighteenth century on.[17]

A regime of sexuality has emerged as part of a series of social struggles over the last two centuries. The transition from feudalism to capitalism in the western countries meant a transition in the way kinship and sexual and class relations were organized. The new ruling class was no longer able to understand itself or organize its social life simply through the old feudal ties of blood or lineage.[18] New forms of family and state formation led to new forms of self-understanding, class consciousness, and notions of moral and social order. Sexuality emerged as an autonomous sphere separate from household production. A proper, respectable sexual and gender identity became an essential feature of the class unity of the bourgeoisie. This process is linked to the emergence of the ideology of individual identity. The regime of sexual definitions was first applied to the bodies of the bourgeoisie itself through its educational and medical systems and through the sexological knowledge that was generated by the new professional groups of doctors and psychiatrists and that served to draw a boundary between bourgeois respectability and the 'bestial' sexual practices of the outcast poor and 'lower orders.' These norms of sex and gender definition helped organize the relations of the bourgeois family and its sexual morality.

Later these same norms of sexual identity and morality were used against the urban working class and poor, who were considered a threat to social order by middle-class and state agencies. The working class both resisted this enforcement of social norms and at the same time adopted them as its own. The male-dominated 'respectable' sections of the working class developed their own norms of family and

sexual life that incorporated the socially dominant norms of masculinity, femininity, and reproductive heterosexuality. The uneven and at
times contradictory development of sexual identity in different classes,
genders, races, and nationalities is a subject that remains to be more
fully explored. [. . .]

The term homosexual itself was not devised until 1869, when
Károly Mária Benkert, a Hungarian, coined the term in an appeal to
the government to keep its laws out of people's lives.[19] The category
of homosexuality was originally elaborated by some homosexuals
themselves, mostly professional men it seems, in order to name their
'difference' and in order to protect themselves from police and
legal prohibitions. The word was taken up by the various agencies of
social regulation from the medical profession to the police and courts.
Homosexuality was defined as an abnormality, a sickness, and a
symptom of degeneracy. The efforts of medical and legal experts

were chiefly concerned with whether the disgusting breed of perverts could
be physically identified for courts and whether they should be held legally
responsible for their acts.[20]

An early Canadian reference—in 1898—to same-sex 'perversion'
among men by a Dr. Ezra Stafford (which refers to the work of Krafft-
Ebing, one of the grandfathers of sexology) linked sex between men
with prostitution in a theory of degeneracy. Stafford wrote that these
things 'may lead to the tragedy of our species.'[21] This connection
between homosexuality and prostitution as stigmatized social and sexual practices continued even to England's Wolfenden report of 1957,
which linked these topics, and it continues to this day, in, for example,
the use by the Canadian police of bawdy-house legislation, originally
intended to deal with houses of female prostitutes, against gay men.

Simultaneously the needs of capitalism for a skilled labor force
and a continuing supply of wage-laborers led to an emphasis on the
heterosexual nuclear family. The rise of modern militarism and the
scramble for colonies by the western powers led to demands for a
larger and healthier supply of cannon fodder at the beginning of the
twentieth century. An intensification of military discipline resulted in
stiff prohibitions against homosexuality, which was seen as subversive
of discipline and hierarchy in the armed forces. As a result, reproductive heterosexuality was reinforced for men, and motherhood
further institutionalized for women.[22]

The category of the male homosexual emerged in sexology as an
'invert' and was associated with some form of effeminacy and 'gender

inversion.' A relation between gender dysfunction and abnormal sexuality was established. [. . .] The categorization of 'perverse' sexual types also provided a basis for resistance. [. . .] Homosexuals themselves used this category to name their experiences, to articulate their differences and cultures, moving this category in a more progressive direction. There has been a century-long struggle over the meaning of homosexuality that has involved sexologists, the police, lawyers, psychiatrists, and homosexuals, a struggle that continues today. The regime of sexuality and the specification of different sexual categories in an attempt to buttress the emerging norm of heterosexuality has unwittingly also provided the basis for homosexual experiences, identities, and cultures. Through these experiences a series of new social and sexual needs, human capacities, and pleasures have been created among a group of men. This homosexual experience, along with the slightly later emergence of a distinct lesbian experience,[23] and the feminist movement have created the basis for contemporary challenges to the hegemony of heterosexuality.

Enter gay liberation and the gay community

Recent social changes in the western capitalist countries have put in question the patriarchal, gender, and sexual relations established during the last century. A prolonged crisis in sexual and gender relations and in the meaning of sexuality has occurred. The feminist and gay liberation movements, for example, have challenged their relegation of sexual relations and particularly 'deviant' forms of sexuality to the socially defined private realm, subverting the public/private categories that have been used to regulate our sexual lives. The development of contraceptive and reproductive technologies has made it more and more possible to separate heterosexual pleasure and procreation, although the struggle continues about who will have access to, and control over, this technology. The expansion of consumer markets and advertising in the post-war period has led to an increasing drawing of sexuality and sexual images into the marketplace and the public realm.[24] This increasing public visibility of sexual images and sexual cultures has led to objections from those who would wish to reprivatize sexuality, in particular its 'deviant' strains. And feminists have challenged the patriarchal values that are visible in much advertising and heterosexual male pornography.

The social ferment of the sixties—particularly the civil rights, black power, and feminist movements—combined with earlier forms of

173

homosexual activism and the expansion of the gay commercial scene and culture to produce the gay liberation movement, which erupted in 1969 in the Stonewall Riot in New York City.[25] The movement developed a new, positive identity that has served as a basis for our resistance to heterosexual hegemony. The movement's most significant achievements were its contesting of the psychiatric definition of homosexuality as a mental illness and its creation of a culture and community that have transformed the lives of hundreds of thousands of men and women. As usual in a patriarchal society, many more opportunities have opened up for men than for women.

In a challenge to the 'universality' of heterosexuality, gays have affirmed that gay is just as good as straight, calling on lesbians and gay men to affirm themselves and their sexualities. This has challenged the gender and social policies of the state, suggesting that sexual activity does not have to be solely for reproduction, but can also be for play, pleasure, love, and support, and questioning the very right of the state to regulate people's sexual lives. We have affirmed our right to sexual self-determination and control over our own bodies and sexuality and have affirmed this right for others as well.

The growth of a visible gay community and the emergence of gay streets and commercial areas in many big cities have led to a reaction from the police, conservative political parties, and the new right. These groups fear the breakdown of 'traditional' sexual and family relations, which they associate with social and moral order, and see the challenge that gay liberation presents to heterosexual hegemony as a threat to the ways in which their lives and institutions are organized. They want lesbians and gay men out of public view and back in the closets, threatening our very existence as a public community.

In a sense the gay ghetto is both a playground and a potential concentration camp. While it provides people a place to meet and to explore and develop aspects of their lives and sexuality, it can also separate people from the rest of the population in a much larger closet that can be isolated and contained. The ghetto can tend to obscure the experiences gay men share with other men in their society. Locking people into the new categorization of gays as minority group or community may weaken the critique of sex and gender relations in society as a whole. As Altman explains, the 'ethnic homosexual' has emerged, 'the widespread recognition of a distinct cultural category which appears to be pressing for the same sort of "equality," in Western society as do ethnic minorities.'[26] However, lesbians and gay men are not born into a minority group, but like heterosexuals assume a sexual identity through social and psychological processes.[27] Gays and lesbians are not only a minority group but also an oppressed and denied sexuality. The position that gays are simply a new minority group can deflect our challenges to the dominant way of life.

In challenging heterosexuality as the social norm gays have brought into question aspects of the institutions of masculinity and male privilege. Over the last decade images of gay men have shifted from the effeminacy of the 'gender invert' to the new macho and clone looks that have dominated the gay men's community. This imagery challenges the previous stereotypes of homosexuals that associated our sexuality with gender nonconformity and has asserted that we can be both homosexual and 'masculine' at the same time.[28] In defining ourselves as masculine we have had to make use of and transform the existing images of straight masculinity we find around us. These new images challenge heterosexual norms that associate 'deviant' gender stereotypes with sexual 'deviancy,' for instance effeminacy with male homosexuality, but at the same time also tend to create new standards and stereotypes of what gay men are supposed to be like. These images and styles themselves continue to be imprisoned within the polarities of gender dichotomy. While gay men often believe we have freed ourselves from the social organization of gender, what we have actually done is exchange 'gender inversion' for a situation where homosexuality can be organized through 'normal' gender identifications. This assertion of masculinized imagery can to some extent lead us away from the critique of the institution of masculinity and its effects in our lives and persuade us that gender is no longer a problem for gay men.

It is ironic that some forms of resistance to past ways in which we were stigmatized can serve to accommodate us to aspects of the existing order of things. It is in this context that some of the challenges to masculinity and gender norms by straight men fighting against sexism will also be valuable to gay men. To be successful, gay liberation must challenge not only the institutionalization of heterosexuality as a social norm but also the institution of masculinity.

GAY LIBERATION AND THE RULING REGIME OF SEX

Gay liberation has emerged from the contradictions within the ruling system of sexual regulation and definition. It is fundamentally a struggle to transform the norms and definitions of sexual regulation. Gay liberation strives for the recognition of homosexuality as socially equal to the dominant social institution of heterosexuality. Yet as Weeks suggests,

the strategic aim of the gay liberation movement must be not simply the validation of the rights of a minority within a heterosexual majority but the challenge to all the rigid categorizations of sexuality. . . . The struggle for sexual self-determination is a struggle in the end for control over our bodies. To establish this control we must escape from those ideologies and categorizations which imprison us within the existing order.[29]

The struggle to transform our sexual norms and to end the control of the institution of heterosexuality over our lives holds out the possibility of beginning to disengage us from the ruling regime of sex and gender. As Foucault suggested,

movements that have been called sexual liberation movements, including gay liberation, are movements that start with sexuality, with the apparatus of sexuality in the midst of which they are caught and which make it function to the limit; but, at the same time, they are in motion relative to it, disengaging themselves and surmounting them.[30]

The struggle for gay liberation can be seen as a process of transformation. The assertion that gay is just as good as straight—which lies at the heart of gay liberation—is formally within the present regime of sexual categorization, for it still separates gay from straight as rigid categories and assigns value to sexuality, thus mirroring the limitations of the current sexual regime. However, the gay liberation movement operates both within and against this regime of sexual regulation. In asserting equal value for homosexuality and lesbianism, it begins to turn the ruling practices of sexual hierarchy on their head. Resistance begins within the present regime of sexual definitions, but it begins to shift the sexual boundaries that they have defined, opening up the possibility of transcending their limitations. By naming our specific experiences of the world, gay liberation provides the basis for a social and political struggle that can transform, defy, cut across, and break down the ruling regime of sex and gender.

The gay and lesbian communities, like other oppressed social groups, oscillate between resistance and accommodation to oppression. This is a struggle on two closely interrelated fronts. First, the gay community itself needs to strengthen cultures of resistance by building on sexual and cultural traditions that question gender norms and the relegation of erotic life to the state-defined private sphere. This will involve challenging the internalization and reproduction of sexism, racism, ageism, and class divisions within the gay community, as well as building alliances with other social groups fighting these forms of domination. Secondly, it requires a struggle outside the gay and lesbian communities for the defense of a community under attack by the police, government, and media. A key part of this strategy would be campaigning for new social policies that uproot heterosexuality as the social norm.

OPENING UP EROTIC CHOICES FOR EVERYONE

In developing a radical perspective we need to draw on the insights of lesbian feminism about the social power of heterosexuality and also on the historical perspectives provided by the new critical gay history, which reveals the social and historical process of the organization of heterosexual hegemony and the present system of sexual regulation more generally. These understandings create the basis for alliances between feminists, lesbians, gay liberationists, anti-sexist men, and other groups against the institution of heterosexuality, which lies at the root of the social oppression of women, lesbians, and gays. This alliance would contest the hegemony of heterosexuality in the legal system, state policies, in forms of family organization, and in the churches, unions, and other social bodies. The struggle would be for women, gays, and others to gain control over our bodies and sexuality and to begin to define our own eroticism and sexuality. A fundamental aspect of such an approach would be the elaboration and exploration of the experiences and visions of those of us living outside institutionalized heterosexuality.

Proposals for new and different ways of living (including collective and nonsexist ways of rearing children) are particularly vital since the new right and moral conservatives in their various incarnations are taking advantage of people's fears about changes in family organization and sexual mores to campaign in support of patriarchal and heterosexist social norms. The defense of a male-dominated heterosexuality is not only central to the policies of the new right and moral conservatives regarding feminism and gay liberation, but is a central theme of their racial and class politics as well.[31] The progressive movement's failure to deal with people's real fears, concerns, and hopes regarding sexual and gender politics is an important reason why right-wing groups are able to gain support. Feminism, gay liberation,

177

and all progressive movements will have to articulate a vision that will allow us to move forward beyond the confines of institutionalized heterosexuality.

Gay liberation enables heterosexual men who question heterosexism to contribute to this new social vision. The issues raised by gay liberation must be addressed by all men interested in fundamental change because heterosexism limits and restricts the lives of all men. This challenge will only be effective, however, if heterosexual privilege is challenged in daily life and in social institutions. This could help begin the long struggle to disentangle heterosexual desire from the confines of institutionalized masculinity and heterosexuality. Together we could begin to redefine and remake masculinity and sexuality. If sexuality is socially produced, then heterosexuality itself can be transformed and redefined and its pleasures and desires separated from the social relations of power and domination. Gay liberation can allow all men to challenge gender and sexual norms and redefine gender and sex for ourselves in alliance with feminism; it can allow all men to explore and create different forms of sexual pleasures in our lives. This redefining of masculinity and sexuality will also help destroy the anxieties and insecurities of many straight men who try so hard to be 'real men.' But the success of this undertaking depends on the ability to develop alternative visions and experiences that will help all people understand how their lives could be organized without heterosexuality as the institutionalized social norm. Such a goal is a radically transformed society in which everyone will be able to gain control of his or her own body, desires, and life.

Notes

1. See G. K. Lehne. 'Homophobia Among Men,' in Deborah David and Robert Brannon, *The Forty Nine Per Cent Majority* (Reading, MA: Addison-Wesley, 1976), 78.
2. On the notion of institutionalized heterosexuality see Charlotte Bunch, 'Not For Lesbians Only,' *Quest* 11, no. 2 (Fall 1975). Also see Adrienne Rich, 'Compulsory Heterosexuality And Lesbian Existence,' in Snitow, Stansell and Thompson, eds., *Powers of Desire: The Politics of Sexuality* (New York: Monthly Review Press, 1983): 177–205.
3. Joe Interrante, 'Dancing Along the Precipice: The Men's Movement in the 80s,' *Radical America* 15, no. 5 (September–October 1981): 54.
4. Ned Lyttelton, 'Men's Liberation, Men Against Sexism and Major Dividing Lines,' *Resources for Feminist Research* 12, no. 4 (December/January 1983/ 1984): 33. Several discussions with Ned Lyttelton were very useful in clarifying my ideas in this section and throughout this paper.

5. Interrante, *op. cit.*, 54.

6. For further elaboration see my forthcoming book entitled *The Regulation of Desire* (Montreal: Black Rose, 1986).

7. See Kinsey, Pomeroy, and Martin, *Sexual Behavior in the Human Male* (Philadelphia: W. B. Saunders, 1948) and Mary McIntosh, 'The Homosexual Role,' in Plummer, ed., *The Making of The Modern Homosexual* (London: Hutchinson, 1981), 38–43.

8. Bunch, 'Not For Lesbians Only.'

9. See Frank Pearce, 'How to be Immoral and Ill, Pathetic and Dangerous all at the same time: Mass Media and the Homosexual,' in Cohen and Young, eds., *The Manufacture of News: Deviance, Social Problems and the Mass Media* (London: Constable, 1973), 284–301.

10. See Andrew Hodges and David Hutter, *With Downcast Gays: Aspects of Homosexual Self-Oppression* (Toronto: Pink Triangle Press, 1977).

11. Gayle Rubin, 'The Traffic in Women: Notes on the Political Economy of Sex,' in Reiter, ed., *Towards an Anthropology of Women* (New York: Monthly Review Press, 1979): 159. I prefer the use of sex and gender relations to sex/gender system since the notion of system tends to conflate questions of sexuality and gender, and suggests that sex/gender relations are a separate system from other social relations rather than an integral aspect of them.

12. See Joe Interrante, 'From Homosexual to Gay to ?: Recent Work in Gay History,' in *Radical America* 15, no. 6 (November–December 1981); Martha Vicinus, 'Sexuality and Power: A Review of Current Work in the History of Sexuality,' *Feminist Studies* 8, no. 1 (Spring 1982): 133–56; and Robert A. Padgug, 'Sexual Matters on Conceptualizing Sexuality in History,' *Radical History Review*, 'Sexuality in History' Issue, no. 20 (Spring/Summer 1979): 3–23.

13. See for instance Michel Foucault, *The History of Sexuality*, vol. 1, *An Introduction* (New York: Vintage, 1980); Jeffrey Weeks, *Sex, Politics and Society: The Regulation of Sexuality since 1800* (London: Hutchinson, 1981); and Jonathan Ned Katz, *Gay/Lesbian Almanac* (New York: Harper and Row, 1983). For recent feminist explorations of sexuality see Snitow, Stansell and Thompson, *Powers of Desire* (New York: Monthly Review Press, 1983); Carol Vance, ed., *Pleasure and Danger: Exploring Female Sexuality* (Boston: Routledge and Kegan Paul, 1984); Rosalind Coward, *Female Desire: Women's Sexuality Today* (London: Routledge and Kegan Paul, 1984); and Mariana Valverde, *Sex, Power and Pleasure* (Toronto: Women's Press, 1985).

14. See Wilhelm Reich, *The Sexual Revolution* (New York: Straus and Giroux, 1974) and Baxandall, ed., *Sex Pol: Essays 1929–1934, Wilhelm Reich* (New York: Vintage, 1972).

15. Unfortunately, over the last few years some anti-pornography feminists have suggested that sexuality is only a realm of danger for women, obscuring how it can also be a realm of pleasure. Some anti-porn feminists have been used by state agencies in attempting to clamp down on sexually explicit material including sexual material for gay men and lesbians. See Vance, *Pleasure and Danger*, Varda Burstyn, ed., *Women Against Censorship* (Vancouver and Toronto: Douglas and McIntyre, 1985), and Varda Burstyn, 'Anatomy of a Moral Panic' and Gary Kinsman, 'The Porn Debate,' *Fuse* 3, no. 1 (Summer 1984).

16. On this see the work of John D'Emilio, for instance his 'Capitalism and Gay Identity,' in Snitow, Stansell and Thompson, eds., *Powers of Desire*, 100–13, and his *Sexual Politics, Sexual Communities* (Chicago: University of Chicago Press, 1983).

17. See Randolph Trunbach, 'London's Sodomites: Homosexual Behaviour and Western Culture in the 18th Century,' *Journal of Social History*, (Fall 1977): 1–33; Mary McIntosh, 'The Homosexual Role,' in Plummer, ed., *The Making of the Modern Homosexual*; Alan Bray, *Homosexuality in Renaissance England* (London: Gay Men's Press, 1982); and Jeffrey Weeks, *Sex, Politics and Society*.

18. See Foucault, *The History of Sexuality*, vol. 1 and Kinsman, *The Regulation of Desire*.

19. John Lauritsen and David Thorstald, *The Early Homosexual Rights Movement* (New York: Times Change Press, 1974), 6.

20. Arno Karlen, *Sexuality and Homosexuality* (New York: W. W. Norton, 1971), 185.

21. Ezra Hurlburt Stafford, 'Perversion,' the *Canadian Journal of Medicine and Surgery* 3, no. 4 (April 1898).

22. On this see Anna Davin, 'Imperialism and Motherhood,' *History Workshop*, no. 5 (Spring 1978).

23. See Lillian Faderman, *Surpassing the Love of Men* (New York: William Morrow, 1981); Christina Simmons, 'Companionate Marriage and the Lesbian Threat,' in *Frontiers* 4, no. 3 (Fall 1979); Martha Vicinus, 'Sexuality and Power;' and Ann Ferguson, 'Patriarchy, Sexual Identity, and the Sexual Revolution,' *Signs* 7, no. 1 (Fall 1981): 158–72.

24. See Gary Kinsman, 'Porn/Censor Wars and the Battlefield of Sex,' in *Issues in Censorship* (Toronto: A Space, 1985), 31–9.

25. See John D'Emilio, *Sexual Politics, Sexual Communities*.

26. Dennis Altman, 'What Changed in the Seventies?' in Gay Left Collective, eds., *Homosexuality, Power and Politics* (London: Allison and Busby, 1980), 61.

27. One prejudice that is embodied in sexual legislation and social policies is the myth that lesbians and gay men are a special threat to young people and that gay men are 'child molesters.' Most studies show, on the contrary, that more than 90 per cent of sexual assaults on young people are committed by heterosexual men and often within the family or home. Breines and Gordon state that 'approximately 92 per cent of the victims are female and 97 per cent of the assailants are males.' See Wini Breines and Linda Gordon, 'The New Scholarship on Family Violence,' *Signs* 8 no. 3 (Spring 1983): 522. Also see Elizabeth Wilson, *What Is to Be Done About Violence Against Women* (London: Penguin, 1983), particular 117–34. We have to eliminate special age restrictions on the right to participate in consensual lesbian and gay sex so that lesbian and gay young people can express their desires and instead challenge the principal source of violence against children and young people—the patriarchal family and straight-identified men. We have to propose changes in family relations and schooling and alternative social policies that would allow young people to take more control over their own lives, to get support in fighting unwanted sexual attention and to be able to participate in consensual sexual activity.

28. See John Marshall, 'Pansies, Perverts and Macho Men: Changing Conceptions of Male Homosexuality' and Greg Blachford, 'Male Dominance in the Gay

World,' in Plummer, ed., *The Making of the Modern Homosexual*; and also Seymour Kleinberg's article elsewhere in this volume for a different approach.

29. Jeffrey Weeks, 'Capitalism and the Organization of Sex,' Gay Left Collective, eds., *Homosexuality, Power and Politics*, 19–20.

30. Michel Foucault, 'Power and Sex,' *Telos*, no. 32 (Summer 1977): 152–61.

31. See Allen Hunter, 'In the Wings: New Right Ideology and Organization,' *Radical America* 15, no. 1–2 (Spring 1981): 127–38.

Masculinity as Homophobia: Fear, Shame, and Silence in the Construction of Gender Identity[1]

Michael S. Kimmel*

We think of manhood as eternal, a timeless essence that resides deep in the heart of every man. We think of manhood as a thing, a quality that one either has or doesn't have. We think of manhood as innate, residing in the particular biological composition of the human male, the result of androgens or the possession of a penis. We think of manhood as a transcendent tangible property that each man must manifest in the world, the reward presented with great ceremony to a young novice by his elders for having successfully completed an arduous initiation ritual. In the words of poet Robert Bly (1990), 'the structure at the bottom of the male psyche is still as firm as it was twenty thousand years ago' (p. 230).

In this chapter, I view masculinity as a constantly changing collection of meanings that we construct through our relationships with ourselves, with each other, and with our world. Manhood is neither static nor timeless; it is historical. Manhood is not the manifestation of an inner essence; it is socially constructed. Manhood does not bubble up to consciousness from our biological makeup; it is created in culture. Manhood means different things at different times to different people. We come to know what it means to be a man in our culture by setting our definitions in opposition to a set of 'others'—racial minorities, sexual minorities, and, above all, women.

Our definitions of manhood are constantly changing, being played out on the political and social terrain on which the relationships between women and men are played out. In fact, the search for a transcendent, timeless definition of manhood is itself a sociological phenomenon—we tend to search for the timeless and eternal during moments of crisis, those points of transition when old definitions no longer work and new definitions are yet to be firmly established.

---

* Reprinted with permission of Michael S. Kimmel.

This idea that manhood is socially constructed and historically shifting should not be understood as a loss, that something is being taken away from men. In fact, it gives us something extraordinarily valuable—agency, the capacity to act. It gives us a sense of historical possibilities to replace the despondent resignation that invariably attends timeless, ahistorical essentialisms. Our behaviors are not simply 'just human nature,' because 'boys will be boys.' From the materials we find around us in our culture—other people, ideas, objects—we actively create our worlds, our identities. Men, both individually and collectively, can change.

In this chapter, I explore this social and historical construction of both hegemonic masculinity and alternate masculinities, with an eye toward offering a new theoretical model of American manhood.[2] To accomplish this I first uncover some of the hidden gender meanings in classical statements of social and political philosophy, so that I can anchor the emergence of contemporary manhood in specific historical and social contexts. I then spell out the ways in which this version of masculinity emerged in the United States, by tracing both psycho-analytic developmental sequences and a historical trajectory in the development of marketplace relationships.

[*Two sections, one on 'Classical Social Theory as a Hidden Meditation of Manhood' and one on 'Masculinity as History and the History of Masculinity' were omitted from this version of the essay. In the first of these sections, Kimmel analyzes four quotes from Marx/Engels, Tocqueville, Weber, and Freud, and demonstrates how these seemingly innocuous statements embody western conceptions of manhood, and in particular the significance of the American ideology of the 'self-made man'. In the second section, Kimmel identifies two prevalent models of American manhood in the late eighteenth and early nineteenth centuries: the 'Genteel Patriarch' and the 'Heroic Artisan'. He explores, also, how these models were eclipsed by 'Marketplace Man', a new masculine identity that emerged in the 1830s. Much of this work is elaborated in* Manhood in America: A Cultural History *(New York: Free Press, 1996).*]

MASCULINITIES AS POWER RELATIONS

Marketplace Masculinity describes the normative definition of American masculinity. It describes his characteristics—aggression, competition, anxiety—and the arena in which those characteristics are deployed—the public sphere, the marketplace. If the marketplace is the arena in which manhood is tested and proved, it is a gendered arena, in which tensions between women and men and tensions among different groups of men are weighted with meaning. These tensions suggest that cultural definitions of gender are played out in a contested terrain and are themselves power relations.

All masculinities are not created equal; or rather, we are all *created* equal, but any hypothetical equality evaporates quickly because our definitions of masculinity are not equally valued in our society. One definition of manhood continues to remain the standard against which other forms of manhood are measured and evaluated. Within the dominant culture, the masculinity that defines white, middle class, early middle-aged, heterosexual men is the masculinity that sets the standards for other men, against which other men are measured and, more often than not, found wanting. Sociologist Erving Goffman (1963) wrote that in America, there is only 'one complete, unblushing male':

a young, married, white, urban, northern heterosexual, Protestant father of college education, fully employed, of good complexion, weight and height, and a recent record in sports. Every American male tends to look out upon the world from this perspective.... Any male who fails to qualify in any one of these ways is likely to view himself ... as unworthy, incomplete, and inferior. (p. 128)

This is the definition that we will call 'hegemonic' masculinity, the image of masculinity of those men who hold power, which has become the standard in psychological evaluations, sociological research, and self-help and advice literature for teaching young men to become 'real men' (Connell, 1987). The hegemonic definition of manhood is a man in power, a man *with* power, and a man of power. We equate manhood with being strong, successful, capable, reliable, in control. The very definitions of manhood we have developed in our culture maintain the power that some men have over other men and that men have over women.

Our culture's definition of masculinity is thus several stories at once. It is about the individual man's quest to accumulate those cultural symbols that denote manhood, signs that he has in fact achieved it. It is about those standards being used against women to prevent their inclusion in public life and their consignment to a devalued private sphere. It is about the differential access that different types of men have to those cultural resources that confer manhood and about how each of these groups then develop their own modifications to preserve and claim their manhood. It is about the power of these definitions themselves to serve to maintain the real-life power that men have over women and that some men have over other men. [. . .]

But we keep trying, valiantly and vainly, to measure up. American masculinity is a relentless test.[3] [. . .] Whatever the variations by race, class, age, ethnicity, or sexual orientation, being a man means 'not being like women.' This notion of anti-femininity lies at the heart of contemporary and historical conceptions of manhood, so that masculinity is defined more by what one is not rather than who one is.

MASCULINITY AS THE FLIGHT FROM THE FEMININE

Historically and developmentally, masculinity has been defined as the flight from women, the repudiation of femininity. Since Freud, we have come to understand that developmentally the central task that every little boy must confront is to develop a secure identity for himself as a man. [. . .]

Masculinity, in this model, is irrevocably tied to sexuality. The boy's sexuality will now come to resemble the sexuality of his father (or at least the way he imagines his father)—menacing, predatory, possessive, and possibly punitive. The boy has come to identify with his oppressor; now he can become the oppressor himself. But a terror remains, the terror that the young man will be unmasked as a fraud, as a man who has not completely and irrevocably separated from mother. It will be other men who will do the unmasking. Failure will de-sex the man, make him appear as not fully a man. He will be seen as a wimp, a Mama's boy, a sissy. [. . .]

The flight from femininity is angry and frightened, because mother can so easily emasculate the young boy by her power to render him dependent, or at least to remind him of dependency. It is relentless; manhood becomes a lifelong quest to demonstrate its achievement, as if to prove the unprovable to others, because we feel so unsure of it ourselves. Women don't often feel compelled to 'prove their womanhood'—the phrase itself sounds ridiculous. Women have different kinds of gender identity crises; their anger and frustration, and their own symptoms of depression, come more from being excluded than from questioning whether they are feminine enough.[4]

The drive to repudiate the mother as the indication of the acquisition of masculine gender identity has three consequences for the young boy. First, he pushes away his real mother, and with her the traits of nurturance, compassion, and tenderness she may have embodied. Second, he suppresses those traits in himself, because they will reveal his incomplete separation from mother. His life becomes a lifelong project to demonstrate that he possesses none of his mother's traits. Masculine identity is born in the renunciation of the feminine not in the direct affirmation of the masculine, which leaves masculine gender identity tenuous and fragile.

Third, [. . .] the boy also learns to devalue all women in his society, as the living embodiments of those traits in himself he has learned to despise. Whether or not he was aware of it, Freud also described the origins of sexism—the systematic devaluation of women—in the desperate efforts of the boy to separate from mother. We may *want* 'a girl just like the girl that married dear old Dad,' as the popular song had it, but we certainly don't want to *be like* her. [. . .]

When does it end? Never. To admit weakness, to admit frailty or fragility, is to be seen as a wimp, a sissy, not a real man. But seen by whom?

MASCULINITY AS A HOMOSOCIAL ENACTMENT

Other men: We are under the constant careful scrutiny of other men. Other men watch us, rank us, grant our acceptance into the realm of manhood. Manhood is demonstrated for other men's approval. It is other men who evaluate the performance. Literary critic David Leverenz (1991) argues that 'ideologies of manhood have functioned primarily in relation to the gaze of male peers and male authority' (p. 769). Think of how men boast to one another of their accomplishments—from their latest sexual conquest to the size of the fish they caught—and how we constantly parade the markers of manhood—wealth, power, status, sexy women—in front of other men, desperate for their approval.

That men prove their manhood in the eyes of other men is both a consequence of sexism and one of its chief props. 'Women have, in men's minds, such a low place on the social ladder of this country that it's useless to define yourself in terms of a woman,' noted playwright David Mamet. 'What men need is men's approval.' Women become a kind of currency that men use to improve their ranking on the masculine social scale. (Even those moments of heroic conquest of women carry, I believe, a current of homosocial evaluation.) Masculinity is a *homosocial* enactment. We test ourselves, perform heroic feats, take enormous risks all because we want other men to grant us our manhood.

Masculinity as a homosocial enactment is fraught with danger, with the risk of failure, and with intense relentless competition. 'Every man you meet has a rating or an estimate of himself which he never loses or forgets,' wrote Kenneth Wayne (1912) in his popular turn-of-the-century advice book. 'A man has his own rating, and instantly he lays it alongside of the other man' (p. 18). Almost a century later, another man remarked to psychologist Sam Osherson (1992) that '[b]y the time you're an adult, it's easy to think you're always in competition with men, for the attention of women, in sports, at work' (p. 291).

....

MASCULINITY AS HOMOPHOBIA

....

If masculinity is a homosocial enactment, its overriding emotion is fear. In the Freudian model, the fear of the father's power terrifies the young boy to renounce his desire for his mother and identify with his father. This model links gender identity with sexual orientation: The little boy's identification with father (becoming masculine) allows him to now engage in sexual relations with women (he becomes heterosexual). This is the origin of how we can 'read' one's sexual orientation through the successful performance of gender identity. Second, the fear that the little boy feels does not send him scurrying into the arms of his mother to protect him from his father. Rather, he believes he will overcome his fear by identifying with its source. We become masculine by identifying with our oppressor.

But there is a piece of the puzzle missing, a piece that Freud, himself, implied but did not follow up.[5] If the pre-oedipal boy identifies with mother, he *sees the world through mother's eyes.* Thus, when he confronts father during his great oedipal crisis, he experiences a split vision: He sees his father as his mother sees his father, with a combination of awe, wonder, terror, *and desire.* He simultaneously sees the father as he, the boy, would like to see him—as the object not of desire but of emulation. Repudiating mother and identifying with father only partially answers his dilemma. What is he to do with that homoerotic desire, the desire he felt because he saw father the way that his mother saw father?

He must suppress it. Homoerotic desire is cast as feminine desire, desire for other men. Homophobia is the effort to suppress that desire, to purify all relationships with other men, with women, with children of its taint, and to ensure that no one could possibly ever mistake one for a homosexual. Homophobic flight from intimacy with other men is the repudiation of the homosexual within—never completely successful and hence constantly reenacted in every homosocial relationship. 'The lives of most American men are bounded, and their interests daily curtailed by the constant necessity to prove to their fellows, and to themselves, that they are not sissies, not homosexuals,' writes psychoanalytic historian Geoffrey Gorer (1964). 'Any interest or pursuit which is identified as a feminine interest or pursuit becomes deeply suspect for men' (p. 129).

Even if we do not subscribe to Freudian psychoanalytic ideas, we can still observe how, in less sexualized terms, the father is the first man who evaluates the boy's masculine performance, the first pair of male eyes before whom he tries to prove himself. Those eyes will follow him for the rest of his life. Other men's eyes will join them—the eyes of role models such as teachers, coaches, bosses, or media heroes; the eyes of his peers, his friends, his workmates; and the eyes of millions of other men, living and dead, from whose constant scrutiny of his performance he will never be free. 'The tradition of all the dead generations weighs like a nightmare on the brain of the living,' was how Karl Marx put it over a century ago (1848/1964, p. 11). 'The birthright of every American male is a chronic sense of personal inadequacy,' is how two psychologists describe it today (Woolfolk & Richardson, 1978, p. 57).

That nightmare from which we never seem to awaken is that those other men will see that sense of inadequacy, they will see that in our own eyes we are not who we are pretending to be. What we call masculinity is often a hedge against being revealed as a fraud, an exaggerated set of activities that keep others from seeing through us, and a frenzied effort to keep at bay those fears within ourselves. Our real fear 'is not fear of women but of being ashamed or humiliated in front of other men, or being dominated by stronger men' (Leverenz, 1986, p. 451).

This, then, is the great secret of American manhood: *We are afraid of other men.* Homophobia is a central organizing principle of our cultural definition of manhood. Homophobia is more than the irrational fear of gay men, more than the fear that we might be perceived as gay. 'The word "faggot" has nothing to do with homosexual experience or even with fears of homosexuals,' writes David Leverenz (1986). 'It comes out of the depths of manhood: a label of ultimate contempt for anyone who seems sissy, untough, uncool' (p. 455). Homophobia is the fear that other men will unmask us, emasculate us, reveal to us and the world that we do not measure up, that we are not real men. We are afraid to let other men see that fear. Fear makes us ashamed, because the recognition of fear in ourselves is proof to ourselves that we are not as manly as we pretend, that we are, like the young man in a poem by Yeats, 'one that ruffles in a manly pose for all his timid heart.' Our fear is the fear of humiliation. We are ashamed to be afraid.

Shame leads to silence—the silences that keep other people believing that we actually approve of the things that are done to women, to minorities, to gays and lesbians in our culture. The frightened silence as we scurry past a woman being hassled by men on the street. That furtive silence when men make sexist or racist jokes in a bar. That clammy-handed silence when guys in the office make gay-bashing jokes. Our fears are the sources of our silences, and men's silence is what keeps the system running. This might help to explain why women often complain that their male friends or partners are often so understanding when they are alone and yet laugh at sexist jokes or even make those jokes themselves when they are out with a group.

The fear of being seen as a sissy dominates the cultural definitions of manhood. It starts so early. 'Boys among boys are ashamed to be unmanly,' wrote one educator in 1871 (cited in Rotundo, 1993, p. 264). I have a standing bet with a friend that I can walk onto any playground in America where 6-year-old boys are happily playing and by asking one question, I can provoke a fight. That question is simple: 'Who's a sissy around here?' Once posed, the challenge is made. One of two things is likely to happen. One boy will accuse another of being a sissy, to which that boy will respond that he is not a sissy, that the first boy is. They may have to fight it out to see who's lying. Or a whole group of boys will surround one boy and all shout, 'He is! He is!' That boy will either burst into tears and run home crying, disgraced, or he will have to take on several boys at once, to prove that he's not a sissy. (And what will his father or older brothers tell him if he chooses to run home crying?) It will be some time before he regains any sense of self-respect.

Violence is often the single most evident marker of manhood. Rather it is the willingness to fight, the desire to fight. The origin of our expression that one has a chip on one's shoulder lies in the practice of an adolescent boy in the country or small town at the turn of the

189

century, who would literally walk around with a chip of wood balanced on his shoulder—a signal of his readiness to fight with anyone who would take the initiative of knocking the chip off (see Gorer, 1964, p. 38; Mead, 1965).

As adolescents, we learn that our peers are a kind of gender police constantly threatening to unmask us as feminine, as sissies. One of the favorite tricks when I was an adolescent was to ask a boy to look at his fingernails. If he held his palm toward his face and curled his fingers back to see them, he passed the test. He'd looked at his nails 'like a man.' But if he held the back of his hand away from his face, and looked at his fingernails with arm outstretched, he was immediately ridiculed as a sissy. As young men we are constantly riding those gender boundaries, checking the fences we have constructed on the perimeter, making sure that nothing even remotely feminine might show through. The possibilities of being unmasked are everywhere. Even the most seemingly insignificant thing can pose a threat or activate that haunting terror. On the day the students in my course 'Sociology of Men and Masculinities' were scheduled to discuss homophobia and male–male friendships, one student provided a touching illustration. Noting that it was a beautiful day, the first day of spring after a brutal northeast winter, he decided to wear shorts to class. 'I had this really nice pair of new Madras shorts,' he commented. 'But then I thought to myself, these shorts have lavender and pink in them. Today's class topic is homophobia. Maybe today is not the best day to wear these shorts.'

Our efforts to maintain a manly front cover everything we do. What we wear. How we talk. How we walk. What we eat. Every mannerism, every movement contains a coded gender language. Think, for example, of how you would answer the question: How do you 'know' if a man is homosexual? When I ask this question in classes or workshops, respondents invariably provide a pretty standard list of stereotypically effeminate behaviors. He walks a certain way, talks a certain way, acts a certain way. He's very emotional; he shows his feelings. One woman commented that she 'knows' a man is gay if he really cares about her; another said she knows he's gay if he shows no interest in her, if he leaves her alone.

Now alter the question and imagine what heterosexual men do to make sure no one could possibly get the 'wrong idea' about them. Responses typically refer to the original stereotypes, this time as a set of negative rules about behavior. Never dress that way. Never talk or walk that way. Never show your feelings or get emotional. Always be prepared to demonstrate sexual interest in women that you meet, so it is impossible for any woman to get the wrong idea about you. In this sense, homophobia, the fear of being perceived as gay, as not a real man, keeps men exaggerating all the traditional rules of masculinity, including sexual predation with women. Homophobia and sexism go hand in hand.

The stakes of perceived sissydom are enormous—sometimes matters of life and death. We take enormous risks to prove our manhood, exposing ourselves disproportionately to health risks, workplace hazards, and stress-related illnesses. Men commit suicide three times as often as women. Psychiatrist Willard Gaylin (1992) explains that it is 'invariably because of perceived social humiliation,' most often tied to failure in business. [. . .]

In one survey, women and men were asked what they were most afraid of. Women responded that they were most afraid of being raped and murdered. Men responded that they were most afraid of being laughed at (Noble, 1992, pp. 105–106).

HOMOPHOBIA AS A CAUSE OF SEXISM, HETEROSEXISM, AND RACISM

Homophobia is intimately interwoven with both sexism and racism. The fear—sometimes conscious, sometimes not—that others might perceive us as homosexual propels men to enact all manner of exaggerated masculine behaviors and attitudes to make sure that no one could possibly get the wrong idea about us. One of the centerpieces of that exaggerated masculinity is putting women down, both by excluding them from the public sphere and by the quotidian put-downs in speech and behaviors that organize the daily life of the American man. Women and gay men become the 'other' against which heterosexual men project their identities, against whom they stack the decks so as to compete in a situation in which they will always win, so that by suppressing them, men can stake a claim for their own manhood. Women threaten emasculation by representing the home, workplace, and familial responsibility, the negation of fun. Gay men have historically played the role of the consummate sissy in the American popular mind because homosexuality is seen as an inversion of normal gender development. There have been other 'others.' Through American history, various groups have represented the sissy, the non-men against whom American men played out their definitions of manhood, often with vicious results. In fact, these changing groups provide an interesting lesson in American historical development.

At the turn of the 19th century, it was Europeans and children who provided the contrast for American men. The 'true American was vigorous, manly, and direct, not effete and corrupt like the supposed Europeans,' writes Rupert Wilkinson (1986). 'He was plain rather than ornamented, rugged rather than luxury seeking, a liberty loving common man or natural gentleman rather than an aristocratic oppressor or servile minion' (p. 96). The 'real man' of the early 19th century was neither noble nor serf. By the middle of the century, black slaves had replaced the effete nobleman. Slaves were seen as dependent, helpless men, incapable of defending their women and children, and therefore less than manly. Native Americans were cast as foolish and naive children, so they could be infantalized as the 'Red Children of the Great White Father' and therefore excluded from full manhood.

By the end of the century, new European immigrants were also added to the list of the unreal men, especially the Irish and Italians, who were seen as too passionate and emotionally volatile to remain controlled sturdy oaks, and Jews, who were seen as too bookishly effete and too physically puny to truly measure up. In the mid-20th century, it was also Asians—first the Japanese during the Second World War, and more recently, the Vietnamese during the Vietnam War—who have served as unmanly templates against which American men have hurled their gendered rage. Asian men were seen as small, soft, and effeminate—hardly men at all.

Such a list of 'hyphenated' Americans—Italian-, Jewish-, Irish-, African-, Native-, Asian-, gay—composes the majority of American men. So manhood is only possible for a distinct minority, and the definition has been constructed to prevent the others from achieving it. Interestingly, this emasculation of one's enemies has a flip side—and one that is equally gendered. These very groups that have historically been cast as less than manly were also, often simultaneously, cast as hypermasculine, as sexually aggressive, violent rapacious beasts, against whom 'civilized' men must take a decisive stand and thereby rescue civilization. Thus black men were depicted as rampaging sexual beasts, women as carnivorously carnal, gay men as sexually insatiable, southern European men as sexually predatory and voracious, and Asian men as vicious and cruel torturers who were immorally disinterested in life itself, willing to sacrifice their entire people for their whims. But whether one saw these groups as effeminate sissies or as brutal uncivilized savages, the terms with which they were perceived were gendered. These groups become the 'others,' the screens against which traditional conceptions of manhood were developed.

Being seen as unmanly is a fear that propels American men to deny manhood to others, as a way of proving the unprovable—that one is fully manly. Masculinity becomes a defense against the perceived threat of humiliation in the eyes of other men, enacted through a 'sequence of postures'—things we might say, or do, or even think, that, if we thought carefully about them, would make us ashamed of ourselves (Savran, 1992, p. 16). After all, how many of us have made homophobic or sexist remarks, or told racist jokes, or made lewd comments to women on the street? How many of us have translated those ideas and those words into actions, by physically attacking gay men, or forcing or cajoling a woman to have sex even though she didn't really want to because it was important to score?

POWER AND POWERLESSNESS IN THE LIVES OF MEN

I have argued that homophobia, men's fear of other men, is the animating condition of the dominant definition of masculinity in America, that the reigning definition of masculinity is a defensive effort to prevent being emasculated. In our efforts to suppress or overcome those fears, the dominant culture exacts a tremendous price from those deemed less than fully manly: women, gay men, nonnative-born men, men of color. This perspective may help clarify a paradox in men's lives, a paradox in which men have virtually all the power and yet do not feel powerful (see Kaufman, 1993).

Manhood is equated with power—over women, over other men. Everywhere we look, we see the institutional expression of that power—in state and national legislatures, on the boards of directors of every major U.S. corporation or law firm, and in every school and hospital administration. Women have long understood this, and feminist women have spent the past three decades challenging both the public and the private expressions of men's power and acknowledging their fear of men. Feminism as a set of theories both explains women's fear of men and empowers women to confront it both publicly and privately. Feminist women have theorized that masculinity is about the drive for domination, the drive for power, for conquest.

This feminist definition of masculinity as the drive for power is theorized from women's point of view. It is how women experience masculinity. But it assumes a symmetry between the public and the private that does not conform to men's experiences. Feminists observe that women, as a group, do not hold power in our society. They also observe that individually, they as women, do not feel powerful. They feel afraid, vulnerable. Their observation of the social reality and their individual experiences are therefore symmetrical. Feminism also observes that men, as a group, *are* in power. Thus, with the same symmetry, feminism has tended to assume that individually men must feel powerful.

This is why the feminist critique of masculinity often falls on deaf ears with men. When confronted with the analysis that men have all the power, many men react incredulously. 'What do you mean, men have all the power?' they ask. 'What are you talking about? My wife bosses me around. My kids boss me around. My boss bosses me around. I have no power at all! I'm completely powerless!'

Men's feelings are not the feelings of the powerful, but of those who see themselves as powerless. These are the feelings that come inevitably from the discontinuity between the social and the psychological, between the aggregate analysis that reveals how men are in power as a group and the psychological fact that they do not feel powerful as individuals. They are the feelings of men who were raised to believe themselves entitled to feel that power, but do not feel it. No wonder many men are frustrated and angry.

This may explain the recent popularity of those workshops and retreats designed to help men to claim their 'inner' power, their 'deep manhood,' or their 'warrior within.' Authors such as Bly (1990), Moore and Gillette (1991, 1992, 1993a, 1993b), Farrell (1986, 1993), and Keen (1991) honor and respect men's feelings of powerlessness and acknowledge those feelings to be both true and real. 'They gave white men the semblance of power,' notes John Lee, one of the leaders of these retreats (quoted in *Newsweek*, p. 41). 'We'll let you run the country, but in the meantime, stop feeling, stop talking, and continue swallowing your pain and your hurt.' (We are not told who 'they' are.)

Often the purveyors of the mythopoetic men's movement, that broad umbrella that encompasses all the groups helping men to retrieve this mythic deep manhood, use the image of the chauffeur to describe modern man's position. The chauffeur appears to have the power—he's wearing the uniform, he's in the driver's seat, and he knows where he's going. So, to the observer, the chauffeur looks as though he is in command. But to the chauffeur himself, they note, he is merely taking orders. He is not at all in charge.[6]

Despite the reality that everyone knows chauffeurs do not have the power, this image remains appealing to the men who hear it at these weekend workshops. But there is a missing piece to the image, a piece concealed by the framing of the image in terms of the individual man's experience. That missing piece is that the person who is giving the orders is also a man. Now we have a relationship *between* men— between men giving orders and other men taking those orders. The man who identifies with the chauffeur is entitled to be the man giving the orders, but he is not. ('They,' it turns out, are other men.)

The dimension of power is now reinserted into men's experience not only as the product of individual experience but also as the product of relations with other men. In this sense, men's experience of powerlessness is *real*—the men actually feel it and certainly act on it— but it is not *true*, that is, it does not accurately describe their condition. In contrast to women's lives, men's lives are structured around relationships of power and men's differential access to power, as well as the differential access to that power of men as a group. Our imperfect analysis of our own situation leads us to believe that we men need *more* power, rather than leading us to support feminists' efforts to rearrange power relationships along more equitable lines.

Philosopher Hannah Arendt (1970) fully understood this contradictory experience of social and individual power:

Power corresponds to the human ability not just to act but to act in concert. Power is never the property of an individual; it belongs to a group and remains in existence only so long as the group keeps together. When we say of somebody that he is 'in power' we actually refer to his being empowered by a certain number of people to act in their name. The moment the group, from which the power originated to begin with . . . disappears, 'his power' also vanishes. (p. 44)

Why, then, do American men feel so powerless? Part of the answer is because we've constructed the rules of manhood so that only the tiniest fraction of men come to believe that they are the biggest of wheels, the sturdiest of oaks, the most virulent repudiators of femininity, the most daring and aggressive. We've managed to disempower the overwhelming majority of American men by other means—such as discriminating on the basis of race, class, ethnicity, age, or sexual preference. Masculinist retreats to retrieve deep, wounded, masculinity are

195

but one of the ways in which American men currently struggle with their fears and their shame. Unfortunately, at the very moment that they work to break down the isolation that governs men's lives, as they enable men to express those fears and that shame, they ignore the social power that men continue to exert over women and the privileges from which they (as the middle-aged, middle-class white men who largely make up these retreats) continue to benefit—regardless of their experiences as wounded victims of oppressive male socialization.[7]

Others still rehearse the politics of exclusion, as if by clearing away the playing field of secure gender identity of any that we deem less than manly—women, gay men, nonnative-born men, men of color—middle-class, straight, white men can reground their sense of themselves without those haunting fears and that deep shame that they are unmanly and will be exposed by other men. This is the manhood of racism, of sexism, of homophobia. It is the manhood that is so chronically insecure that it trembles at the idea of lifting the ban on gays in the military, that is so threatened by women in the workplace that women become the targets of sexual harassment, that is so deeply frightened of equality that it must ensure that the playing field of male competition remains stacked against all newcomers to the game.

Exclusion and escape have been the dominant methods American men have used to keep their fears of humiliation at bay. The fear of emasculation by other men, of being humiliated, of being seen as a sissy, is the leitmotif in my reading of the history of American manhood. Masculinity has become a relentless test by which we prove to other men, to women, and ultimately to ourselves, that we have successfully mastered the part. The restlessness that men feel today is nothing new in American history; we have been anxious and restless for almost two centuries. Neither exclusion nor escape has ever brought us the relief we've sought, and there is no reason to think that either will solve our problems now. Peace of mind, relief from gender struggle, will come only from a politics of inclusion, not exclusion, from standing up for equality and justice, and not by running away.

Notes

1. This chapter represents a preliminary working out of a theoretical chapter in [*the book that became* Manhood in America: A Cultural History]. I am grateful to Tim Beneke, Harry Brod, Michael Kaufman, Iona Mara-Drita, and Lillian Rubin for comments on earlier versions of the chapter.

2. Of course, the phrase 'American manhood' contains several simultaneous fictions. There is no single manhood that defines all American men: 'America' is meant to refer to the United States proper, and there are significant ways in which this 'American manhood' is the outcome of forces that transcend both gender and nation, that is, the global economic development of industrial capitalism. I use it, therefore, to describe the specific hegemonic version of masculinity in the United States, that normative constellation of attitudes, traits, and behaviors that became the standard against which all other masculinities are measured and against which individual men measure the success of their gender accomplishments.

3. Although I am here discussing only American masculinity, I am aware that others have located this chronic instability and efforts to prove manhood in the particular cultural and economic arrangements of Western society. Calvin, after all, inveighed against the disgrace 'for men to become effeminate,' and countless other theorists have described the mechanics of manly proof. (See, for example, Seidler, 1994.)

4. I do not mean to argue that women do not have anxieties about whether they are feminine enough. Ask any woman how she feels about being called aggressive; it sends a chill into her heart because her femininity is suspect. (I believe that the reason for the enormous recent popularity of sexy lingerie among women is that it enables women to remember they are still feminine underneath their corporate business suit—a suit that apes masculine styles.) But I think the stakes are not as great for women and that women have greater latitude in defining their identities around these questions than men do. Such are the ironies of sexism: The powerful have a narrower range of options than the powerless, because the powerless can *also* imitate the powerful and get away with it. It may even enhance status, if done with charm and grace—that is, is not threatening. For the powerful, any hint of behaving like the powerless is a fall from grace.

5. Some of Freud's followers, such as Anna Freud and Alfred Adler, did follow up on these suggestions. (See especially, Adler, 1980.) I am grateful to Terry Kupers for his help in thinking through Adler's ideas.

6. The image is from Warren Farrell, who spoke at a workshop I attended at the First International Men's Conference, Austin, Texas, October 1991.

7. For a critique of the mythopoetic retreats, see Kimmel and Kaufman, Ch. 14, Brod, Harry and Michael Kaufman (eds.) *Theorizing Masculinities*, Thousand Oaks, CA: Sage, 1994.

References

Adler, A. (1980). *Cooperation between the sexes: Writings on women, love and marriage, sexuality and its disorders* (H. Ansbacher & R. Ansbacher, Eds. & Trans.). New York: Jason Aronson.

Arendt, H. (1970). *On revolution.* New York: Viking.

Bly, R. (1990). *Iron John: A book about men.* Reading, MA: Addison-Wesley.

Connell, R. W. (1987). *Gender and power.* Stanford, CA: Stanford University Press.

Farrell, W. (1986). *Why men are the way they are.* New York: McGraw-Hill.

Farrell, W. (1993). *The myth of male power: Why men are the disposable sex.* New York: Simon & Schuster.

Freud, S. (1933/1966). *New introductory lectures on psychoanalysis* (L. Strachey, Ed.). New York: Norton.

Gaylin, W. (1992). *The male ego.* New York: Viking.

Goffman, E. (1963). *Stigma.* Englewood Cliffs, NJ: Prentice-Hall.

Gorer, G. (1964). *The American people: A study in national character.* New York: Norton.

Kaufman, M. (1993). *Cracking the armour: Power and pain in the lives of men.* Toronto: Viking Canada.

Keen, S. (1991). *Fire in the belly.* New York: Bantam.

Kimmel, M. S. (in press). *Manhood: The American Quest* [which became Manhood in America: A Cultural History, *New York: Free Press, 1996*].

Leverenz, D. (1986). Manhood, humiliation and public life: Some stories. *Southwest Review, 71,* Fall.

Leverenz, D. (1991). The last real man in America: From Natty Bumppo to Batman. *American Literary Review, 3.*

Marx, K., & F. Engels. (1848/1964). The communist manifesto. In R. Tucker (Ed.), *The Marx-Engels reader.* New York: Norton.

Mead, M. (1965). *And keep your powder dry.* New York: William Morrow.

Moore, R., & Gillette, D. (1991). *King, warrior, magician, lover.* New York: HarperCollins.

Moore, R., & Gillette, D. (1992). *The king within: Accessing the king in the male psyche.* New York: William Morrow.

Moore, R., & Gillette, D. (1993a). *The warrior within: Accessing the warrior in the male psyche.* New York: William Morrow.

Moore, R., & Gillette, D. (1993b). *The magician within: Accessing the magician in the male psyche.* New York: William Morrow.

Noble, V. (1992). A helping hand from the guys. In K. L. Hagan (Ed.), *Women respond to the men's movement.* San Francisco: HarperCollins.

Osherson, S. (1992). *Wrestling with love: How men struggle with intimacy, with women, children, parents and each other.* New York: Fawcett.

Rotundo, F. A. (1993). *American manhood: Transformations in masculinity from the revolution to the modern era.* New York: Basic Books.

Savran, D. (1992). *Communists, cowboys, and queers: The politics of masculinity in the work of Arthur Miller and Tennessee Williams.* Minneapolis: University of Minnesota Press.

Seidler, V. (1994). *Unreasonable men: Masculinity and social theory.* New York: Routledge.

Tocqueville, A. de. (1835/1967). *Democracy in America.* New York: Anchor.

Wayne, K. (1912). *Building the young man.* Chicago: A. C. McClurg.

Weber, M. (1905/1966). *The Protestant ethic and the spirit of capitalism.* New York: Charles Scribner's.

What men need is men's approval. (1993, January 3). *The New York Times*, p. C-11.

Wilkinson, R. (1986). *American tough: The tough-guy tradition and American character*. New York: Harper & Row.

Woolfolk, R. L., & Richardson, F. (1978). *Sanity, stress and survival*. New York: Signet.

15 What Is Problematic about Masculinities?[1]

Kenneth Clatterbaugh*

THE TEMPTATION OF MASCULINITIES

The old *Men's Studies Review* became *masculinities* in the winter of 1993. The name change is politically and methodologically significant. Politically, the new title seeks to allay 'suspicions that "men's studies" is some ill-defined reaction against women's studies' (*masculinities* 1:1,2). Methodologically, this change represents an effort to be inclusive and, thereby, to gain a more honest appraisal of the lives of men.

This effort at inclusion also seeks to avoid the false universalization and oversimplification that is characteristic of much of the work in gender studies. Thus, essays featuring adjectival masculinities such as Jewish masculinity, Black masculinity, Chicano masculinity, gay masculinity, and even middle-class masculinity have appeared in the literature (Clatterbaugh 1990; Segal 1990; Zinn 1992; Brod 1994; Kimmel 1994; Hearn and Collinson 1994). At the same time, to speak of masculinities does not preclude the effort to understand hegemonic masculinity (in the singular) (Carrigan, Connell, and Lee 1987; Connell 1987).[2] Hegemonic masculinity (vs. alternate) is described as 'the image of masculinity of those men who hold power' (Kimmel 1994). That image is presumably 'young, urban, white, northern heterosexual, Protestant father of college education, fully employed, of good complexion, and a recent record in sports' (Kimmel 1994, 125).[3]

Whatever masculinity is or masculinities are, they are subjects of theorizing (Brod and Kaufman 1994). While some think that masculinities are biologically grounded, it is generally agreed that they are 'socially and historically constructed' (Brittan 1989; Hearn and Morgan 1990, 4; Hearn and Collinson 1994; Kimmel 1994). Some concept of masculinity has been central in most contemporary writings about

* Reprinted with permission of Michael S. Kimmel.

men (Clatterbaugh 1990). Masculinities are important because it is hoped that by understanding what creates and maintains a masculinity, new and healthier ways of being masculine can be found.

While I applaud these efforts to understand contemporary masculinities, to discover their historical and social differences, and, perhaps most important, to change their most noxious and harmful aspects, without destroying their positive qualities, I have for some time entertained several philosophical worries about launching these discussions on the back of the terms masculinity and masculinities. My concerns are that these terms carry a lot of historical baggage, which unless great care is exercised in their use, leads to confusion and careless thinking. If part of profeminist political responsibility is to clearly communicate with men about their lives and the forces that act on them, then we are ill served by the careless use of this term. [. . .]

THE SECRET—AND HOW IT'S BEEN KEPT

It may well be the best-kept secret of the literature on masculinities that we have an extremely ill-defined idea of what we are talking about. In recent literature, the only piece I know of that makes this secret public is by Coleman (1990), who concludes: 'The theorist has a need . . . for some rigorously defensible criterion for what is to count as "masculinity." None seems forthcoming' (p. 190). In this section, I want to explore how this conceptual problem arises and how it is that we have been able to carry on in spite of it.

The literature in gender studies, psychology, sociology, and anthropology typically distinguishes between the sex of an individual and that individual's sex role (Spence and Helmreich 1978, 12; Reinisch, Rosenblum, and Sanders 1987, 16–17; Doyle and Paludi 1995, 6–7). Spence and Helmreich (1978) note that the sex of an individual is biological and, with rare exceptions, 'individuals retain this biological status through the life span' (p. 12). Sex is considered unambiguous and readily apparent. The sex role is a much more amorphous entity made up of social, cultural, and psychological components (Doyle and Paludi 1995, 6). Sex roles may not be constant throughout a lifetime (Maccoby 1987, 231). [. . .]

With few exceptions, the writings on masculinities continue to distinguish gender role (sometimes sex role or simply gender), on one hand, from sex, on the other (Brittan 1989, 2–3). Masculinity is a role;

maleness is the sex. Some authors prefer expressions like 'manhood,' 'being a man,' 'masculine affirming' to refer to the complex social, cultural, and psychological components that make up the gender role; some simply prefer gender (Kimmel 1994, 20; Doyle 1989). A significant number of writers, especially sociobiologists, argue that there is a causal link between being genetically male and having a certain gender role. Or, they argue that a significant proportion of the gender role is sex derivative. Most authors, however, deny this causal link, and if masculinity is cultural, it must be kept distinct from maleness, which is biological. As Kimmel (1994) expresses it: 'Manhood does not bubble up to consciousness from our biological makeup; it is created in culture' (p. 120; cf. Brittan 1989, 6–11).

The separation of masculinities from male genetics is both scientific and political. Scientifically, there are many reservations about what, if any, behaviors, attitudes, and abilities are located in genetic materials (Hubbard and Lowe 1979; Fausto-Sterling 1985; Clatterbaugh 1990). Politically, the hope is that once we come to understand what sustains or causes a masculinity, we will be in a better position to secure socially and personally healthy masculinities. Furthermore, there are many candidates for the causes that (individually or collectively) sustain masculinities—socialization, economic rewards, ideology, athletics, military experience, homophobia, role models, male stereotypes, psychoanalytic factors, Jungian archetypes, and racism, to name only some of the purported causes (Coleman 1990, 188).

Because the cause offers an explanation of its effect, we do not want to beg the question of which causes we identify by defining an effect through its causes; for example, think how trivially circular it would be to define a masculinity as that which is produced by a certain archetype, which, in turn, is defined as the cause of that masculinity.[4] Thus, we need a characterization of any particular masculinity that is logically independent of our characterization of its causes. What we require is a description of those traits or properties that constitute a masculinity that is free of speculation as to their causes.

Here, however, is where the trouble begins. Assuming that masculinity is some complex of behaviors, attitudes, and abilities, which may include various powers and privileges or limitations on these, how are we to decide which properties to include in this complex? Of course, once we know which properties to include in a definition of a masculinity—once we have an idea of it—we can begin to identify the different masculinities. We can also begin to identify those groups of individuals who exhibit a particular masculinity. [. . .]

The most common strategy is not to talk about gender roles at all. Instead, masculinity itself is identified with the stereotype or the norm, that is, what a sample of persons believe to be masculine attitudes, behaviors, and abilities or what a sample of persons consider should be masculine attitudes, behaviors, and abilities. [. . .]

The obvious difficulty in talking about ideas and norms is that we are not talking about actual traits; we are talking instead about beliefs about these. [. . .] Such studies are of great interest, but they are about perceptions of gender, not gender roles. [. . .]

A related strategy is to talk about male images that occur in the media, in literature, and even religion. For example, Gerzon's (1982) *A Choice of Heroes* is a fascinating look at the images that have dominated American culture at different historical epochs. Images vary from time to time, among groups and subgroups and over the lifetime of individuals. Much excellent work in cultural studies is concerned with such images (Jeffords 1989). The hegemonic masculinity defined in the first section as White, northern, Protestant, and so on, is an image of hegemonic masculinity; it is not about the behaviors, attitudes, and beliefs that constitute the hegemonic gender role. [. . .]

The next strategy for breaking the circle is also widely found in writings on masculinities. [*The 'circle' referred to here comes from an earlier discussion that was dropped from the essay in which Clatterbaugh points out that 'we cannot identify a group prior to having an idea of the appropriate masculinity. Thus, we are caught in a circle of needing an idea A to determine a group B and needing a group B to determine an idea A. How then can we ever begin? How do we break out of the circle?'*] It defines gender role as those behaviors, attitudes, and abilities that are exhibited by groups of individuals that conform to a stereotype or norm (Maccoby 1987, 227–8). Thus, a masculine individual is someone who is stereotypically masculine, or, a masculine individual is someone who is normatively masculine. This strategy at least has the advantage of getting us back to gender roles, that is, behaviors, attitudes, and abilities actually exhibited. What this strategy allows us to do is to select an idea, by sampling people's beliefs, and then to identify a group via that idea, that is, the group that exhibits conforming behaviors. This strategy breaks out of the circle by identifying the idea independently of the group. [. . .]

A definition that omits any reference to stereotype or norm is the following [*Prior to identifying M7, Clatterbaugh lists M1–M6, which are six other definitions of masculinity he uses to investigate strategies that have been used to talk about masculinity*]:

M7: A masculine person is one who exemplifies those characteristics that have been shown to differentiate the sexes. A particular masculinity is the set of differentiating characteristics of a particular group of individuals determined by sex and some other set of ascriptive characteristics.

[. . .] M7 breaks out of the circle by starting with a group, defined usually by physical or behavioral traits, or social status. M7 is, of course, statistical. If most men behave aggressively relative to women, then aggressiveness is a characteristic to be included among the defining traits of masculinity. If upper middle-class men value a certain kind of rationality, then rationality is to be included in their masculinity. If men are privileged in being hired as firefighters, then this privilege is included in masculinity. This definition does not assume that all men are aggressive or rational; it does not assume that no women are aggressive, rational, or privileged. It simply looks for differentiating characteristics.

To look at differentiating characteristics does not preclude noting what characteristics are common; commonalities are revealed by seeking differences. Differentiating characteristics can also be time tagged and/or culture tagged to allow that they may change. Definition M7 does not beg any causal questions since the characteristic used to identify the group may not turn out to be causally significant. For example, gay, African American men in 1969 in urban America may exhibit a set of beliefs that may be caused largely by socioeconomic status rather than being gay or African American. M7 does not preclude such a finding.

M7 clearly links the power men have and masculinity; indeed, having a particular power may be the identifying trait of a group of individuals. Diverse masculinities can be approached in the same way. Black masculinity includes those characteristics that differentiate Black men from non-Black men. One could further talk of those characteristics that differentiate middle-class Black men from other classes of Black men, and so on. Of course, [. . .] such characterizations would be historically and culturally varied. In short, if a particular trait by a specific test at a specific time in a specific culture is characteristic of members of a group of men, then that trait is characteristic of that group's masculinity. This definition lends itself well to cross-cultural perspectives on masculinity (Gilmore 1990).

The strengths of M7 seem to outweigh its weaknesses, of which there are several. [. . .] Groups to be studied will, to some extent, be arbitrarily chosen or chosen for political gain. In using M7, one must not assume that every division will produce a distinct masculinity.

It must be at least possible that young men and older men share a masculinity, all of which presupposes, contrary to the definition, that masculinities can be identified apart from the group. Furthermore, this assumption requires that the characteristics that identify the group are not necessarily the traits that cause the masculinity. In short, listing distinct characteristics such as age, wealth, race, and so on is insufficient to show that those so catalogued do in fact display distinct masculinities—groups do not necessarily line up one to one with masculinities. [. . .]

THE POSTMODERN OPTION: DISCOURSE

Efforts to usefully define or identify gender roles have been openly abandoned by writers who seek to ground masculinity in discourses about men and masculinity (Hearn and Collinson 1994, 97–8). The failures of the old (modernistic) social science to provide a coherent structure in which to discuss masculinities seem to demand a new approach. Among the various kinds of postmodern efforts is to treat the individual 'as being produced by a multitude of discourses' (Gutterman 1994, 220).

Not only are individuals to be thought of as subjects of various discourses, but also being male, being masculine, being masculine in a particular way are also subjects of various discourses. 'As members of any particular culture, community, or group, individuals are given a vast array of scripts that together constitute them as social subjects. Some scripts are branded onto individuals more emphatically than others' (Gutterman 1994, 223). As subjects, however, these discourses will be internally contradictory with one another as well as contradictory with each other, regardless of whether the discourses are about individuals or types of individuals. [. . .]

According to the discourse strategy, polarities play an important discursive role. Thus, masculinity is constantly contrasted with what is not masculine (Gutterman 1994, 226). Familiar dichotomies include masculine-feminine, strong-weak, and dominant-submissive; even among masculinities there are dichotomies that help to identify particular discourses.

The importance of treating masculinity as a subject of discourse is, in the end, partially political. It seeks to undermine masculinity as a special subject. 'These conflicts (inconsistencies) in turn create an area where the governing conceptions of a particular discourse suffer a sort of slippage wherein predominant roles and values lose their claims to absolute authority and subsequently can be altered' (Gutterman 1994, 220).

The central question is whether by shifting to talking about discourses, we leave behind any of the problems that beset earlier efforts to define masculinities. In fact, it would seem that we are beset by almost exactly the same set of problems under slightly different descriptions.

First, if masculinities are produced by discourses and 'produced' means anything like 'caused,' then we need some independent description of the masculinities caused or we run the risk of asserting trivialities. For example, if M (masculinity$_x$) is caused by D (discourse$_y$), and M is identified as that which is caused by D, then we say nothing informative when we claim that M is produced by D.

Second, discourses are like stereotypes and norms, they are human artifacts strongly influenced by what people believe the world is like. The question arises as to whether discourses are accurate in representing that which they purport to represent. Of course, one can always argue that masculinities are nothing but discourses. And, once masculinity is identified with discourses, then there is no representation problem; discourses, by definition, are accurate. But this move destroys the causal story, since cause and effect are usually taken to be distinct things; once discourses are identified with masculinities, they can no longer be the cause of masculinities.

Third, there seem to be serious problems as to how we identify a discourse. It seems likely that a discourse is identified through its subject. If a discourse is so identified, how is the subject identified? It seems likely that a subject is identified by being the subject of an identifiable discourse. We now have the problem of the circle reappearing within the realm of discourses and subjects instead of ideas and groups.

Fourth, given the inconsistency and slippage and the belief that each individual is the subject of multiple discourses—however they are determined—we seem to have a recurrence of the problem that there are as many masculinities as there are individuals; in which case, we should give up talking about masculinities at all and stick to individuals. Related to this point of inconsistency and slippage, the above construction of masculinity seems incoherent. This view maintains that, on one hand, masculinities are filled with inconsistencies and slippage and that, on the other hand, discourses about masculinities are produced by rigid use of dichotomies. But inconsistency and slippage are precisely the enemies of dichotomy; slippage and inconsistency are the ways in which dichotomies are denied. Thus, the construction of the construction of masculinity in terms of discourse is incoherent.

THE OPTION OF SUBJECTIVITY

One of the common strategies is to talk about how masculinity is perceived by an individual, either oneself or another. Such stories are of great interest and can be filled with empathetic insights. We often see ourselves in others or others in ourselves. Masculinity then becomes a personal achievement, something we do, something we accomplish, an undeniable truth for any male who has grown to manhood. Coleman (1990) describes this approach as dramaturgical. 'Here "masculinity" is seeable as sustained by a continual work of "presentation management" on the actor's part. The model is dramaturgical' (p. 186).

The dramaturgical model that focuses on actors' accounts of the actions they take, and the reasons they give for taking those actions, seems to have a number of advantages over the previous accounts; chiefly, it avoids the circle because it has no need for a clear independent conception of masculinity. Masculinity is whatever the actor thinks it is or says it is. This account is connected to the study of gender formation, or what is the same, gender identity. Gender identity can be studied by taking a number of accounts of how different actors form their roles and looking for similarities and differences.

But the escape from the previous problems is only partial. What makes some dramaturgical accounts more interesting than others is that they seem to hit closer to social reality than others. Part of what makes them interesting is that they are illustrative of the struggle to become masculine, they are not simply or idiosyncratically autobiographical. Indeed, the actors themselves are generally convinced that there is some standard of masculinity that they are trying to achieve. Part of what makes them interesting is that as individuals or observers of individuals, we can assert that the actor missed the role or mistook what masculinity is. If masculinity were exhausted by what individuals said it was that they were trying to achieve, this notion of correcting them would make no sense. Thus, we are once again faced with the difficulty of articulating what masculinity is.

THE OPTION OF STIPULATION

The last strategy is the most highly charged politically. This view of masculinity is that masculinity is the set of behaviors, attitudes, and abilities that have been identified as important from a particular political point of view. It is commonplace in writings about men to identify men as competitive, emotionally stilted, violent, homophobic, and/or racist. These taken-for-granted understandings of masculinity are ill suited for scientific work, although they are excellent material for rhetorical essays (Hearn and Morgan 1990, 9). Stipulated masculinities have no trouble breaking out of the circle, but one wonders why they should be taken seriously. Are they grounded in reality? Do they have anything to do with men?

The dangers of stipulations are many. First, if, as profeminists have argued, men have enjoyed a sustained period of choice and privilege, then men should exhibit the greatest diversity of behaviors, attitudes, and abilities. Indeed, talking about masculinities was, in part, motivated by a belief in this radical diversity of men. The resurrecting of a political stereotype seems to undercut the effort of talking about a multiplicity of masculinities; it is a throwback to essentialism. The men's rights literature, for example, that focuses on men as victims and as not having choices is explicitly hostile to the view that there is a plurality of masculinities (Clatterbaugh 1990, 61–83).

Second, there is a tendency in the stipulation view to approach the scientific literature in a grab bag fashion and to cite only that literature that supports the politically determined stereotype. For example, studies that show that users of pornography are characteristically male are used to support the conclusion that use of pornography is characteristic of men (Stoltenberg 1993, 272–99). Indeed, the fact that some men are the consuming class puts pornography at the essence of masculinity for some writers (Funk 1993, 50–1). Oddly enough, such inferences are made even in the face of evidence that beyond periods of brief exposure most men are not users of pornography and that the attitudes of men although slightly more favorable toward pornography are not radically dissimilar to the attitudes of women (Berger, Searles, and Cottle 1991, 3–4). But when the motivation is political, it becomes unimportant whether men have the traits attributed to them. Indeed, most literature on pornography is interested only in the effect of pornography on users and not at all on the question of how men are users and to what extent. Perhaps the question of degree of use is irrelevant because the point of stipulation is to establish an image of masculinity and by fiat apply it to men; thus, essays are indifferent to the distinction between the author's image of men and men; they slide back and forth as if they are interchangeable (Stoltenberg 1993; Funk 1993; Kimmel 1994).

MASCULINITIES AS A SUBTERFUGE

A cursory look at the literature on masculinity and masculinities will probably convince a reader that these terms are a subterfuge—that by 'masculinity' is meant '(adult) male' and by 'masculinities' is meant '(adult) males in different situations.' Masculinity is a term to be put in the title of an article—men are the subject. Thus, an uncautious reader might become concerned about 'migrant masculinity' if she or he were not aware of the 'fuzzy collapse' of 'masculinity' into 'man' (Margold 1994; Wiegman 1994, 2). [. . .]

Since it is apparently men that we want to talk about, if masculinity becomes a kind of synonym for men or adult male, and masculinities becomes a synonym for adult males in different situations, then [. . .] we must be careful to distinguish these terms from the many meanings [. . .] that were intended in the first place to distinguish being masculine from being a man, meanings that were intended to treat masculinity as something social and historical whereas being a male adult was biological. Even if we adapt masculinities to this use, we still need a term for whatever it is that is culturally imposed. To try to make masculinity or masculinities do both jobs invites all of the confusions noted above, together with a conflation that we set out to avoid, a mistake, which constructionists think that biological determinists make. [. . .]

[*A section on 'Political Consequences' was dropped from the essay.*]

TALKING ABOUT MEN

Writings by women, in contrast to much of the writing by men, talk about men, not masculinities (Friedan 1963; Frye 1983; Sargent 1981; Jaggar 1983; Tong 1989; cf. Brod and Kaufman 1994, vii). The same focus on men occurs in the pioneer essays by men (Brod 1987;

Kimmel 1987). Talking about men seems to be what we want to do. Is not one of the major issues in the feminist movement why so many positions of privilege and power in the Congress, in major corporations, and so on are held by men? (If there were 100 countable masculinities and these masculinities were distributed equally among the men who hold these positions, the situation would still be intolerable and unjust.) Another problem is that so many of the most violent acts in our society are done by men. It seems most appropriate that the National Organization for Men Against Sexism (NOMAS) has a task group for ending men's violence. Is not a third critical problem where to locate men in feminist theory and practice, that is, what role do men play in creating and maintaining the oppression of women and what role can men play in ending that oppression? [. . .]

The objective conditions of power in society favor men in precisely the ways that have been identified variously by feminist writers (Frye 1983; Sargent 1981; Jaggar 1983; Tong 1989). Studying images of men is important in revealing the ways we represent power, as are discourses about men. Thus, I am not asking that these tasks be abandoned, as long as we are clear about what we are doing and about the limits of these enterprises in contributing to an understanding of men. We should be reasonably clear that we are not talking about men when we are talking about images, stereotypes, or norms, and that we are not talking about images when we talk about men, male behaviors, privileges, and attitudes. This sorting out can be done; Walker (1994) provides an excellent example of a paper in which images versus behaviors and men versus masculinity are kept clear and their relationships clearly defined. Indeed, she manages to reveal a great deal about how men construct and think about friendship without ever using the terms masculinity or masculinities.

This essay is not a sustained argument for a return to men studies, if that label is offensive to those in women studies, although I have yet to see an argument to that effect. It is a call for some degree of conceptual clarity, especially around foundational concepts. My concern is that we shall be unable to build the kind of discipline that we need, unable to articulate the goals that we seek, and unable to generate the kinds of political change, which we agree needs to occur, if we persist in the kinds of equivocations that are pervasive in our literature. I am concerned that our language contributes to our becoming more isolated and more elitist—more distanced from men and women in general.

As profeminist men, our goal is certainly captured by Kimmel's citation from James Baldwin: 'We, with love, shall force our brothers to see themselves as they are, to cease fleeing from reality and begin to change it' (Baldwin 1962, 21). My argument in this article is that, given the current conceptual tangle around masculinities, we are more likely to maintain our bearings by flagging this troublesome concept and, at least for the present, talking about men, male behaviors, attitudes, and abilities, on one hand, and images, stereotypes, norms, and discourses, on the other. If our goal really is to change reality, we can at least guard against the further mystification of it.

Notes

1. Author's note: I wish to thank Jean Roberts, Audre Brokes, Susan Jeffords, and Mike Dash for comments on earlier drafts of this article.
2. There is no apparent reason why hegemonic masculinity should be in the singular; given the history of choices available to men and different ways to realize life, there is likely a multiplicity of acceptable hegemonic masculinities.
3. Although if one looks at images of power in mass media today, a different description emerges, namely, older (forty to fifty years old), rural or small town, southern, heterosexual family man, evangelical, no recent record of sports, indifferent complexion, overweight, indifferent employment record.
4. A commonly defended triviality in mythopoetic writings. See Moore and Gillette (1990).

References

Baldwin, J. 1962. *The fire next time.* New York: Dell.

Berger, R. J., P. Searles, and C. E. Cottle. 1991. *Feminism and pornography.* New York: Praeger.

Brittan, A. 1989. *Masculinity and power.* Oxford, U.K.: Basil Blackwell.

Brod, H. 1987. *The Making of masculinities: The new men's studies.* Boston: Allen & Unwin.

Brod, H. 1994. Some thoughts on some histories of some masculinities: Jews and other others. in *Theorizing masculinities,* edited by H. Brod and M. Kaufman. Thousand Oaks, CA: Sage.

Brod. H., and M. Kaufman, eds. 1994. *Theorizing masculinities.* Thousand Oaks, CA: Sage.

Carrigan, T., R. Connell, and J. Lee. 1987. Hard and heavy: Towards a new sociology of masculinity. In *Beyond patriarchy: Essays by men on pleasure, power, and change,* edited by M. Kaufman. Toronto: Oxford University Press.

Clatterbaugh, K. 1990. *Contemporary perspectives on masculinity: Men, women, and politics in modern society.* Boulder, CO: Westview.

Coleman, W. 1990. Doing masculinity/doing theory. In *Men, masculinities, and social theory,* edited by J. Hearn and D. Morgan. London: Unwin Hyman.

Connell, R. W. 1987. *Gender and power*. Stanford, CA: Stanford University Press.

Curtis, B. 1994. Men and masculinities in American art. *masculinities* 2 (2): 10–37.

Doyle, J. and M. Paludi. 1995. *Sex and gender*. Madison, WI: Brown and Benchmark.

Doyle, J. A. 1989. *The male experience*, 2nd edn. Dubuque, IA: William C. Brown.

Fausto-Sterling, A. 1985. *Myths of gender*. New York: Basic Books.

Friedan, B. 1963. *The feminine mystique*. New York: Dell.

Frye, M. 1983. *The Politics of reality: Essays in feminist theory*. Trumansburg, NY: Crossing Press.

Funk, R. E. 1993. *Stopping rape: A challenge for men*. Philadelphia: New Society.

Gerltner, D. M. 1994. *Experiencing masculinities: Exercises, activities and resources for teaching and learning about men*. Denver, CO: Everyman Press.

Gerzon, M. 1982. *A choice of heroes: The changing face of American manhood*. Boston: Houghton Mifflin.

Gilmore, D. D. 1990. *Manhood in the making: Cultural concepts of masculinity*. New Haven, CT: Yale University Press.

Gutterman, D. S. 1994. Postmodernism and the interrogation of masculinity. In *Theorizing masculinities*, edited by H. Brod and M. Kaufman. Thousand Oaks, CA: Sage.

Hearn, J. and D. L. Collinson. 1994. Theorizing unities and differences between men and between masculinities. In *Theorizing masculinities*, edited by H. Brod and M. Kaufman. Thousand Oaks, CA: Sage.

Hearn, J. and D. Morgan, eds. 1990. *Men, masculinities, and social theory*. London: Unwin Hyman.

Hubbard, R., and M. Lowe. 1979. *Genes and gender II*. New York: Gordian.

Jaggar, A. 1983. *Feminist politics and human nature*. Totowa, NJ: Rowman and Allanheld.

Jeffords, S. 1989. *The remasculinization of America*. Bloomington: Indiana University Press.

Kimmel, M. S. 1987. *Changing men: New direction in research on men and masculinity*. Newbury Park, CA: Sage.

Kimmel, M. S. 1994. Masculinity as homophobia: Fear, shame, and silence in the construction of gender identity. In *Theorizing masculinities*, edited by H. Brod and M. Kaufman. Thousand Oaks, CA: Sage.

Kimmel, M. S., and M. A. Messner. 1992. *Men's lives*, 2nd edn. New York: Macmillan.

Maccoby, E. E. 1987. The varied meanings of 'masculine' and 'feminine.' In *Masculinity/femininity: Basic perspectives*, edited by I. M. Reinisch, L. A. Rosenblum, and S. A. Sanders. Oxford, U.K.: Oxford University Press.

Majors, R. G., and J. U. Gordon. 1994. *The American Black male*. Chicago: Nelson-Hall.

Margold, J. A. 1994. Migrant masculinity in the transnational workplace. *masculinities* 2 (3): 18–36.

Moore, R., and D. Gillette. 1990. *King, warrior, magician, lover*. San Francisco: Harper.

Pleck, J. H. 1981. *The myth of masculinity*. Cambridge, MA: MIT Press.

Reinisch, I. M., L. A. Rosenblum, and S. A. Sanders. 1987. *Masculinity/ femininity: Basic perspectives*. Oxford, U.K.: Oxford University Press.

Sargent, L. 1981. *Women and revolution*. Boston: South End.

Segal, L. 1990. *Slow motion: Changing masculinities, changing men*. New Brunswick, NJ: Rutgers University Press.

Seidler, V. I. 1990. Men, feminism and power. In *Men, masculinities, and social theory*, edited by J. Hearn and D. Morgan. London: Unwin Hyman.

Spence, J. T., and R. L. Helmreich. 1978. *Masculinity and femininity: Their psychological dimensions, correlates, and antecedents*. Austin: University of Texas Press.

Stoltenberg, J. 1993. *The end of manhood: A book for men of conscience*. New York: Dutton.

Tong, R. 1989. *Feminist thought: A comprehensive introduction*. Boulder, CO: Westview.

Walker, K. 1994. Men's friendships: 'I'm not friends the way she's friends.' *masculinities* 2 (2): 38–55.

Wiegman, R. 1994. Feminism and its mal(e)contents. *masculinities* 2 (1): 1–7.

Zinn, M. B. 1992. Chicano men and masculinity. *In Men's lives*, edited by Michael S. Kimmel and Michael A. Messner, 67–77. New York: Macmillan.

Displaying the Phallus: Masculinity
and the Performance of Sexuality
on the Internet

Marjorie Kibby and Brigid Costello*

The structure of the look defines visual pleasure, as the relationship between the subject of the gaze and its object is based in the pleasure of control and consumption. The directing and direction of the look controls the desire, and hence the fulfillment, of the desire. Film theorists in the 1970s saw the look of the cinema as structured around the male gaze (Mulvey 1975), and Berger (1972) asserts that 'men act and women appear. Men look at women. Women watch themselves being looked at' (p. 47), but later writers suggested that both male and female subject positions have access to a controlling gaze (Rodowick 1982; Neale 1986). Until the late 1970s, the male body was infrequently available as the object of the female gaze. 'There are plenty of pinups for women—moviestars, pop singers—but they are rarely nude,' Walters (1978, 229) wrote. However, a consumerization of male sexuality occurred during the late 1970s and 1980s and combined with an empowerment of women through feminism to produce a demand for images of men offered as a sexual spectacle. Contemporary advertising images, pin up calendars, and soft porn 'play girl' magazines present sexualized images of the male body for public consumption. But a certain instability is produced around the male body sexually displayed. The male nude disappeared from Western art in the nineteenth century, and the female body took on the role as signifier of the erotic. As Walters (1978) explained,

The male nude fades out in the nineteenth century. The male body is determinedly and nervously covered up; and as the male goes out of focus, the female nude becomes the central symbol of art. For the first time nude is automatically taken to mean a woman. (p. 228)

* Reprinted with permission of Marjorie Kibby and Sage Publications, Inc., from *Men and Masculinities*, vol. 1, no. 4 (April 1999).

The male nude reappeared in art and popular culture in the late 1970s, but it has been a nervous uncovering. New codes of masculine display are not fully written, and certainly not comfortably accepted, as a result of the unanswered questions around women's desire, the gendered norms of activity and passivity, the construction of male sexuality in performance, and the symbolism of the phallus.

This instability is evidenced in adult video-conferencing sites, in which an interactive pornography subverts traditional regimes of pleasure and desire. Participants in CU-SeeMe erotic exchanges are both the subject and the object of the consuming gaze, as the interactive performance enables a blurring of the distinction between the consumer and the consumed. Heterosexual males in our society might lack a cultural framework for sexual exhibition, but video conferencing is providing one space for the working through of an erotics of masculine display.

CU-SeeMe

CU-SeeMe is a software facility that turns a desktop computer into the long-awaited picture phone. To access the technology, an individual needs a newer model Macintosh or PC and an Internet connection. The software can be downloaded for free, and together with a video card and camcorder, or a $200 digital video camera, it enables a video/text/audio connection between any number of parties, anywhere in the world. CU-SeeMe transmissions occur out of 'reflector' sites. These are high-end 'broadcasting' computer servers, each 'ref' theoretically determining what you can transmit, or view, when connected to that particular site. Most reflectors are open access, regulated only by etiquette, or agreed codes of practice. Many are tied to corporate or educational institutions, with varying degrees of regulated access; the majority cater to ad hoc conferencing, although some set up special events or performances. The CU-SeeMe medium is rich in entertainment, artistic, educational, and informational possibilities. However, like any new technological development from telephones to videotape, CU-SeeMe sites have been rapidly colonized by those seeking erotica.

Adult CU-SeeMe reflectors such as Biker Street, Anything Goes, Jack Off Live, or Stacker's Place provide spaces in which anywhere from fifteen to twenty-five people can 'meet.' Many reflectors have a public 'room' that anyone can enter and a selection of private rooms that require membership fees and/or have restricted password access. These rooms are often coded as oriented toward heterosexual, homosexual, or lesbian sexualities, or as having a specific focus. At Stacker's Place, there are eight members-only rooms with names like the Dressing Room, the Locker Room, the Rack, and the Game Room. At Jack Off Live, there are five rooms including M4M Muscle, Bi-Curious, and Dark Alley. Users of CU-SeeMe log on to these rooms to make initial contact and then establish a more private one-on-one direct connection (DC) with each other.

CU-SeeMe conferencing consists of a video image and text-based chat. The software is capable of processing color images and audio signals, but the low bandwidth of modem connections means that color and audio are effectivety lost. In practical terms, CU-SeeMe exchanges are based on typed text and jerky, several-frames-per-second black and white video. Image information appears in blocks that can take anywhere from ten seconds to five minutes to appear, depending on transmission speeds. When someone moves, only the blocks of information that have changed are replaced, and if a participant moves quickly, the screen becomes a blur. The poor quality of the images means that active interpretation is needed to decode them and imagination required to 'flesh' them out.

The users on a ref are represented on the CU-SeeMe interface by a list of names. Participant's names range from the simple (CU-User, M, Joe, Mary) to the expressive (Farm Boy, Countess, Coach & Blondie). Selecting a person's name opens a video window to display their image. Some refs also allow 'lurkers,' someone who can see other participants and chat but who cannot transmit video of themselves. These are also listed by name. The interactions of participants are regulated by information and formal codes of behavior, and most reflectors have methods of banishing those who transgress. The rules vary from the general, 'if ALL agree that it is fun' (Bikers Street) to the specific 'DC'ers WILL BE BANNED FOR LIFE!' (Anything Goes, Party Room). These codes are usually enforced by ref operators, whose ability to hand out passwords and ban users can give them substantial power within a conference. The personality and disciplinary style of each reflector operator often plays a large part in creating a ref's atmosphere and attracting participants. Commercial refs charge a monthly membership fee, and many show porn videos or have paid 'performers' and structured interaction. Public sites offer a performance space in which consumers present themselves to each other.

The examples in this article come from public, heterosexual or noncoded, adult reflectors. As with other forms of Internet communication, the majority of users of these reflectors are white, male, and American. However, there is a strong female presence, and, in line with recent trends in the consumption of pornography, there are a large number of couples. Women as consumers of sexual images necessitate the construction of a male sexual spectacle, a construction that suggests that regimes of sexual representation are much more dynamic and unstable than is generally acknowledged in discussions of pornography.

WHAT DO WOMEN WANT?

Where pornography is traditionally organized around spectator, spectacle, and specimen, the interactive nature of CU-SeeMe subverts the traditional objectification of women in pornography. CU-SeeMe allows women to look actively and speak powerfully to control the discourses of sexuality. It does enable a female erotic gaze. The minority representation of women on heterosexual refs gives them a power to direct the sexual encounter. Ref operators are at pains to cater to the needs of women so that they are retained as participants, and many refs have explicit rules that ensure women's protection and pleasure: 'You may not request a DC from a lady for any reason. Doing so will get you kicked' (Stacker's Place). Women's minority representation on these refs leads to a competition between men for women's attention, giving women the power to manipulate the sexual exchange to cater to their own desires.

Pleasure is determined within social conditions that have seen the figurative disappearance and reappearance of the clitoris as women's sexual pleasure has been denied or admitted at different periods in history. The current acknowledgement of female sexual desire is evidenced by the growing market in women's erotica: novels, magazines, strip shows, videos, and pinups. However, the question that Freud asked, 'What do women want?' (Jones 1955, 421) is still not wholly answerable. It may be, though, that the safety, anonymity, and personal expression offered by CU-SeeMe is stimulating a more free expression of women's desires than has been heard in other forums. What we see on CU-SeeMe refs is a desire to bridge the distance between subject and object in an exploration of the range of scopophilic pleasures— the pleasures of looking and being looked at.

Although erotic chat is an element of CU-SeeMe, the primary pleasures of the medium are those of the gaze. There may be fifteen to twenty-five people on a ref, it is usually only possible to see about four people at once, so there is an active competition to attract the gaze of other participants. For males on heterosexual refs, there is a high level of competition for the attention of the few women, and they usually need to signal via chat that their display is worthy of attention:

* \<leicester\>: want to see me naked Suze? (Digital Curl, 11 May 1997)
* \<shade\>: Open my vid Pam (Stackers, 21 May 1997)

This gives women the opportunity to direct men's displays in line with their own sense of the erotic. Where men tend to restrict sensuality in favor of genital performance (cf. Brod 1990), women are demanding displays that recognize whole-body sensuality. Part of the pleasure for women seems to be the potential dislocation of phallic mastery in sexual encounters that can bypass gendered relations of penetration in favor of shared sensual exploration and mutual masturbation. Women's interest in participating in a polymorphous set of sexual exchanges that situate the male as the object of the gaze is stimulating new forms of male sexual performance.

ACTIVE/PASSIVE

The picture of infantile sexual life drawn by Freud ([1905] 1981) saw activity and passivity as coexisting, describing a phase in which 'opposing pairs of instincts are developed to an approximately equal extent' (p. 97). Pleasure is actively sought through the instinct for mastery of the somatic musculature and passively received through the erotogenic membrane of the mouth and anus. As the ego develops, active and passive modes of gratification are subsumed into the general orientations of the ego, or personality types. Psychoanalytic theory stresses that in the first years of life, the two modes exist in both males and females and 'cannot be described as "masculine" and "feminine" but only as "active" and "passive" ' (p. 96). By maturation though, instincts have been overlaid with social meanings as the ego tests 'reality' and directs responses to the external environment. In our society, a boy comes to see the penis as representing activity and, through activity, power. In a patriarchal, heterosexist society, boys must abandon passivity to retain 'masculinity.' But, as Freud shows, what is repressed is not erased, and sexuality for many men is a site of tension and conflict. Many men sense, and some actively explore, sexuality as a relaxed, whole-body pleasure (Connell, Radican, and Martin 1987, 13), but popular culture forms depict normative masculinity as being connected to an active, genital sexuality. 'What men want, as often as not, is to be sexually passive. What men do not want, by and large, is for women (and certainly other men) to know this' (Segal 1994, 290).

Mulvey (1975) described how 'in a world ordered by sexual imbalance, pleasure in looking has been split between active/male and passive/female' (p. 6). In discussing the male pinup, Dyer (1992) referred to the problematic of the maintenance of power within the active/passive nexus of looking, saying that where males are situated as the object of the gaze, the element of passivity must necessarily be disavowed if men are to conform with dominant ideas of masculinity as activity. In the pinup, this is done by capturing a pose that suggests the man is midaction, or using sports equipment or other props that imply activity, and in most cases through a depiction of tensed muscles that connote immanent activity. Although women are now demanding sexualized images of men, the way in which men are represented erotically is in no way equivalent to the way in which women are so represented. There is no obverse image of the 'pink bits' shot of women; no standard image of the nude male that depicts so graphically his availability for female use or consumption. Women are only just beginning to formulate what such an image might be and to what extent it might rely on the codes of imaging women or on existing gay aesthetics, and to what extent it will demonstrate new codes of masculine erotic display.

CU-SeeMe enables women's consumption of images of the male body and legitimizes a male sexual exhibitionism. Male conferencees set up their space, their cameras, and their bodies to provide visual representations of themselves as objects of the erotic gaze. The way the picture is framed, placing the figure at the center or edge of the image; the way the setting is lit to emphasize or disguise aspects of the body or the space; the use of superimposed titles; and the choice of backgrounds are all conscious decisions designed to set up an image of the male body for the consumption of others. That men have a desire to display themselves as a sexual object is demonstrated by the large number of men who submit their naked images to reader's pages in magazines such as *Australian Women's Forum* and even to heterosexual male journals such as *The Picture*. Although many of the men do so to please/excite their female partners, and some profess to 'advertising' their desirability, many explain their participation in terms of the pleasure of the display, for example, 'It seemed like a fun thing to do' (McCathie 1996, 8–11). However despite the potential the CU-SeeMe offers for a passive male exhibitionism, and the positive responses of women to their display, proportionately few men avail themselves of the opportunity. There is still a sense in which taking up the place of the imaged implies a loss of potency for the male. The overt display of the naked male body seems to generate insecurities that may have their origin in links between self-exposure and vulnerability and a consequent questioning of masculine identity. Passivity and vulnerability need not necessarily imply weakness or powerlessness, but they are directly associated in normative versions of masculinity.

On CU-SeeMe heterosexual sites, the display of the male body is coded in ways that avoid passivity or that refigure identity to account for passivity. The images are often framed to include signifiers of action, such as bicycles or other sporting equipment, and many include the keyboard in the shot so that the image includes the action of typing. Men often depict themselves standing or moving about. On 'couples' refs, the man is more likely to be at the keyboard, while the woman is shown reclining, and when a couple sets up a show, the man is more likely to play an active role in the performance, while the woman is acted on. Although the men on these sites often urge women to display their faces, men rarely show their faces in conjunction with a sexualized display. Men who set up shots of their genitals do not often simultaneously reveal their faces.

The display often seems to be less directed at and for women than as constituting a narcissistic reflection of conventional masculinity. The exhibition is primarily a declaration of normative masculinity, and in many cases any conflation of intent with female erotic desires is solely coincidental. As Diamond (1991) points out, it is a misconception to see penile display as being aimed at women:

Many women say that they are turned on by a man's voice, legs and shoulders more than the sight of his penis. . . . While we can agree that the human penis is an organ of display, the display is intended not for women but for fellow men. (p. 64)

The possession and display of a large penis is a sign of masculinity in good working order and is directed (if only implicitly) at other men.

The visual plays a major role in the way that contemporary male sexuality is constructed. Williams (1989) theorizes that this is a legacy of the impossibility of representing female sexual pleasure visually in the same way that the physical pleasure of the male is depicted by showing erection and ejaculation. Male sexual fantasy becomes, in essence, a search for the parallel confession of female pleasure but finds male ejaculation as the only objective measurement of orgasm (pp. 49–50). In discussing the money shot in hardcore porn as an indicator of the fulfillment of desire, Williams notes the highly ambivalent identification implicit in a presumably heterosexual male viewer gazing with rapt interest on another man's ejaculating penis (p. 101). The homosocial subject position requires the woman as a switching station between trajectories of male desire. The literal or figurative presence of the woman legitimates the narcissistic gaze—the male looking at the self through the same-sex other. The male body can be presented as a pleasurable object on adult reflectors, but that pleasure is primarily contained within a narcissistic/autoerotic framework. What develops in male/female exchanges is a 'look don't touch' sensibility in which the visual is prioritized over the sensual. Male sexuality becomes a sort of self-conscious badge of masculinity rather than the object of female pleasure and desire.

This narcissistic eroticism involves a slippage into and from homoerotica. While the sites are designated heterosexual, on 'singles' refs often the majority of conferencees are male and frequently are all male. So it is common for heterosexual males to have positioned themselves as sexual objects for an audience that is entirely male. It is not unusual to find a group of heterosexual males sitting at their computers displaying their genitals to each other while they discuss their wives and girlfriends or their computer program. The image of the sexualized male body is derived in both form and composition from a long tradition of soft-core homoerotica. The popular images of the nude male on calendars and posters are borrowed from a gay aesthetic and co-opted by the desires of women. Thus 'heterosexualized,' the nude male is appropriated by a heterosexual discourse that enables a narcissistic gaze between males. The anxiety felt by many men that to show an awareness of the male body is to express homoerotic feelings is evidenced by a bantering chat, or a studied disavowal of the situation. Where a man is initially assumed to be a woman, the discovery of his masculine gender is generally responded to with expressions of aversion or of collusion in the joke. For example,

* <Inge & Blaine>: Nice butt huh?
* <Petman>: oh wow that's great
* <Jay from LA>: mmmInge

* \<Inge & Blaine>: It's not Inge it's Blaine
* \<Jay from LA>: Oh yuck
* \<Jay from LA>: NOT fair Inge
* \<Petman>: tricky
* \<Joe>: I thought so! (Adult Exchange, 26 May 1997)

Ref operators on heterosexual sites display a concern with the implications of the predominance of males on the sites, often offering warnings on the type of activities accommodated, or saying explicitly 'This reflector is a HETEROSEXUAL reflector' (Digital Curl). But CU-SeeMe does offer a safe arena for men to explore homoerotica. On uncoded or heterosexual refs, the anonymity, physical security, and emotional distance provided by the medium enable men aroused by each other's display to explore the situation on a one-to-one basis by direct connecting. Designated gay sites provide further opportunities for experiencing virtual gay sex without the negative aspects that such an exploration might involve in the real world and with the added pleasures of the game or the performance.

PERFORMING MASCULINITY

CU-SeeMe involves a performance, both visual and verbal. In staging and framing the image and in chatting via rapidly established conventions of exchange, participants perform a sexualized self. For men, what is being performed is primarily the normative aspects of masculinity. Although some exploit the potential of the medium to present aspects of self that might be considered deviant or perverse in the real world, for most the display involves performing themselves as heterosexual in that they enact sexual difference along normative gender lines.

Performed sexual displays on adult CU-SeeMe refs are referred to as 'shows.' People are complemented on doing a great show or asked whether they show. On heterosexual refs, these shows are usually performed by women or by couples. Males in these couples often perform an active sexual role, positioning their female partner's body to be the primary focus of the erotic display. Lone males are usually content to watch these performances and to direct them via chat:

* \<Rastaman>: you might move the cam back a bit though Cyn . . . kinda out of focus. (Biker Street, 24 May 1995)

Although males often masturbate, this is not regarded as a show, perhaps because this is one of the most common activities of males on
these refs, and it is interpreted as being primarily for the pleasure of
the participant, not the viewers.

A state of nakedness requires a specific, culturally learned etiquette
of being looked at, and conventions of masculine erotic display are not
well developed. The codes of the male pinup are yet to be effectively
translated into heteromale performance. Women are able to draw on
established signifiers of the erotic: settings, costumes, and poses elaborated for erotic purposes. Similar props for men (the leather jacket,
military caps, cowboy boots, sneakers and socks, or the windbreaker),
despite, or because of, their active macho associations, carry the
connotations of the gay porn culture within which they developed.
However, the changing regimes of sexual representation in response to
women's articulated desires are opening a space for a creation/
depiction of heterosexual masculine erotics of appearance. On adult
CU-SeeMe sites, males dress up and pose for the camera, wearing a
different hat each night, showing off their leopard-spotted under-
pants, displaying their well-toned bodies, or performing a butt dance.
The usual aim of these displays is to persuade female participants to
DC, or make a direct, one-to-one connection with them. The interactions on CU-SeeMe foreground the male body and the erotics of
performance as the object of attraction. There is little scope for men
to use more established devices such as their position, occupation,
wealth, or social power to attract the sexual interest of women. The
medium insists that men arouse women's attention through attractive
appearance or erotic display. However, heterosexual males have little
tradition of public sexualized display. Such performances are usually
reserved for private erotic encounters. Even in the anonymous
environment of CU-SeeMe, many men seem uncomfortable displaying their naked bodies in other than one-on-one connections. It is not
unusual for men to refuse to undress or perform while on a public
connection. For example, Robyn, while showing a close-up of her self
masturbating, asks PvtSins to lower his camera to show his genitals
(X mission, 18 May 1997). He refuses, but when she repeats the
request, he suggests that they make a DC.

Men's most common mode of display is an anonymous chest shot
until they have an erection, and then the camera is lowered to frame
the genitals. Any forms of display that invoke feelings of passivity,
vulnerability, or homosexuality generally take place in DCs rather
than public spaces. However, during one-on-one connections, and

occasionally in public spaces, some men are responding to women's demands for a visually exciting show by dressing up, showing their buttocks, caressing their bodies, and in other ways consciously presenting themselves as objects of display. The interactive nature of CU-SeeMe makes it difficult for men to completely avoid being positioned as erotic objects. Exchanges usually evolve as 'tit-for-tat' interactions between participants, in which men who wish to look at women's bodies must present their own as an erotic display.

THE PHALLUS

Tensions around the display of the naked male body arise from the fact that, fully naked, males reveal that which they hold in greatest secret, the penis. The penis is central to cultural concepts of masculinity: its length, shape, appearance, and performance are held to be critical indicators of essential aspects of masculinity. The crucial myth of masculinity remains intact by not being subjected to visual testing. Because the penis is 'proof' of masculinity, keeping it hidden from view maintains the mythology of masculine strength and power; revealing it as small, flaccid, and vulnerable exposes the myth. The significance of the penis in revealing the 'truth' about masculinity is related to the conflation of the mythology of the penis and the mystique of the phallus. The male body functions as a phallic symbol; its difference is marked by the penis. Although the penis is not the phallus, in a patriarchal society those with power generally have a penis, and the penis has become the object in which notions of power are grounded. So the penis has a complex mythology of masculine power surrounding it, much of which is dependent on it remaining safely hidden. As Dyer (1992) says, 'A limp penis can never match up to the mystique that has kept it hidden from view for the last couple of centuries' (p. 116).

Making male genitals visible on CU-SeeMe causes considerable risk to a fragile male identity, an identity that is culturally constructed around sexual parts to which heroic feats and colossal proportions are assigned. 'Crotch cam' is used to protect identity while displaying the penis. Genital display is often consciously performed or staged, with men adopting poses such as lying back, legs spread out, squatting on a chair, or framed from behind to reveal both buttocks and genitals. Most of the penises that are displayed in a flaccid state are significantly proportioned, and the majority of men appear not to reveal their penis unless or until they have an erection. The display of a limp penis seems to invoke anxieties about male potency and the ambivalence that many men feel about their sexuality.

Identity on the refs is primarily constructed and revealed through the names chosen by participants, and a significant number of men use names that establish their identities in terms of their penises: 8½, Hard 4U, Tool, Firehose. Computer-mediated contact between individuals always leaves gaps in their experience of each other, and these gaps are filled by the images, desires, and emotions evoked by the on-line name. The use of names such as Stiffie focuses identity on genital performance.

Masculinity is a negotiated system of identities, one aspect of which is the ritual display of phallic attributes. The erect penis stands in for the phallus, celebrating the primacy of the male subject, symbolizing power by demonstrating sexual prowess in public rituals. Cathy Waldby (1995) comments that 'The penis does not act the phallus unless it is lived by one or both partners as the phallus' (p. 270). The possession of an erection is perceived by men to give them a certain authority to direct the sexual encounter, and the power relationships on CU-SeeMe often revolve around the display of an erection as a visible sign of sexual potency. However, an erection confers sexual authority only if the women agree to concede it. Power is an active relationship, established through control over the discourses of sexuality on the ref—a control that is relational, and shifting, in that the exchanges of power in the sexual encounters are determined both by those 'presenting,' and by those 'reading.' Generally, on the refs men control the course of the exchange:

* <JJF>: If you would lean back a little Ame it would get even more eXXciting! (Stackers Place, 25 May 1997)
* <Zardoz>: EO would you please stand up so we can see a little more of that lovely body (World Ear, 24 May 1997)

But women do have the ability to refuse men's requests, set their own agendas, and make suggestions or specific demands without the constraints of a real-world social occasion.

* <Joe>: Pam, would you like to see my cock?
* <Autodoc>: boy you're a charmer
* <PamelaSue>: no I have seen enough cocks tonight (Stackers, 23 May 1997)
* <tony>: katie . . . would you like to dc to chat
* <katie>: no thanks not right now

225

* <ann>: good call katie probably a crotch cam boy (Digital Curl, 26 April 1997)

Ultimately, it is impossible to categorically assign power, to designate a particular image or line of chat, as indicating the relations of power in the sexual exchange. However, the interactive, yet detached, nature of the medium subverts lived relations of power, enabling the fulfillment of desires to have the phallus, or to be the phallus, regardless of gender, and sexuality is experienced across the boundaries of power and desire. CU-SeeMe enables the transformation of the female object into an active subject of desire and pleasure, therefore if not completely inverting established power relationships of subject/object and active/passive, then at least rendering those relationships ambivalent.

CONCLUSION

The erotic display on public, adult CU-SeeMe refs is a working through of changing modes of male sexuality. Although it is primarily a performance of normative masculine sexuality for and by men, it also offers a space for the sexual empowerment of women. Within this space exists the possibility of a polymorphous masculine sexuality that articulates active and passive regimes of looking, a celebratory display of the eroticized male body, and the exploration of marginalized sexualities. As a type of interactive pornography, CU-SeeMe provides the opportunity for both men and women to construct positions that are simultaneously the subject and the object of the consuming gaze. In opening up a space in which men can explore the erotic pleasures of sexualized display, the adult refs augment the development of male sexual identities that incorporate passivity and vulnerability. The sexual exchanges on CU-SeeMe provide one avenue through which an erotics of masculine display is being developed. As such, the adult refs are not simply a cyberspace reenactment of 'lived' sexual relations but a reinterpretation of the possibilities.

References

Berger, J. 1972. *Ways of seeing*. Harmondsworth, UK: Penguin.
Brod, H. 1990. Pornography and the alienation of male sexuality. In *Men, masculinities and social theory*, edited by J. Hearn and D. Morgan, 124–39. London: Unwin Hyman.

Connell, R., N. Radican, and P. Martin.1987. The changing faces of masculinity. Typescript, Department of Sociology, Macquarie University.

Diamond, J. 1991. *The rise and fall of the third chimpanzee*. London: Radius.

Dyer, R. 1992. Don't look now: The instabilities of the male pin-up. in *Only entertainment*, 103–19. London: Routledge.

Freud, S. [1905] 1981. *Three essays on the theory of sexuality*. Pelican Freud Library, Vol. 7. Harmondsworth, UK: Penguin.

Jones, E. 1955. *Life and work of Sigmund Freud*, Vol. 2. New York: Basic Books.

McCathie, W. 1996. Great big cocks . . . and the blokes who have them. *The Picture* 29:8–11.

Mulvey, L. 1975. Visual pleasure and narrative cinema. *Screen* 16:6–18.

Neale, S. 1986. Sexual difference in the cinema: Issues of fantasy, narrative and the look. *Oxford Literary Review* 8:123–32.

Rodowick, D. N. 1982. The difficulty of difference. *Wide Angle* 5:4–15.

Segal, L. 1994. *Straight sex: The politics of pleasure*. London: Virago.

Waldby, C. 1995. Destruction: Boundary erotica and refigurations of the heterosexual male body. In *Sexy bodies: The strange carnalities of feminism*, edited by E. Gross and E. Probyn, 266–77. London: Routledge.

Walters, M. 1978. *The nude male: A new perspective*. New York: Paddington.

Williams, L. 1989. *Hard core: Power; pleasure and the 'frenzy of the visible.'* Berkeley: University of California Press.

17 Racial Warriors and Weekend Warriors: The Construction of Masculinity in Mythopoetic and White Supremacist Discourse

Abby L. Ferber*

[. . .] In both academic and mainstream circles, the idea that masculinity, especially white masculinity, is in crisis is widespread. [. . .] Because men benefit most from traditional definitions and proscriptions of gender, they are less likely to initiate change. Instead, women's inroads into the workplace, increased political and economic autonomy, and questioning of male domination have historically been perceived as threats to male privilege. Since the 1960s and the second wave of the women's movement, many males have responded with fear, anger, and feelings of loss. [. . .] Many white males feel under attack by movements for both gender and racial equality.

[. . .] Both the contemporary white supremacist movement and the mythopoetic movement have been able to attract some of these disillusioned white males, who now believe that their interests are not being represented. As Ezekiel (1995) describes the sentiments of white supremacist activists, 'White rule in America has ended, members feel. A new world they do not like has pushed aside the traditional one they think they remember' (p. xxv).

Identities once taken for granted as secure and stable are in flux, challenged by the Civil Rights movement, women's movement, and gay and lesbian movements. [. . .] As David Wellman argues, the declining position and wages of all Americans means that white men are correct when they perceive themselves to be losing ground. In fact, the United States is experiencing greater income inequality than ever before. As a result of both cultural and structural changes, white men do not see themselves as possessing power and are increasingly joining social movements to represent their interests. Rather than exploring the real sources of economic dislocation in the United States today,

---

* Reprinted with permission of Abby L. Ferber and Sage Publications, Inc., from *Men and Masculinities*, vol. 3, no. 1 (July 2000).

many of these movements instead blame the losses of white men on women and minorities. [. . .]

On the surface, the white supremacist movement presents itself as primarily concerned with race relations. Scholars studying the movement have explored its racist and anti-Semitic ideologies, but there has been little discussion of the role of gender in its ideology. The mythopoetic movement, on the other hand, is about gender, masculinity in particular. However, sympathetic observers point out that the movement is centrally concerned with helping men to rediscover their 'deep' masculinity, which, in contrast to hypermasculinity, aims to help men become more in touch with their feelings and emotions, to examine negative and narrow social definitions of masculinity, to balance their masculine and feminine sides, and to become better fathers and husbands. The goals of the mythopoetic movement are certainly laudable and seem well-intentioned, in sharp contrast with the motivations of the white supremacist movement, easily recognized as despicable to most casual observers. It is for this reason that it is all the more surprising to find such striking similarities in their discourses. [. . .]

READING WHITE MASCULINITY

[. . .] As Kimmel (1995) points out, 'The mythopoetic men's movement [is] as much a textual phenomenon as it [is] a ritual process' (p. 4). The mythopoetic men's movement formed around certain key texts, especially Robert Bly's *Iron John: A Book About Men* (1990). The movement's gatherings and retreats are a means of making the messages of the texts real for people, a means of gathering men together to discuss the ideas and issues generated within the written works. For the white supremacist movement as well, written works bind together a range of people and organizations. As Ezekiel (1995) found in his study of members of the movement, 'The agreement on basic ideas is the glue that holds the movement together . . . the ideas are important to the members. The white racist movement is about an idea' (p. xxix). It is in the written texts that we find the most comprehensive and persistent explication of these ideas.

How many people do these ideas actually reach? The Intelligence Project of the Southern Poverty Law Center, established to monitor hate group activity, identified 462 white supremacist hate groups in existence throughout the United States in 1997 (Intelligence Project of The Southern Poverty Law Center 1998, 6). It is difficult to estimate the membership of these groups, which is often concealed. Daniels conservatively estimates the general membership in white supremacist organizations to be around forty thousand, while Ezekiel reports that hard-core members number twenty-three thousand to twenty-five thousand. Another 150 thousand purchase movement literature and take part in activities, however, and an additional 450 thousand actually read the movement literature, even though they do not purchase it themselves (Daniels 1997; Ezekiel 1995). The Anti-Defamation League (1988) estimates that fifty white supremacist periodicals continue to publish, and there are at least 2000 'hate sites' on the Internet (p. 1; Roberts 1997).

At its peak, it was estimated that approximately one hundred thousand men participated in some sort of mythopoetic event (Schwalbe 1996, 4). Robert Bly's book *Iron John* spent months among the top ten national best-sellers. These two discourses, then, reach a far wider audience than only those men (and some women) who consider themselves members of these movements. From this perspective, these discourses reach huge numbers of people and have far wider implications than only what they mean for those actively involved in the movements. [. . .]

....

THE MOVEMENTS

....

The mythopoetic men's movement

Beginning even before the 1990 publication of *Iron John*, retreats, workshops, and conferences were being organized across the country. As Kimmel (1995) observes, men 'were trooping off to the woods on weekend retreats to drum, chant, be initiated, bond, and otherwise discover their inner wildmen or retrieve their deep masculinity' (p. 4).

The mythopoetic men's movement is a world of and for men. Its leaders, authors, and followers are all men. Workshop attendees are overwhelmingly white, middle class, middle aged, heterosexual men. While race is not an overt feature of their ideology, they nevertheless appeal primarily to white men.

Bly argues that men are experiencing an identity crisis; numerous forces, especially men's lack of relationships with their fathers, have prevented men from discovering their deep masculinity. According to Bly, men can only get in touch with their true being with other men. Throughout the discourse, as well as in retreats and workshops, men are encouraged to reclaim their authentic masculinity through initiation ceremonies, rituals, stories, and myths, guided by other men. [. . .]

The white supremacist movement

The white supremacist movement is also overwhelmingly a movement of and for white men. Despite the efforts of some organizations to increase the number of women involved, white men make up the bulk of the membership of the movement and serve as the writers, publishers, and editors of white supremacist discourse (Blee 1996). Ezekiel (1995) notes that the organizations he observed remain almost exclusively male, and tasks within the organizations are strictly segregated by gender. He notes, 'A few women are around, never as speakers or leaders; usually they are wives, who cook and listen. Highly traditional ideas of sex roles, and fears of losing male dominance, fill the conversation and speeches' (p. xxvii). Reading white supremacy alongside mythopoetic discourse reveals that it is not just a racist, anti-Semitic movement, but a patriarchal one as well.

Most white supremacist organizations share a number of unquestioned beliefs. They believe that races are essentially and eternally different, not only in terms of visible characteristics, but also behaviorally and culturally, and that races are ranked hierarchically based on these supposedly innate differences. They believe the white race is superior and responsible for all of the advances of Western civilization. They also mobilize against a common threat: they believe the white race faces the threat of genocide, orchestrated by Jews and carried out by blacks and other nonwhites. White supremacist discourse asserts that this genocidal plan is being carried out through forced race mixing, which will result in the mongrelization, and therefore annihilation, of the white race. Interracial sexuality is defined as the 'ultimate abomination,' and images of white women stolen away by black men are the ever present symbol of that threat (Ridgeway 1990, 19). In stark contrast to the images of active, sexually independent women put forth by the women's movement, white supremacist discourse depicts white women as passive victims at the hands of Jews and blacks, and in dire need of white men's protection. The protection of white womanhood comes to symbolize the protection of the race; thus, gender relations occupy a central place in the discourse.

While the contemporary white supremacist movement is concerned with rearticulating a white identity in response to the challenges of racial and ethnic social movements, this white identity is most certainly a gendered identity. Both the white supremacist and the mythopoetic movements represent responses to the second wave of the feminist movement and the challenges it has presented to traditional gender identities. Responding to what is perceived as a threat to what were once believed to be stable identities, both movements are primarily concerned with rearticulating white male identity and privilege. Both movements appeal to similar constituencies of white males who feel vulnerable, victimized, and uncertain about the meaning of masculinity in contemporary society; the white supremacist movement attempts to redeem a specifically white, racial masculinity, whereas the mytho-poetic movement couches its version of masculinity in nonracial terms. Nevertheless, their visions of masculinity and their analyses of the problems faced by men share much in common.

ESSENTIAL MASCULINITY

[. . .] Despite decades of scholarship demonstrating that gender is a social construction, both the mythopoetic and white supremacist movements reassert an essentialist notion of gender identity. Essential-ism is the centerpiece of both ideologies, and their other similarities revolve around this shared central assumption. Ken Clatterbaugh (1995) explains that essentialism assumes that 'social differences such as those between men and women, people of different races, or social classes are due to intrinsic biological or psychic differences between the members of the different groups' (p. 49). These differences are believed to be innate and immutable, and are seen as more significant than environmental factors in explaining differences among people. [. . .]

There are, nevertheless, differences between the two essentialist revisions of masculinity. Both respond in different ways to our cul-ture's definition of hegemonic masculinity, an ideal based on an image of white, middle- or upper-class, heterosexual men. This image serves as the ideal that all men are expected to live up to, and against which all men are measured, but that few can achieve. [. . .] Both movements suggest that men today are betrayed by such ideals, but in very different ways: white supremacists argue that white men are prevented from achieving this ideal, while the mythopoets argue that the definitions themselves are problematic.

The white supremacist movement promises its recruits that it will enable them to prove themselves real men according to the vision of hegemonic masculinity. They argue that white men have been unfairly prevented from achieving this ideal (by Jews, nonwhites, and women) and denied their rightful position of power. Join the white supremacist movement, they reassure, and regain the powerful masculinity that should be yours. Key to achieving this vision of masculinity is reasserting control over women and other men. The mythopoetic movement, on the other hand, to some extent challenges hegemonic masculinity, at least the part of it that says men must be unfeeling, must never show emotion, must be independent, violent, and dedicated to competitive work. They argue that men must explore their wounds and emotions. Yet, rather than exploring masculinity as a social construction, they argue that those aspects they despise represent 'toxic' masculinity, or hypermasculinity, not the real, true, deep masculinity that men must discover. In *Knights Without Armor*, Aaron Kipnis (1992) presents a 'New Male Manifesto,' where he states, 'A man doesn't have to live up to any narrow, societal image of manhood. . . . Masculinity does not require the denial of deep feeling. . . . Violence springs from desperation and fear rather than from authentic manhood.'

Like the white supremacist movement, mythopoets present their movement as men's salvation—join our retreats, read our books, and find your real masculine self. Unfortunately, this deep masculinity nevertheless retains many other features of hegemonic masculinity, as we shall see. Both movements, then, promise to help men discover their true masculinity and prove to the world that they are real men.

Despite these differences, the similarities are striking. To enable men to discover their masculinity, both movements are concerned with creating community among men, 'drawing men together . . . breaking isolation . . . for the development of community' (Bliss 1995, 296). Both see men as out of touch with their true masculinity. [. . .] Masculinity is characterized as unchanging and universal, merely needing to be recovered. [. . .] Describing the process by which a boy becomes a man, Bly (1996) concludes, 'That is the way it has been for hundreds of years' (p. 127). Mythopoetic authors Moore and Gillette (1992) claim that masculinity has 'remained largely unchanged for

233

millions of years,' because it is 'hard wired' and 'genetically transmitted' (p. 33).

Men and women are depicted as opposites possessing complementary natures. [. . .] Not only do men and women possess essential natures, then, but these natures are dichotomous and timeless. [. . .]

Like mythopoetic discourse, white supremacist discourse rearticulates essentialist notions of identity. The discourse insists that racial and gender differences are essential and immutable, secured by either God or genetics. While race is the most overt preoccupation of the white supremacist movement, gender identity remains central to the discourse and is intertwined with the construction of racial identities. While whiteness is repeatedly defined in terms of visible, physical differences in appearance, differences in intelligence, morality, character, and culture are all posited as racially determined. As *The NSV Report* (National Socialist Vanguard) proclaims, 'Racists believe that values and ideals are a manifestation of race and are thus biologically inherited' (*NSV Report* 1991, 3). Physical characteristics and culture are linked here, both determined by race and unchanging.

Gender differences are also posited as inherent. White supremacist discourse, like mythopoetic discourse, often relies on stories of the past to demonstrate the immutability of these natures. For example, a *White Power* article explains that 'our ancestors wisely realized that women were different from men not just biologically, but psychologically and emotionally as well. They recognized that the sexes had distinct but complementary roles to play in society . . . ordained by natural law' (*White Power* no. 105, 4). As in mythopoetic discourse, sexual difference is depicted as oppositional and complementary. [. . .]

These identities are always at risk and never secure. The endless repetition through which these identities are constructed suggests that they require this repetition for their existence; they are neither innate nor essential. It is at this historical juncture, when both racial and gender identities are increasingly revealed to be unstable, that those who have the most invested in these categories and their hierarchical construction react by reasserting their unwavering foundations.

WHITE MEN UNDER ATTACK

Both movements argue that their existence is necessary to protect men (and for white supremacists, only white men), who are depicted as under attack in contemporary society. As suggested by the title of David Duke's National Association for the Advancement of White People, women and minorities have organizations to protect their interests, why not white men?

These sentiments are overt throughout white supremacist publications. As an article in the *White Patriot* asserts, 'the White people of America have become an oppressed majority. Our people suffer from discrimination in the awarding of employment, promotions, scholarships, and college entrances' (*White Patriot* no. 56, 6). Similarly, an *Instauration* article echoes, 'we are now becoming a minority in a land which we tore from the vines and tangle of the wilderness' (*Instauration* 1985, 14).

As these passages suggest, the contemporary white supremacist movement depicts the white race, and men in particular, as under attack. In *The Racist Mind*, Raphael S. Ezekiel (1995) suggests, 'white rule in America has ended, members feel. A new world they do not like has pushed aside the traditional one they think they remember' (p. xxv). Trivializing and dismissing the enduring reality of both race and gender oppression, white masculinity is often depicted as the new minority, the only truly oppressed group.

Issues such as affirmative action, which have increasingly been reframed in the terms of 'reverse racism,' are rallied around to garner support. For example, *The NSV Report* contends that affirmative action is not really about giving jobs to disadvantaged minorities but part of a bigger conspiracy against white men. [. . .]

Both movements encourage men to see themselves as victims, depicting men as under attack in today's world and arguing that 'those who hold the reins of power pile abuse, distortion, ridicule and hatred' on white men (begging the question, Who then holds the reins of power?) (*Instauration* 1985, 14). According to Bly (1996),

The ridicule of masculinity that has poured out of comic strips, from Dagwood Bumstead to Homer Simpson, from sitcoms and Letterman monologues, and from university classrooms, has had a profoundly damaging effect on young men. Gender feminists have contributed to this problem, encouraging stereotypes of masculinity that would be totally unacceptable if directed toward any other group . . . the new equation, male equals bad, has given rise to a loss of identity for a whole generation of men. (p. 129)

Both movements attack women and minorities for playing the 'victim' role, arguing that it is a ruse used against white men, the 'real' victims. 'How obvious it is,' Bliss (1995) explains, 'once we look—men die eight years younger than women in the U.S. today: they have higher rates of cancer, heart attacks, and suicide. More substance abuse, risk-taking, and automobile accidents' (p. 303).

Kipnis (1995) argues that 'male-bashing is de rigueur in today's academy' and describes feminism as 'male-denigrating. . . . After decades of unrestrained male-bashing, men have good cause for anger toward the women's movement. This is not backlash; it is a legitimate response to abuse of academic, social, media, and literary power' (pp. 278–80). [. . .] Kipnis describes a conspiratorial environment where women are in control and patriarchy is a relic of the past.

Wherever patriarchy is referred to, it is in the past tense. For example, Bly (1996) admits, 'We know that women paid a huge price in self-respect, in violence, in slavery, in shame, in the old paternal society. Almost no woman in the world wants to return to that' (pp. 113–14). Elsewhere Bly (1995) explains, 'None of us wants to reestablish patriarchy' (p. 272).

We find in both discourses a reversal of the reality of inequality. Both movements assert that the days of white male power are over and that the playing field has been leveled. Within this framework, then, any attempts to aid women or minorities are seen as giving them unfair advantages, and perceived as unfair attacks against white males. Whether affirmative action or women's studies programs, they are depicted as attempts to privilege women and minorities. Because they assume that white men receive no power or privilege in contemporary society, they reverse the balance of power, seeing all attempts to remedy inequality as actually attacks against white men, as instances of reverse discrimination. Kipnis (1992) suggests it is now men who must fight for equal rights. In his 'New Male Manifesto,' he declares, 'Men deserve the same rights as women for custody of children, economic support, government aid, education, health care, and protection from abuse.'

Sociologists, however, continue to document white male privilege (Coppock, Haydon, and Richter 1995; Wellman 1997). While some men (white, middle/upper class, heterosexual, able bodied) are more privileged than others, generally speaking, all men have greater access to valued resources in our society than women as a group. As Coppock et al. (1995) painstakingly demonstrate, 'the proclamation of "post-feminism" has occurred at precisely the same moment as acclaimed feminist studies demonstrate that not only have women's real advancements been limited, but also that there has been a backlash against feminism of international significance' (p. 3). They point out that 'criticizing feminism for oppressing men has become positively fashionable' (p. 5). That is precisely what we find in these two discourses.

The reality of power relations is further eclipsed with the mythopoets' emphasis on wounding. [. . .] Inequality and power are erased, and instead both men and women are said to be 'wounded.' According to this logic, both men and women must explore their wounds and 'reconcile' with each other.

[. . .] There is no patriarchy, only sexism, which is equally harmful to women and men. There is no power, only differences that must be reconciled. [. . .] Structural power imbalances are reduced to a matter of miscommunication, to psychological obstacles to be worked through. [. . .]

While Kipnis (1995) argues that 'it is important to create a forum where . . . proactive male perspectives are not paranoically distorted as implicitly anti-feminism' (p. 275), the mythopoetic movement is not that forum. This discourse is clearly antifeminist, and the 'pro-male' language distorts this fact. Like the white supremacist movement, the mythopoetic movement presents itself as not 'anti' anyone, simply pro-male. They simply love and seek to protect their own kind. This logic mirrors white supremacist logic, evident in a *Western Guardian* article that argues that the purpose of the white supremacist movement is merely 'the restoration of a healthy interest in and love of the achievements of White Western man' (*Western Guardian* 1980). Another publication proclaims that the social problems they address have 'very little to do with the black man rising . . . rather it is about the white man falling' (*Instauration* 1980, 14). The language used here is part of a broader effort to remake the image of the movement. Rather than be seen as haters, white supremacists are attempting to present themselves simply as defenders of the white race. In many articles, they insist that they hate no one, but simply wish to promote and protect the white race, and white men in particular, today's truly oppressed. [. . .]

DEMASCULINIZATION AND FEMINIZATION

Both mythopoetic and white supremacist discourse suggests that misery and destruction result when men and women try to deny their essential natures, and they argue that this is precisely what has been occurring in contemporary America.

Both discourses argue that contemporary social problems are due to the women's movement and the breakdown of traditional gender roles. [. . .] The women's movement is blamed for distorting the natural gender order and, according to both discourses, this has led to the demasculinization of men.

What is wrong with America? Men have become wimps. [. . .]

The problems facing us today, then, are a result of this demasculinization, which both Bly and the white supremacists trace to the widespread questioning of authority during the 1960s and the rise of new social movements. Now, men are no longer willing to stand up and assert their masculinity. [. . .]

Like mythopoetic discourse, white supremacist discourse sees contemporary society as sick and blames this decline on the demasculinization of white men. [. . .] Mirroring mythopoetic discourse, the demasculinization of white men is defined as the root of our problems. [. . .]

Throughout both discourses, contemporary social problems are blamed on the supposed demasculinization of white males by women and feminism. Both movements believe that the questioning of traditional gender roles and identities has led men to become more like women, breaking down the natural order of essential sexual difference. Both movements argue that men can no longer stand up and protect women and the community (for white supremacists, the racial community), and so chaos and social disorder prevail. Both movements offer themselves as alternatives to help men rediscover their masculinity and save the community.

SHAME

Throughout both discourses, shame is presented as a primary tool relied on to demasculinize and attack (white) men. Both movements seek to redeem masculinity and help men overcome the shame leveled against them: 'many young men . . . are ashamed of being men . . . To be ashamed of your gender is not healthful for anyone' (Bly 1995, 274).

Once again, women, and especially the women's movement, are targeted for the downfall of manhood. [. . .]

Bly [*equates*] the unjust blame of parents and mothers with the blame leveled against patriarchy and white privilege by the women's and minority movements. In doing this, he trivializes the concerns of these movements, dismisses their claims, and ignores the fundamental issues of power they raise. He sympathizes with white males, whom he sees as unfairly under attack. As he writes, 'Men in general are not good enough, fathers are not thoughtful enough, sons are not pacific enough, men don't express their feelings enough: there's a lot of "not enough." But some harsh criticisms are softening' (p. 173).

[. . .] Shame also plays a central role in white supremacist discourse. For example, a *Thunderbolt* article asserts in its title that ' "Destroy Racism" Means Mongrelize Whites.' [. . .] Here as in mythopoetic discourse, it is argued that guilt and shame are primary weapons used to demasculinize men. [. . .]

....

THE SOLUTION
....

[. . .] According to both discourses, all of society is threatened when masculinity is lost. Society can only be saved if men reclaim their authority and reassert their masculinity. 'Men thus need a movement to reconnect with the "Zeus energy" that they have lost. And "Zeus energy is male authority accepted for the good of the community" ' (Messner 1995, 103; Bly 1990, 22).

Through the use of myths, Bly and others lead men in search of this 'deep masculinity.' Men are invited to reclaim their lost masculinity by attending mythopoetic retreats and workshops. Male initiation ceremonies and gatherings are designed to substitute for the absent father and restore masculinity. 'At weekend retreats . . . they can feel a sense of intimacy and connectedness to other wounded and searching men. They can discover the depths of their manhood' (Kimmel and Kaufman 1995, 24). These retreats and the discourse draw on male initiation rituals over thousands of years to establish the permanence and essence of manhood.

The discourse argues that these rituals require separation from women and the world of women. As Kimmel and Kaufmnn (1995) argue, 'the demonstration of manhood becomes associated with a relentless repudiation of the feminine,' reasserting the oppositional nature of sexual difference (p. 24).

White supremacist discourse, like mythopoetic discourse, turns to the past for its vision of a healthy society. Stories about the past are offered as evidence to bolster the assertions of inherent racial and gender differences. White supremacist discourse is filled with stories about the past, yet these stories are never simple retellings of some static history. Historical memory is thoroughly political, reflecting the interests and position of those who write it. The process of excavating the past is, instead, the construction of the past. Both depict a past where men were secure in their masculinity and the hierarchical gender order remained firmly entrenched.

For example, one article presents a picture of the past to redefine white masculinity [*designed*] [. . .] to encourage white men to reclaim their rightful role as patriarchs who will protect white women from the advances of nonwhite men (*National Vanguard* 1983, 17).

Like mythopoetic discourse, white supremacist discourse venerates the past by honoring 'fathers' and male ancestors. White supremacists argue that we must turn to the rules and laws of our fathers, and our fathers' times, to solve the problems of the present. [. . .]

For both movements, restoring what they see as the natural gender order is the key to solving what they see as our most pressing social problems. A *National Vanguard* article highlights this, warning, 'Unless a healthy relationship between the sexes is reestablished in the West, the White race certainly will not survive' (*National Vanguard*, 1983, 21–2). [. . .]

CONCLUSION

While the mythopoetic men's movement and the white supremacist movement are very different, with different tactics and purportedly different goals, they have much in common. They both construct masculinity as an essence; they both posit the demasculinization of white men as a primary cause of the problems facing our society today; they both blame women and the women's movement for that demasculinization; and they both posit a conspiratorial, politically correct environment where men are under attack. For both movements, men today are no longer in touch with their true natures, and this natural order must be restored if we are to combat the ills that plague us. Both movements offer themselves as the solution, claiming to help men rediscover their true masculinity, reclaim authority, protect the community, and solve our social ills. [. . .]

[. . .] Both of these movements are part of a backlash against the women's movement, changing ideas about gender, and other social movements that have destabilized taken-for-granted notions of identity. Both the mythopoetic and white supremacist movements seek to reassert traditional notions of authentic masculinity and reclaim and maintain white male authority and privilege.

Given the very obvious differences between these two movements, the similarities are all the more striking. [. . .] Both movements may be appealing today not because they are extreme or outrageous but because they resonate with widely held assumptions about essential gender and racial identity, which have been increasingly subject to interrogation.

While race is not central to the mythopoetic movement's ideology, both movements appeal to privileged white men who feel they have been denied what they were taught they were entitled to. For the mythopoets, this birthright is framed in terms of masculinity; for the white supremacists, it is a specifically white masculinity. Whether racialized or not, both movements' visions of masculinity are similar.

The most significant feature of each construction of masculinity is its essentialist nature. [. . .] Both movements appeal to white men tired of being blamed for gender and racial inequality, especially given their own declining class position. Both discourses provide them with easy outs: on one hand, if men are violent or abusive, it is because they have been wounded; on the other hand, men should, by nature, be in power. Relegating behavior to the realm of human nature relieves us of responsibility—if it is nature, it cannot be changed, or so we assume. How can we possibly blame someone for acting according to their nature? Recognizing race and gender as social constructs, however, requires that we accept responsibility for these categorizations and the consequences once assumed to follow. [. . .]

[. . .] Both the mythopoetic men's movement and the white supremacist movement should be situated within this broader trend, the recurring attempt to make socially constructed identities and relations of inequality appear inevitable and rooted in nature.

References

Anti-Defamation League. 1988. *Hate groups in America: A record of bigotry and violence.* New York: Author.

Blee, K. 1991. *Women of the Klan: Racism and gender in the 1920s.* Berkeley: University of California Press.

Bliss, S. 1995. Mythopoetic men's movements. In *The politics of manhood,* edited by M. S. Kimmel, 292–307. Philadelphia: Temple University Press.

Bly, R. 1990. *Iron John: A book about men.* Reading, MA: Addison-Wesley.

Bly, R. 1995. Thoughts on reading this book. In *The politics of manhood*, edited by M. S. Kimmel, 271–4. Philadelphia: Temple University Press.

Bly, R. 1996. *The sibling society.* New York: Vintage.

Clatterbaugh, K. 1995. Mythopoetic foundations and new age patriarchy. In *The politics of manhood*, edited by M. S. Kimmel, 44–63. Philadelphia: Temple University Press.

Coppock, V., D. Haydon, and I. Richter. 1995. *The illusions of 'postfeminism': New women, old myths.* London: Taylor and Francis.

Daniels, J. 1997. *White lies: Race, gender and sexuality in white supremacist discourse.* New York: Routledge.

Ezekiel, R. S. 1995. *The racist mind: Portraits of American Neo-Nazis and Klansmen.* New York: Viking.

Ferber, A. L. 1998. *White man falling: Race, gender and white supremacy.* Lanham, MA: Rowman and Littlefield.

Instauration. 1985. Edited by Wilmot Robertson. Cape Canaveral, FL: Howard Allen Enterprises, Inc.

Intelligence Project of The Southern Poverty Law Center. 1998. *Intelligence report* 89 (Winter).

Kimmel, M. S. 1995. *The Politics of manhood: Profeminist men respond to the mythopoetic men's movement (and the mythopoetic leaders answer).* Philadelphia: Temple University Press.

Kimmel, M. S., and M. Kaufman. 1995. Weekend warriors: The new men's movement. In *The politics of manhood*, edited by M. S. Kimmel, 15–43. Philadelphia: Temple University Press.

Kipnis, A. 1992. *Knights without armor.* New York: Putnam.

Kipnis, A. 1995. The postfeminist men's movement. In *The politics of manhood*, edited by M. S. Kimmel, 275–86. Philadelphia: Temple University Press.

Messner, M. A. 1995. 'Changing men' and feminist politics in the United States. In *The politics of manhood*, edited by M. S. Kimmel, 97–111. Philadelphia: Temple University Press.

Moore, R., and D. Gillette. 1992. *The king within: Accessing the king in the male psyche.* New York: William Morrow.

The NSV Report. 1983–93. Edited by Rick Cooper and Dan Stewart. National Socialist Vanguard.

Ridgeway, J. 1990. *Blood in the face.* New York: Thunder's Mouth Press.

Schwalbe, M. 1996. *Unlocking the iron cage.* New York: Oxford University Press.

The Thunderbolt. 1974–84. Edited by I. B. Stoner and Edward Fields. National States Rights party.

Wellman, D. 1997. Minstrel shows, affirmative action talk, and angry white men: Marking racial otherness in the 1990s. In *Displacing whiteness: Essays in social and cultural criticism*, edited by R. Frankenberg, 311–31. Durham, NC: Duke University Press.

The Western Guardian. 1980. Roanoke, VA: Western Guard America.

White Patriot. 1979–84. Edited by Thomas Rabb. Knights of the Ku Klux Klan.

White Power. 1969–78. Edited by Matt Koehl. Arlington, VA and New Berlin, WI: National Socialist White People's Party.

18 'Muslim Brothers, Black Lads, Traditional Asians': British Muslim Young Men's Constructions of Race, Religion and Masculinity

Louise Archer*

Despite the growth of academic interest in masculinity, issues around black masculinity remain largely undertheorized. British Muslim men are noticeably absent in the literature, despite their increasing representation in public discourses as fundamentalist, 'ultimate Others' (Phoenix, 1997). This article uses a critical feminist approach to explore young Muslim men's construction of racialized, gendered identities. Discussion groups were conducted with 24 young British Muslims, aged 14–15 years. Half of the groups were conducted by the white, British, female author, and the other half by a British-Pakistani female researcher. Particular attention is given to the young men's use of discourses of hegemonic masculinity in their negotiations between 'Muslim', 'black' and 'Asian' masculinities. Issues are also raised with regard to the role of the researcher(s) and the interaction of 'race' and gender between interviewers and participants in the production of research.

[. . .] In academic literature issues around 'race' and gender have been largely addressed as separate and distinct identity spheres, subsuming gender within 'race', or vice versa: for example, Mirza (1992) has argued that 'blackness' has been treated as synonymous with 'male' and questions of 'gender' have been addressed in the context of 'whiteness'. Gilroy (1993: 7) has also argued that gender is often collapsed into race, so that, for example, the 'crisis of black social life' has been presented as a crisis of masculinity alone. Consequently, as Mirza suggests, 'Black masculinity is not something we consciously talk about much in academic study' (1999: 137). Within this general neglect of 'black' (ethnic minority) masculinity there is a particular dearth of research concerned with British Muslim identities.

* Reprinted with permission of Louise Archer and Sage Publications Ltd., *Feminism and Psychology*, vol. 11, no. 1 (February, 2001).

Over the past decade there has, however, been a considerable growth in literature concerned with 'masculinity' per se (see Coltrane, 1994; Gough, 1998; Newton, 1998). This interest in the topic of masculinity is thought to follow from a combination of factors, including the increasing 'mainstreaming' of feminist issues in academia, the rise of postmodernist theories, the pervasiveness of 'crisis' in the contemporary social world, the 'feminization' of the labour market and the emergence of 'race' as a central site of critique (Newton, 1998). Indeed, many writings on masculinity are underpinned by the notion that somehow contemporary masculinity is 'in crisis'—for example, Gough (1998) critically summarizes how 'celebratory' approaches to masculinity state the need to 'rebuild' men's damaged sense of self and increase men's sense of power (see Bly, 1990). In contrast, critical approaches attempt to dismantle and disrupt naturalizing notions of masculinity by showing the various workings of patriarchal power (for example, Wetherell, 1993; Brod, 1994). It is from this critical perspective that this article is written.

[*Sections on 'The public "crisis" of masculinity and ethnic minority men as "problematic"' and on 'Theorizing Asian and Black Masculinities' were dropped from this edition due to page constraints.*]

A DISCURSIVE APPROACH

[. . .] The discursive approach taken in this article is based on the work of Wetherell and Potter (1992) and Billig (1991; Billig et al., 1988). In this article, analysis is orientated to identifying various shared patterns of meaning (referred to here as 'discourses') in respondents' talk and the ways in which speakers draw on different meanings and linguistic resources to construct and justify (or argue against) different accounts, arguments and subject positions. The analysis pays particular attention to how talk does not occur 'in a vacuum', but is contextually produced and negotiated in relation to different audiences, through gendered, racialized relationships between researchers and participants. It is also assumed that talk is ideological, and performs actions/ functions, such as justifying particular power relations. Subsequently, analysis considers possible implications of the young men's discursive positions and constructions for themselves and others. This form of analysis can also be used to point to possibilities for critical and political projects, such as supporting a feminist exploration of the

245

ways in which class, gender and race interact, and how particular dominant ideologies maintain and reproduce particular power relations. Thus, in this article, discursive analysis is used to examine the various ways in which young Muslim men construct, negotiate and justify multiple identity positions, identifying the discourses they draw on and the implications of their talk.

ROLE OF THE RESEARCHER(S)

[. . .] [*Particular*] attention is paid to the context of what the young men said to which researcher. Thus the position is taken that the young men's 'thoughts and feelings, their actions, their experiences, cannot be separated from their audience—from the relationships that sustain and support them, or from the patriarchal lens through which they are filtered' (Brown, 1998: 91–2).

FINDINGS

The young men constructed plural and contradictory identity positions, locating themselves in relation to Muslim girls, African Caribbean boys and white boys. The following analyses are organized into three main sections: the first examines the discourses drawn on by the young men in their construction of 'Muslim' identities. The second section considers the young men's constructions of 'black' male identities, and the third section discusses their constructions of 'Asian' masculinities.

[*Actual interview dialogue was dropped from this section on 'Muslim Masculinities and "Muslim Brothers".'*]

[. . .] Across all of the discussion groups, all the young men identified themselves first and foremost as 'Muslim'. Various researchers have pointed to how British Muslim young people are increasingly defining themselves in terms of their religion, as opposed, for example, to parental country of origin (Gardner and Shukur, 1994; Shaw, 1994). Gardner and Shukur explained this increasing use of Muslim identities as a response to racism, suggesting that Islam provides a strong, positive identity, in comparison with being defined in negative, racist terms. Similarly, the young men's commitment to, and assertion of, Muslim identities may at first seem to mirror media concerns with the rise of 'militant' Islam in Britain. However, I would suggest that analysis reveals a more complex picture—the young men do not seem to be merely reacting to, and resisting, racism. Instead, in constructing Muslim identities the young men seemed to perform a number of actions through their talk and I would suggest that their constructions have consequences for some theories of ethnic minority identity, as will be explained below.

Rather than just being a reaction to white racism, I would suggest that the young men's talk could be read as actively engaging with white society, rejecting 'whiteness' and British identity through identification with a 'strong' religion (Gufter [*one interviewee*]) that unifies young Muslims from different Pakistani and Bangladeshi backgrounds, such that 'you're all *one*' (Jamil [*another interviewee*]). In addition to implying the importance of this unity at a local level, elsewhere in the discussion groups one young man (Rahan) pointed to the potential for global brotherhood ('you got Muslim brothers all over the world so wherever you go a Muslim brother will help you'). However, it is important to note here that although the young men emphasized how religious identification (as a Muslim) supersedes nationality, none of them explicitly talked about white male Muslims or included them in notions of Muslim masculinity. Discussions about 'white men' generally assumed a non-Muslim British male (although elsewhere in the discussions various boys mentioned the possibility of converting white women to Islam in order to marry them).

The association of Islam as 'strong' and Muslims as 'all one' could imply conversely that the boys were challenging 'British' ('white'?) cultures as 'weak' and divided. For example, a few of the boys did distinguish between themselves and white men in terms of perceived differences between cohesive Muslim families and unstable, constantly reconstituted white families. Furthermore, I would suggest that the young men could be read as using Muslim identity as a point against which to resist 'British' identity and the West, asserting that identity is more than just 'where you're born' (most of the young men were born in England). In fact, by rejecting country of birth as an important defining factor of identity, Gufter uses a powerful anti-assimilationist argument whereby religion is reified and essentialized as the marker of identity, and the central role accorded to 'majority culture' (as one axis of identity formation) is completely rejected (cf. Hutnik, 1991).

[. . .] The young men constructed their Muslim identities in specifically 'male' terms, both in their references elsewhere in the discussions to 'Muslim brothers', and by drawing divisions between themselves (as 'authentic' Muslims) and Muslim women (as 'inauthentic'—see below). The young men's assertion of Muslim identities contrasted with findings from discussion groups conducted with young women (in the same schools) where the women negotiated and argued for British Muslim identities (reported in Archer, 1998). Whereas the young women attempted to 'shrug off' race (Wetherell and Potter, 1992: 122), the young men actively 'took up' race, using religion as the defining feature of 'race'. As the following analyses will hopefully elaborate, I suggest that the young men's active 'taking up' of race worked to assert themselves as powerful men in relation to Muslim women (by controlling the boundaries and definition of gendered Muslim identities) and simultaneously assert themselves in relation to white men.

[*Actual interview dialogue was dropped from this section on 'Male Muslim Voices as Authentic'.*]

[. . .] in various [. . .] discussion groups, the young men defined themselves against women. In other words, unlike themselves, their female peers were constructed as not 'real' Muslims. By identifying the 'real' markers of Muslim identity (of what constitutes taking Islam 'seriously'), Gufter controls the parameters of 'Muslim' identity. This can be interpreted as the young men positioning themselves as 'authentic' speakers, by questioning and undermining women's legitimacy to call themselves Muslim (Wetherell and Potter, 1992).

However, the young men can also be read as asserting identities against western society. For example, [. . .] the boundaries of western and Islamic societies are identified and defined in terms of the status accorded to women. I would therefore suggest that, using arguments based in 'culture', the young men use 'women' as a particular discursive arena for drawing divisions and negotiating power between themselves and other (white) men. For example, Gufter simultaneously asserts patriarchy as a definitive aspect of Muslim identity and rejects the possibility of convergence between British and Muslim identities by positioning Islam as incompatible with 'western' notions of feminism and women's 'higher status'. Thus Muslim women's inauthenticity is rooted in their 'British-ness' and Britain/western life (as defined by its accordance of 'higher status' to women) is positioned as incompatible with Islam. The young men are also able to place themselves as the necessary protectors of women/culture (Wetherell, 1993), without themselves requiring protection. This theme is continued and expanded below in the context of the use of 'Asian' and the struggle to control culture/identity through the control of Asian women.

[*Actual interview dialogue was dropped from this section on '"Black" Masculinities'.*]

[. . .] in response to an initial question about whether the boys had experienced racism at school, Deepak [*a student*], reproduces a discourse of black boys as 'messed up' by racism. As bell hooks (1992) has argued, black masculinity has been conceptualized as psychologically 'fucked up' (1992: 89) and, as suggested earlier in this article, ethnic minority males have been labelled as 'failures' in school and as suffering from various degrees of identity conflict. However, rather than explaining being 'messed up' in terms of cultural identity conflict, Deepak argues that it is a result of structural racism in schools, whereby the 'white lad' is always privileged and the 'black lad' is always wrong.

In contrast, Yasser [*another student*] talks about the growing 'pupil power' of 'the blacks' who are 'taking over' in school. Yasser's talk echoes the findings of Alexander (1996), in which young African Caribbean men also referred to how 'the black guys run the school' (1996: 54). However, Alexander found that the young men also recognized that this power was only partial, because while they were running the school, the white boys were securing academic success in the classroom ('the white boys were studying in classes', Alexander, 1996: 54).

Yasser also equates 'whites' as 'the British', effectively positioning him and other 'non-whites' ('us') as 'not British'. Gilroy (1987) suggests that discourses of cultural racism position blackness and Englishness as mutually exclusive categories; the young men in this study could be read as using and subverting this discourse by asserting its 'truth' in order to define themselves relationally and oppositionally to white men.

Across all the discussion groups the young men used 'black' identities when talking about racism, although in discussions with myself the young men positioned themselves as black only more indirectly, when describing racist incidents (for example, where whites were racist to blacks) or in the description of racial insults (being called 'black bastard'). In contrast, the young men in Tamar's groups positioned themselves as 'black lads' in a number of ways, although, as will be discussed further below, this sometimes entailed negotiations around the authenticity of this identity.

[*Actual interview dialogue was dropped from this section on* '"*Black Racism*"?']

Across the groups young men referred to conflicts with white (predominantly male) peers and teachers in school, but it was only in Tamar's groups that such strong views were voiced. [. . .] Yasser in particular argues that whereas whites are inevitably racist, he and his friends were 'adopting' racist attitudes as an active response to white racism ('they can't do nothing about it, we can though'). The emphasis on agency and retaliation in this statement could also be interpreted as a response to racist discourses that position ethnic minorities as passive victims of racism.

Most of the young men drew on black identities when talking about common experiences of white racism. By positioning themselves as black, they constructed racism as a general pervasive phenomenon, perpetrated by whites on to all blacks, regardless of differences between black groups. . . .

[*Actual interview dialogue was dropped from this section on* '"*Black*" *or* "*Brown*"?']

[. . .] In the struggle for authenticity and control of meaning, the young men could be read as challenging and undermining the authenticity of African Caribbeans, by criticizing them for 'mixing in with white' and 'diluting' their blackness or, alternatively, for failing to maintain the boundaries of black and white. Abdul [*a student*] locates blackness as an internal, physiological and natural quality, which dissociates skin colour from signifying blackness and thus protects his own assertion of a black identity from potential challenges. His identification as black seems to be further justified through his use of a religious discourse in which 'race' is divinely ascribed at birth ('God creates your heart black or white'). This use of religion can be read as giving extra weight to Muslim definitions of the boundaries of black masculinity. The young men's chastising of African Caribbeans for not recognizing racism ('they should realize') could be interpreted as drawing on a notion of 'culture as therapy' (Wetherell and Potter, 1992: 131), because it implies that black people who mix with whites are going against their 'nature' and require enlightenment. The consequence of such a discourse would be to allow the young men to justify their identities as 'authentic' black men. [. . .]

[*Actual interview dialogue was dropped from this section on 'Traditional Asians'.*]

Across many of the discussion groups the young men drew on Asian identities primarily when making generalizations about social relations and to talk about issues concerning women. 'Asian' identities were used particularly in conjunction with discourses of 'change' and 'westernization', and the young men argued that particular forms of 'sexism' were in fact 'cultural'. For example, Sham uses a 'two-handed' rhetorical technique (see Billig et al., 1988; Van Dijk, 1984) to argue that although the control of Asian women's sexuality and behaviour is not 'fair', it is something that all 'Asian lads' do. He thus draws on a discourse of a culture to present the sexual division of power as 'natural' and intrinsic of Asian masculinity and (therefore) as 'non-problematic'.

I would suggest that the discursive struggles around identity through the control of women can be explained in terms of the argument made by Yuval-Davis and Anthias (1989), that women are constructed as cultural carriers through their embodiment of collective honour. As Cynthia Enloe (1989) argues (cited in Alexander, 1996), women have been co-opted into the nationalist struggle 'both as symbols of cultural continuity and solidarity, and of external colonial possession' (Alexander, 1996: 157). Alexander discusses this in the context of black men's resistance to black women's relationships with white men, but I would suggest that the young men's resistance to the 'westernization' of Muslim women could be read here as resistance to the internal, psychological 'colonizing' of Asian/Muslim women by the dominant (white male) culture. As Alexander asserts, 'the ability to control and exploit another group's women is seen as the ultimate expression of power' (Alexander, 1996: 157). Thus the control of Asian women in the domestic and social sphere can be 'best understood within the context of power relations with wider social forces' (Alexander, 1996: 157). In other words, I suggest that the young men's discursive attempts to assert control over their Muslim female peers through 'tradition' (opposing the influence of 'British' [white/western] values among Asian women) should be read in conjunction with the boys' positioning of themselves in relation, and opposition, to white men.

The implied concerns with asserting 'ownership' of 'our women' seems to reproduce Wetherell's (1993) suggestion that the 'protection of femininity' is a defining feature of masculinity. The young men's cultural framing of this protection and their enactment of such behaviours becomes a way of 'being' an 'Asian lad'. Consequently, feminist ideas (and 'western culture') are resisted through discourses of culture and particular gender relations are reified as 'natural' and unchangeable because of culture and 'tradition'. The young men's assertion of powerful, patriarchal Asian masculinities could also be interpreted in terms of Brown's (1998) finding that working-class girls distanced themselves from 'weak' conventional femininity in order to seem powerful. By aligning themselves with hegemonic masculinities, the young men could be seen to distance themselves from stereotypical notions of Asian masculinity (for example, as effeminate, victim of racism and so on).

DISCUSSION

In this article I have attempted to show how 'race', gender, religion and cultural discourses were intermeshed in young Muslim men's identity constructions. The young men drew on a range of fluid, shifting identities (Bhavnani and Phoenix, 1994) in order to position themselves in relation to other men and to women. I interpreted their constructions of various specifically racialized masculinities as an engagement with power. As Claire Alexander suggests: ' "culture" becomes a site for struggle over meaning, constructed through the relations of power, in which identities are created, negotiated and contested as part of an ongoing search for control' (Alexander, 1996: 191).

For example, the young men in this study used black, Asian and Muslim masculine identities in quite different ways; as a shared site of solidarity against racism, as a resistance to whiteness but also as a means of drawing divisions between black groups, and as an assertion of masculine power. Thus the young men's identity discourses can be read as part of a process of 'imagined' construction which is constantly reinvented and challenges traditional notions of essentialized cultural or racial entities' (Alexander, 1996: 199). I would also suggest that the young men's carving out of Muslim male identities in this specifically British context could be read as an example of Back's suggestion that 'new ethnicities' are produced through tensions between global and local influences, in which the meaning of 'black' and 'British' identities are questioned (Back, 1996). Furthermore, as Brown (1998) (using Bakhtin's notion of 'ideological becoming') suggests, young people may draw on and appropriate particular discourses to perform social actions, and subsequently make such discourses 'their own'. By exploring the range, content and variability in the young men's identity constructions I hope also that this work goes some way towards countering negative public stereotypes and academic theories of Muslim/Asian male identity.

References

Alexander, C. (1996) *The Art of Being Black: The Creation of Black British Youth Identities.* Oxford: Oxford University Press.

Archer, L. (1998) 'The Social Construction of Identities by British Muslim Pupils Aged 14–15 years', unpublished PhD thesis, University of Greenwich.

Back, L. (1996) *New Ethnicities and Urban Culture: Racisms and Multiculture in Young Lives.* London: UCL Press.

Bhavnani, K. and Phoenix, A., eds (1994) *Shifting Identities, Shifting Racisms: A Feminism & Psychology Reader.* London: Sage.

Billig, M. (1991) *Ideology and Opinions: Studies in Rhetorical Psychology.* London: Sage.

Billig, M., Condor, S., Edwards, D., Gane. M., Middleton, D. and Radley, A. (1988) *Ideological Dilemmas: A Social Psychology of Everyday Thinking.* London: Sage.

Bly, R. (1990) *Iron John: A Book about Men.* Reading, MA: Addison-Wesley.

Brod, H. (1994) 'Some Thoughts on some Histories of some Masculinities: Jews and Other Others', in H. Brad and M. Kaufman (eds) *Theorizing Masculinities.* London: Sage.

Brown, L.M. (1998) 'Voice and Ventriloquation in Girls' Development', in K. Henwood, C. Griffin and A. Phoenix (eds) *Standpoints and Differences: Essays in the Practice of Feminist Psychology.* London: Sage.

Coltrane, S. (1994) 'Theorizing Masculinities in Contemporary Social Science', in H. Brod and M. Kaufman (eds) *Theorizing Masculinities.* Thousand Oaks, CA: Sage.

Enloe, C. (1989) *Bananas, Beaches and Bases: Making Feminist Sense of International Politics.* London: Pandora.

Gardner, K. and Shukur, A (1994), '"I'm Bengali, I'm Asian and I'm Living Here": The Changing Identity of British Bengalis', in R. Ballard (ed.) *Desh Pardesh: The South Asian Presence in Britain.* London: Hurst.

Gilroy, P. (1987) *Problems in Anti-racist Strategy.* London: Runnymede Trust.

Gilroy, P. (1993) *Small Acts.* London: Serpent's Tail.

Gough, B. (1998) 'Men and the Discursive Reproduction of Sexism: Repertoires of Difference and Equality', *Feminism & Psychology* 8(1): 25–49.

hooks, b. (1992) *Black Looks.* London: Turnaround Press.

Hutnik, N. (1991) *Ethnic Minority Identity: A Social Psychological Perspective.* Oxford: Clarendon Press.

Mirza, B.S. (1992) *Young, Female and Black.* London: Routledge.

Mirza, B.S. (1999) 'Black Masculinities and Schooling: A Black Feminist Response', *British Journal of Sociology of Education* 20(1): 137–47.

Newton, J. (1998) 'White Guys', *Feminist Studies* 24(3): 574–98.

Phoenix, A. (1998) 'Dealing with Difference: The Recursive and the New', *Ethnic and Racial Studies* 21(5).

Shaw, A. (1994) 'The Pakistani Community in Oxford', in R. Ballard (ed.) *Desh Pardesh: The South Asian Presence in Britain.* London: Hurst.

Van Dijk, T.A. (1984) *Prejudice and Discourse: An Analysis of Ethnic Prejudice in Cognition and Conversation.* Amsterdam: Benjamins.

Wetherell, M. (1993) 'Masculinity as Constructed Reality', paper for the plenary in feminist issues in research and theory at conference on *Constructed Realities: Therapy, Theory and Research.* Lofoten: Norway, June.

Wetherell, M. and Potter, J. (1992) *Mapping the Language of Racism: Discourse and the Legitimation of Exploitation.* London: Harvester Wheatsheaf.

Yuval-Davis, N. and Anthias, F., eds (1989) *Woman-Nation-State.* London: Macmillan.

Envisioning (Black) Male Feminism: A Cross-Cultural Perspective

Samuel Adu-Poku*

INTRODUCTION

The question of men's presence in feminism has always been a controversial one. Some feminists have portrayed men's intrusion in feminism as an attempt to appropriate women's experiences and discursive spaces to sustain patriarchal representations of women as 'other' (Klein, 1983; Smith, 1987). The presence of black men in feminism is a complex and conflicting issue, particularly in a Euro-Canadian/ American context. A black man's place in (black) feminist criticism has been a questionable one, emanating from a traditional patriarchal perspective on gender and culture. 'Why then would men want to be in feminism if it's about struggle [against patriarchy]? What do men want to be in—in pain?' (Jardine, 1987, p. 58).

The irony in contemporary discussions of masculinities lies in the borders separating the critical discourses of race, gender, and sexuality from each other, and often from black males as subjects. Gender intersects with racial, ethnic, sexual, and regional modalities of discursive constituted identities. As a result, it becomes impossible to separate out 'gender' from the practical and cultural intersections in which it is invariably produced and maintained. Too often, feminists (e.g. Bart *et al.*, 1991; Klein, 1983; Showalter, 1987) have lumped all 'men' together as a uniform category without due consideration to individual differences, or differences in race, ethnicity, class, or sexuality that crisscross the landscape of masculinities, and which affect and shape the lives and destinies of individual men. The presence of black men in feminism opens up sites for exploring the intersection of gender with race.

Theorists devoted to exploring the subject of men's place in feminism generally, agree on the uses and usefulness of the autobiographical

* Reprinted with permission of Samuel Adu-Poku and Taylor and Francis Books Ltd, from *Journal of Gender Studies*, vol, 10, no. 2 (July 2001).

male 'I'. Such scholars suggest that citing the male critical self reflects a response to (apparent) self-difference with and from the traditional androcentric perspectives of his gender and culture (e.g. Boone, 1989; MacLean, 1989; Moi, 1989). As a black male of African origin, my motivation in envisioning (black) male feminism is grounded in my personal, ethnocultural and cross-cultural experience. My conviction is that speaking autobiographically, and from a cross-cultural perspective, will enable me to address the challenges in envisioning (black) male feminism.

ETHNOCULTURAL AND CROSS-CULTURAL EXPERIENCE

During the course of my graduate studies in Canada, I was attracted to a course—EDST 576, *Seminar on Women and Education*. As the only male and black student, I was confronted with many challenges. In our first class session, I was taunted by a student that I would need to alter my gender before I would be welcomed into the course. I felt that the unspoken part of her taunt was that I needed to alter my race as well in order to gain credibility as a feminist scholar. I was thus reminded of my problematic position and the 'threat' I posed as a black male and an 'outsider' to feminism. I began to reflect on the impact my presence would make in an all-white, all-female, and a women-centred course. In spite of the initial intimidation, and contrary to my expectation, I found an active space in *Women and Education* that transformed my experience in several ways. With its women-centred ideological base, it resonated with familiar themes and experiences in my previous cultural encounter. My thoughts on gender equity education took a new turn. *Women and Education* stimulated my intellectual interest in gender studies as well as my understanding of 'what a man against patriarchy could be, and do' (Awkward, 1996, p. 17). It was here that postmodern theory, the phenomenon of institutional discrimination, and gender politics became meaningful to me. I began to understand the political cause of my discontent with my parents' treatment of my sisters during my formative years. *Women and Education* assured me that while 'masculinity' poses a problem for male feminism, it does not at all preclude such a vision.

Growing up in Ghana, I was socialised to believe that boys and girls were predestined to fulfil distinctly different roles in society. For many years, I witnessed the unceasing discriminatory practices against females, both within the family and within the Ghanaian cultural and educational milieus. As a woman, my mother played multiple roles as wife, farmer, educator, trader, and mother of five children. My father, as a professional educator, spent most of his time working in the public service. When my parents were confronted with the issue of deciding which of their five children (three girls and two boys) to provide with tertiary education, they invested their limited financial resources in the education of their sons at the expense of their daughters. Their decision was grounded in prevailing patriarchal cultural practices and the modern economy which present men as husbands, breadwinners, leaders, administrators, public service workers, soldiers, politicians, with women as wives, mothers, sexual aids, and domestic workers. In Ghana, then, formal education for boys was perceived to be a viable economic investment. Females, generally, are socialised to internalise that marriage and procreation is what a woman was created for and that higher education was an unfortunate postponement of her self-fulfilment (Aidoo, 1984). The overarching effect of male dominance in the colonial state became a legacy in post-independent African states where women were virtually reduced to second-class citizens, unfit to determine their own destinies.

At an early age, I was initiated into the cult of male chauvinism. As a boy, I enjoyed many privileges that my social position afforded. Unlike my sisters who were overtasked with household chores and childcare responsibilities, I usually had ample time for studies and recreation. It was obvious that my parents were more involved and interested in their sons' educational achievement than in their daughters'. Even though my sisters spent much of their time and energies with our mother, generating extra income to supplement family resources, much of this income went into our (boys') educational costs. Ultimately, while my brother and I acquired university education, the highest level any of my sisters attained was a secondary education. As a self-fulfilling prophecy, my sisters have taken up their 'God-given' roles as wives and are striving to raise their own families under difficult economic conditions. To demonstrate my objection to their plight, and my vision of feminism, I have, as an adult, not only adopted three of my sisters' children as dependants, but also contributed immensely toward their efforts to reinvest in their lives and achieve self-empowerment.

The story of my parents' discriminatory treatment of their female children is not a unique case. It is a common practice within many modern Ghanaian families. Until recently, official policies, both written and unwritten, served to reinforce the colonial tradition of male dominance in the educational and political spheres. The educational system was deeply entrapped in gendered colonial histories, despite attempts to transform it toward a more neutral identity. The famous quotation from Kwegyir Aggrey: 'If you educate a man, you educate an individual. If you educate a woman, you educate a nation' (Aidoo, 1984, p. 259) evidently points to the fact that some individuals perceived formal education as the answer to the limitations of the untrained mind, and to the definite waste that was the sum of female lives. The disadvantage of females in formal education in most African states has engendered women's continuous subordination and lack of access to resources in the postcolonial era. While I acknowledge my privileges and power under such a system, I harbour a shadowy hope that, one day, my spouse and daughter(s) may not encounter similar gender discrimination and domination within the domestic and public spheres. Deep within my spirit, I reject the lure of hegemonic male domination entrenched in patriarchal culture and colonial legacies. Internally, I strive for new ways of relating to and interacting with females. I yearn to be part of the struggle to give voice to the many silenced girls and women, but I have no idea as to where and how to begin. Having internalised androcentric perspectives, I have become sceptical of my vision of (black) male feminism. Whilst my betrayal of hegemonic masculinity and passion for feminism is viewed as a failure in the eyes of patriarchy, the prevailing discourse of gender also vividly and painfully circumscribes my position as 'Other'. Thus, the pathways opened to men professing a feminist consciousness are fraught with many obstacles, in view of our structural locations and identities.

My autobiography may yield but only a part of the truth(s) of my life experience. Incomplete though it may be, the story continues to shape my perspective in gender discourse and social justice. My preoccupation with feminism is a transformative process grounded in my personal and cross-cultural experience. This process, according to Collins (1991), is 'a self-conscious struggle . . . to develop new interpretations of familiar realities . . . in order to reject patriarchal perceptions of women and to value women's ideas and actions' (p. 27). I do not appoint myself a spokesperson for women but, rather, I seek to appropriate my experience of 'Otherness' to enable 'me' to speak on issues of academic, political, social and personal concern. Postmodern feminist thought provides a framework within which marginalised voices could find spaces to express the repressed self.

It is undeniable that we live in a sexist culture; nevertheless, men are far from monolithic in support of its sexism. The reality of multiple sites and sources of marginalisation and oppression challenges the monolithic focus on gender. In the Western world, where feminism has gained ground, and where some space exists for pro-feminist men to express their repressed desires, feminism often reads to men as an accusation. Living in North America, I have come to terms with my own failure to confront the power structures of society and my personal relationships. Having undergone a personal transformation, I strive to confront sexism not only in the public sphere, but also in the personal arena. I have wittingly become part of the reconstruction of domestic life: sharing childcare, cleaning and cooking, and decision making. My aim is to become sensitive, nurturing, domestically proficient, emotionally expressive, and to develop mutually supportive relationships with both women and men. Convinced that women, as mothers, are primary educators and central to a family's or country's overall education, I could not waver in support of my spouse's quest for 'liberation' and self-determination through higher education. Evidently, these principles could not be achieved without yielding some of the privileges my social position as a black male affords. Douglas (1994) indicates that pro-feminist men need to accept the ambiguity of their adopted positions and be willing to critically interrogate their theory and practice. They must listen to and respect not only the voices of women who welcome their works, but also those who criticise and dismiss them. Nevertheless, pro-feminist men need not take abuse in order to gain feminist acceptance.

COLONISATION AND THE SUBVERSION OF GENDER ROLES AND RELATIONS IN AFRICA

Colonisation played a major role in the subversion of traditional gender roles and relations in many African societies. An analysis of the sociopolitical organisation among the Akans of southern Ghana will reveal the impact of colonisation and Western gender discourses on the creation of local gender systems. This is important because present-day 'customs' are not always rooted in ancient traditions.

Colonial custom and practice evolved from a worldview which believes in the absolute superiority of the coloniser over the colonised, the *masculine* over the *feminine*, and the modern or progressive over the traditional or the 'primitive' (Nandy, 1983). The cultural logic of Western social categories is rooted in philosophical discourses about the distinctions between body, mind, and soul, and in the ideology of biological determinism. Two social categories that emanated from Western philosophical thought were the 'men of reason' (the thinker) and the 'women of the body' (Oyèwùmi, 1997). These categories were appositionally constructed, reductionist and oversimplified—swallowing up all distinctions in their rigid binary structure. By contrast, feminist articulation of gender difference as social construction repudiates the philosophy of binary opposition engrained in Eurocentric male discourses. However, this concept is embedded in the framework of European-derived categories of knowledge, which is foreign to many African societies. Arhin (1983), Atkins (1993) and Oyèwùmi (1997) have indicated that gender was not the foundational social thought and identity among the Akans of Ghana, Zulus in southern Africa, and Ondo Yorubas of Nigeria, respectively. Nevertheless, due to imperialism, this debate, or 'the women question', has been universalised and uncritically imposed on African cultures, making it difficult for Akan and other black/African males to assert their traditional roles and relations with their female counterparts, relations grounded on indigenous principles of complementarity and mutual respect. By analysing African societies through Western gendered perspectives, feminists and other scholars have largely ignored the fact that gender categories in many African societies are neither precultural nor fixed in historical time and cultural space. From a cross-cultural perspective, then, white feminism becomes an accomplice to the imperialistic tendencies of the Eurocentric male discourses it seeks to subvert. It is relevant to emphasise the hierarchical race and gender relations of the colonial situation because white women did not occupy the same position in the colonial order, or in the era of slavery, as black women, and men.

The degree to which gender hierarchy is manifested today in Ghanaian institutions differs from the way it was played out during the precolonial period. Women, generally, occupy the lower echelon in postcolonial Ghanaian society. In the precolonial period, however, gender role differentiation among the Akans did not result in an increasing disparity in power and influence between women and men. The ranking of individuals depended first and foremost on seniority, which was usually defined in accordance with actual or presumed order of the arrival of their earliest maternal ancestors in the community, and by relative age (Arhin, 1983; Oyèwùmi, 1997). Women from both the Akans of Ghana and the other matrilineal peoples of West Africa held high status and important political positions within their communities (Clarke, 1984; Farrar, 1997). Similarly, the Ondo Yoruba kingdom of eastern Nigeria is known for passing on kingship to either the female or male descendant of a deceased king.

The Akan sociopolitical communities were inhabited by members of groups of matrilineages, localised segments of seven or eight matrilineal clans. Members of one clan were held to be related to each other by blood because they traced their origin from one female ancestor. Of the localised matrilineages in the villages, towns or autonomous political community, members of one clan were the *adehye*, royals, because it was understood by the whole community that their maternal ancestors were the first settlers. They were the owners of the land, the principal stool, and holders of the principal political office known as the chief, *ohene* or *odekro* (male), and the queenmother, *ohemma* (female). Subordinate stools and political power were vested in the other matrilineages, which were ranked according to seniority. Ranking carried with it commensurate command of the local resources. In Akan culture, the stool encodes the philosophical construct of territoriality. It exists in relation to specific laws of custody of the ancestral land, *asase*. Because the stool is believed to enshrine ancestral power, it becomes a sacred symbol of the occupant's political and religious authority.

Under the Akan sociopolitical organisation, females were major political players in a dual-sex political system. The Akan state was an organised hierarchy of councils that passed laws and administered the state according to the 'custom' of the ancestors. Female stools usually complemented the hierarchy of male stools. Members of the village, town or community council usually included the *aherewa* or *ohemma*, queenmother, who was responsible for the affairs of women including female stool-holders. As members of their respective councils, female stool occupants and clan leaders participated in the legislative and judicial processes, the making and unmaking of war, the distribution of land and basic resources, and the general administration of the community. An *ohemma* of a state also administered her own judicial process and had her own *okyeame*, a spokesperson who in the Akan court acted as prosecutor and judge (Arhin, 1983). The *ohemma* was wisdom personified; she was the 'mother' of the *ohene*, as well as the latter's most effective adviser. She was the refuge for a fugitive from the *ohene*'s court who often successfully sought her intervention in cases of the death penalty. The *ohemma* was the custodian of 'custom', the foremost authority on the genealogy of the royal matrilineage, and hence the first and final arbiter on who was qualified by blood to be a

ruler. The peace, order and stability of the political community, therefore, depended largely on the *ohemma*. The *ohemma* was not only a
maker of the occupants of male stools; she could herself occupy a
male stool and have male servants. Female occupants of male stools
performed the duties of their male counterparts, including their
military responsibilities. The queenmother also served as the centre
around which the potential opposition to the chief could be safely and
non-divisively collected.

In Akanland, there was no intrinsic relationship between gender
role differentiation and gender subordination. Gender subordination
occurs when a society attaches power and prestige to men's work
and devalues women's work or vice versa. The Akan state relied on
built-in customs and practices, and a system of gender differentiation
with a high degree of balance in power to contest patriarchy. The high
degree of checks and balances within the political system undermined
the expression of hegemonic male domination. This situation also
enabled women and men to work together as partners, with their roles
complementing each other.

The prevalence of female political and social power under the institution of queenmother in ancient Africa has generated some debates
over a theory that matriarchy is the most ancient family form in Africa
and the rest of the world (Clarke, 1984; Farrar, 1997). Currently, few
scholars in the academic 'mainstream' believe that a 'true' matriarchy
ever existed. Those who do are dismissed as proponents of feminist
propaganda, or simply people who are confusing matrilineality (the
practice of tracing descent through the maternal line) with matriarchy
(a form of social organisation dominated by women). The concern
here is not to determine whether a genuine matriarchy ever existed in
Africa or elsewhere. What is worth emphasising is an understanding
of traditional roles, structural relations, political power, and range of
social statuses that were available to women in ancient and later precolonial African societies, and how these were impacted under colonisation. Though it is quite conceivable that a great majority of women
outside the royal clan could have been relatively powerless in society, a
significant number of women from the various clans of the Akans
were in possession of considerable political authority and social status
within the matrilineal and extended family structure (Clarke, 1984;
Farrar, 1997).

The political role of females in the Akan state apparently became
submerged in colonial rule and its supporting institutions. Colonisation brought about an increasing differentiation in power and influence

between women and men through the displacement and devaluation of traditional practices that empowered women. The modern economy became a way of renewing male power, which now became crassly economic, instead of being submerged under indigenous sociopolitical systems. The British colonial government, for instance, recognised the authority of the traditional (male) chiefs at the local level, but did not acknowledge the existence of queenmothers (Arhin, 1983; Oyèwùmi, 1997). Gender identity was employed to determine policies and practices in administration, education, trade, legal matters, defence and religious systems.

The exclusion of women from politics by the colonial state was a new development that was in sharp contrast to the Akan political organisation, in which women were major players. Male dominance in colonial and postcolonial African politics, and the existence of certain cultural practices, such as female circumcision, polygamy, and arranged infant marriages in parts of Africa, has created an erroneous impression that gender identities are fixed in historical time and cultural space. The inclusion of a cross-cultural perspective in the analysis of gender could illuminate feminism which, in many ways, intersects African-centred ideals of democracy, group unity, mutuality, collective responsibility, and social bonding.

ADDRESSING THE CHALLENGES OF REPRESENTATION IN FEMINISM

Attempts especially, by white feminists, to excommunicate men from feminism pose some troubling issues for (black) males who engage in feminist critical discourse. Should all men be denied access to feminism? Are the issues of gender and sociopolitical concerns of women the prerogative of feminists? Or, to draw parallels—do all heterosexuals have to stay out of sexuality theory? Are white people ineligible to engage in critical 'race' theory? The answers to these questions are dependent on individual political and ideological positions on these issues. Bart *et al.* (1991) assert that 'one must inhabit a female body to have the experience that makes one feminist' (p. 191). Clearly, there are differences between what is required of a black male thinking about anti-racism and a (black) male professing feminist politics. Becoming and being a feminist, like an anti-racist, involves a transformative process that is experientially grounded (Steinem, 1992).

Schacht and Ewing (1997) stress the need to recognise the realities of individual women and men, each as valid within the particularistic context. Though men cannot experience women's oppression by patriarchy, they can perceive through imagination. Pro-feminist men could travel on different pathways to the same destination. Denying men the promise of feminism does not only evoke an essentialist argument, but also falls into the trap of the imperialistic tendencies of a Eurocentric male discourse of binaries, which most feminists reject.

Critics of feminism have demonstrated that universal generalisations about women and men are almost certain to be false. Leach and Davies (1990) argue that 'the female subject of feminism is one constructed across a multiplicity of discourses, positions, and meanings, which are often in conflict with one another and inherently (historically) contradictory' (p. 325). Mohanty (1991) points out that the underlying conception of 'global sisterhood' is a notion of universal patriarchy operating in a cross-cultural way to subordinate all women. Third World feminists and some white liberal feminists have opposed the stand by radical Western feminists that women are equally oppressed by patriarchy, arguing that the experience and life chances of poor and minority women are at least as much shaped and limited by class oppression and racism as they are by their sex (Knowles & Mercer, 1992). Jaggar (1983) examines the radical feminist claim that all men have a shared interest in the subordination of women, and argues that:

it obscures the fact that men are also staggeringly unequal with each other in the amount of control that they are able to exert over their own lives and over the lives of women. Most men, in fact, are victims of a small, white ruling class that maintains its domination through the interrelated structures of racism, imperialism and class society. Similarly, the view that women as such constitute a class draws attention to certain commonalties in women's experience of oppression, but it also obscures wide differences in the oppressive experiences of different women and even the fact that some women dominate others. (p. 118)

With this understanding, it could be unjustified to appeal to a common cultural experience of women as a legitimate ground for men's exclusion from feminism and gender studies. To do this could be ignoring the diverse and varied concerns of individuals within the categories of 'women' and 'men'.

The unique social location of black men in Western societies, that is, their simultaneous experience of gender privilege and race oppression, makes their presence in feminism ambiguous. Power imbalances, the cultural domination of Africans and the Diaspora, place black men in situations which legitimise their claim to be part of a collective struggle for social change. This does not mean that a white able-bodied heterosexual man has no role to play in feminism. What it means is that, for a male to profess a feminist consciousness, he needs to declare his motivation, as well as the particularity of his human situation in the context of history and the present. It is pertinent in our analyses of racial and gender identities, to situate the debates 'within all those historically specific developments and practices which have disturbed the relatively "settled" character of many populations and cultures' (Hall, 1996, p. 4). Boone (1989) implores feminists to pay particular attention to 'those marginalized male voices whose interests may intersect with, or move along paths that are congruent to, but not the same as those already marked out by feminist interests to date' (p. 174). Opening up ways we think about gender and feminism will allow us to develop models that make room for new understandings of internal and external actualities.

WORKING FROM THE MARGINS: BLACK MEN'S PLACE IN FEMINISM

Interests and goals in feminism may intersect with anti-racism, but they are not the same as those espoused in anti-racism. Despite the extensive scope of feminist analyses, the relationship between feminist and anti-racist politics remains obscure and contentious. For instance, black women have criticised goals advanced within white feminist politics, which blatantly ignore or misrepresent their concerns. Many black women, both in America and Europe, feel that the main analytical categories employed in white feminism to demarcate women's oppression, the family, patriarchy, and reproduction, do not provide an adequate account of the realities of black women who, as a category, are oppressed both by racism and sexism (Carby, 1982; Knowles & Mercer, 1992). The bone of contention lies in the decision as to which of the two social realities—feminism or anti-racism—must be eminent in the social struggle. What is often overlooked in this debate is the recognition that the experience of one form of oppression is influenced by and influences another form of experience. Therefore, it is an illusion to approach a larger social struggle in isolation.

As a black, African, middle-aged, able-bodied, heterosexual, academic, male of Akan ethnicity, I present multiple identities and political positions within a multiracial society. With my heterosexuality, I occupy a privileged position in relation to other sexual identities within a normative heterosexual society. Likewise, my educational attainment gives me leverage in academia. With my gender, I am portrayed as a biological man, the enforcing agent of domination and oppression against women. On one hand, my association with feminism becomes problematic, demanding an apologetic defence of my motivation in feminism and a rejection of patriarchy. On the other hand, however, race places me at the margin of demographic groups in a white dominant society. As a black male, my gender intersects with race and ethnicity to limit my access to the full expression of a hegemonic masculinity. Why then should white feminism be exclusionary to black me(n) if it appropriates the experience of 'difference' and 'otherness' as a legitimate political ideology? Black feminism, generally, does not exclude black men due to intersectionality of race, class, and cultural histories.

A cornerstone of feminist discourse is the notion that gender is socially constructed, and that its categories are mutable (Kessler & McKenna, 1978). This idea is significant from both a cross-cultural and black male feminist perspective. With this concept, it is possible to see the Akan culture and descriptions of other cultures as evidence for alternative, but real, conceptions of 'femininity' and 'masculinity'. My identity as a black male suggests that my concerns are not those of the white males, even though we share a common ground where we can engage in feminist critical discourse. This is borne out as a result of my assimilation into Western educational and institutional structures. The point of departure lies in our different historical and structural locations, which places me in a unique position in the struggle against racism and sexism. On the race issue, I share an enabling solidarity with other black men and women. Nevertheless, I subscribe to multiple black identities and varied black experience, since blackness is not a homogeneous entity, but defined across situations even within the same sex. Loyalty to gender and race has often been construed as unquestioning allegiance to the feminist or anti-racist cause for freedom and the refusal to betray that quest to the pursuit of other goals. The presumed primacy of opposing racism as a common black cultural goal, however, need not obscure the voices of individual black me(n) and women who are eager to oppose black patriarchy. Black women grapple with a quadruple burden of discrimination by social class, black patriarchy, white patriarchy and white racism.

The power relations between white women and black men within a white dominant culture, in many ways mimic the relationship between white feminism and anti-racism. Power imbalances inherent in racism nullify any real 'threat' a black male might pose to white feminism. White women are able to 'buy off' some of their sexist oppression with class and racial privilege (hooks, 1989; Jaggar, 1983). Because some white women benefit from the exploitation of black people and, historically, because they have been inheritors of colonial gain, white feminism is linked to the perpetuation of racial oppression (Carby, 1982). Boone (1989) notes that: 'In exposing the latent multiplicity and difference in the word "me(n)", we can perhaps open up a space within the discourses of feminism where a male feminist can have something to say beyond impossibilities and apologies and unresolved ire' (p. 159).

Masculinity is never a fixed core, although it can acquire specific meaning in a given social context. Social phenomena such as sexism and racism seek to fix, universalise and naturalise gender and create impervious boundaries between groups. Recognition of the implications of black men working in and around feminism has the potential of rewriting feminism. Awkward (1996), Dyson (1994) and hooks (1990) alert us to reconceptualise our notions of identity based on essentialism, in order to explore marginal locations as spaces where we can best become whatever we want to be while we remain committed to a collective struggle. There is a clear distinction between the marginality imposed by oppressive structures and the marginality which I choose as a site of resistance, an epistemic privilege, location of radical openness and possibility.

THE PARADOX OF REPRESENTATION IN FEMINISM

My family's story vividly portrays that, within certain contexts, cultural norms discourage some groups like women and children from speaking out, especially on matters concerning education, leadership, property ownership and economic development. When my sisters were denied the opportunity to acquire higher education, they were also denied their rights to self-determination, and the right to claim their own voices and spaces from which they could speak with people who make the policies that affect their health, education, economic, and personal development. Salazer (1991) argues that, even though representing others is problematic, it remains crucial in the struggle for political and cultural empowerment for those groups who have remained silenced, owing to specific material, intellectual, and social circumstances. In view of this, it is justifiable for (black) men to join hands with marginalised women in their struggle for cultural and political empowerment.

As opinion shapers and social activists, the significance of our positions makes it difficult to retreat whilst the disempowered remain in their position of oppression. How can women's situations be reformed if (black) men continue to be silent accomplices to sexism, by shying away from the opportunity to join the women's struggle? How can one become an effective advocate of anti-racism if sexism is unchecked? According to Alcoff (1991), the social location of the person who speaks or writes, determines how the message is heard, and the impact it makes upon its audience and readers. Black males have a unique role to play in feminism by virtue of their cultural, political and historical experience. Through feminist discourses, it is possible for individual (black) males to confront the power structures of their personal relationships in order to build a strong foundation for social change. Building bridges between women and men is crucial not only for gaining access to and exploring exclusive masculine settings (Schacht & Ewing, 1997), but also for the discovery of paths that are congruent to those already outlined by feminist interests.

CONCLUSION

Feminism is helpful to people who are seeking to understand the ways in which difference is constructed through various representations and practices that name, legitimate, marginalise, and exclude the cultures and voices of subordinate groups in society. The writing/(re)writing of definitions of 'woman' and 'man' is imperative for developing a fuller understanding of the complex formulation of black manhood found in diverse (con)texts. By incorporating a cross-cultural dimension to the analysis of gender, feminists could explore alternative conceptions of identity, and their implications for theory and praxis. In envisioning (black) male feminism, I utilised the possibilities provided by the differences that feminism has exposed and created. Pro-feminist (black) men must demonstrate how their auto-biographical lenses illuminate feminism: in other words, what feminism could gain from inclusion of their visions. They should strive to confront power structures of their personal relationships and of society. Furthermore, they should assume a role in educating women and men not only about the depth of women's oppression, revealed through an array of feminist publications, and the realities of individual women, but also about how oppressive structures in white feminism and patriarchy could be interrogated. A productive alliance between women and pro-feminist (black) males could advance the struggle against sexism, racism and systemic power imbalances in society. This could be achieved through a collective action rather than isolation and competition. The forging of new relationships between feminist and anti-racist educators, based on perceived differences and common interests, could engender meaningful educational and social change.

References

Aidoo, A. A. (1981) Ghana: to be a woman, in: R. Morgan (Ed.) *Sisterhood is Global: the International Women's Movement anthology* (New York: Anchor Press).

Alcoff, L. (1991) The problem of speaking for others, *Cultural Critique* (Winter), pp. 5–31.

Arhin, K. (1983) The Political and Military Role of Akan Women, in: C. Oppong (Ed.) *Female and Male in West Africa* (London: George Allen & Unwin).

Atkins, K. (1993) *The Moon is Dead! Give us our money! The cultural origins of African Work Ethics, Natal, South Africa, 1843–1900* (London: Heinemann).

Awkward, M. (1996) A Black Man's Place(s) in Black Feminist Criticism, in: M. Blount & G. Cunningham (Eds.) *Representing Black Men* (New York: Routledge).

Bart, P.B., Freedman, L.M. & Kimball, P. (1991) The Different Worlds of Women and Men: attitudes toward pornography and responses to a love story—a film about pornography, in: M. Fonow & J. A. Cook (Eds) *Beyond Methodology: feminist scholarship as lived research* (Bloomington: Indiana University Press).

Boone, J.A. (1989) Of Me(n) and Feminism: who(se) is the sex that writes, in L. Kaufmann (Ed.) *Gender and Theory: dialogues on feminist criticism* (New York: Basil Blackwell).

Carby, H. (1982) White Women Listen. Black feminism and the boundaries of sisterhood, in Center for Contemporary Cultural Studies. *The Empire Strikes Back* (London: Hutchinson).

Clarke, H. (1984) African Warrior Queens, in I.V. Sertima (Ed.) *Black Women in Antiquity* (New Brunswick, NJ: Transaction Books).

Collins, P.H. (1991) *Black Feminist Thought: knowledge, consciousness, and the politics of empowerment* (New York: Routledge).

Douglas, P. (1994) 'New Men' and the tensions of pro-feminist men, *Social Alternatives*, 12(4), pp. 32–5.

Dyson, M.E. (1994) Essentialism and the Complexities of Racial Identity, in D.T. Goldberg (Ed.) *Multiculturalism: a critical reader* (Boston: Blackwell).

Farrar, T. (1997) The queenmother, matriarchy, and the question of female political authority in precolonial West African monarchy, *Journal of Black Studies*, 27(5), pp. 579–97.

Hall, S. (1996) Introduction: who needs 'identity?', in S. Hall (Ed.) *Questions of Cultural Identity* (London: Sage).

hooks, b. (1989) *Talking Back: thinking feminist/thinking black* (Boston, South End Press).

hooks, b. (1990) *Yearning: race, gender and cultural politics* (Boston, South End Press).

Jaggar, A. (1983) *Feminist Politics and Human Nature* (Totowa: Rowman & Littlefield).

Jardine, A. (1987) Men in Feminism: odor di uomo or compagnons de route?, in A. Jardine and Paul Smith (Eds) *Men in Feminism* (New York: Methuen).

Kessler, S. & McKenna, W. (1978) *Gender: an ethnomethodological approach* (New York: John Wiley).

Klein, R. (1983) The men-problem in women's studies: the expert, the ignoramus and the poor-dear, *Women's Studies International Forum*, 6(4), pp. 413–21.

Knowles, C. & Mercer, S. (1992) Feminism and Anti-racism: an exploration of the political possibilities, in J. Donald & A. Rattansi (Eds) *Race, Culture and Difference* (California: Sage).

Leach, M. & Davies, B. (1990) Crossing the boundaries: educational thought and gender equity, *Educational Theory*, 40(3), pp. 321–31.

MacLean, G. (1989) Citing the Subject, in L. Kaufmann (Ed.) *Gender and Theory: dialogues on feminist criticism* (New York: Basil Blackwell).

Mohanty, C. (1991) *Third World Women and the Politics of Feminism* (Bloomington: Indiana University Press).

Moi, T. (1989) Men Against Patriarchy, in: L. Kaufmann (Ed.) *Gender and Theory: dialogues on feminist criticism* (New York: Basil Blackwell).

Nandy, A. (1983) *The Intimate Enemy: loss and recovery of self under colonialism* (Delhi: Oxford University Press).

Oyèwùmi, O. (1997) *The Invention of Women: making an African sense of western gender discourse* (Minneapolis: University of Minnesota Press).

Salazer, C. (1991) A third world woman's text: between the politics of criticism and cultural politics, in: S.B. Gluck & D. Patai (Eds) *Women and Words: the feminist practice of oral history* (New York: Routledge).

Schacht, S.P. & Ewing, D. (1997) The many paths of feminism: can men travel any of them? *Journal of Gender Studies*, 6(2), pp. 159–76.

Showalter, E. (1987) Critical Cross-dressing: male feminists and the year of the women, in: A. Jardine & P. Smith (Eds) *Men in Feminism* (New York: Methuen).

Smith, P. (1987) Men in Feminism: men and feminist theory, in: A. Jardine & P. Smith (Eds) *Men in Feminism* (New York: Methuen).

Steinem, G. (1992) *Revolution from Within: a book of self-esteem* (Boston: Little, Brown and Company).

Further Reading

ADAMS, RACHEL, and SAVRAN, DAVID (eds.), *The Masculinity Reader* (Malden, Mass.: Basil Blackwell, 2002).

ALTMAN, DENNIS, *Homosexual: Oppression and Liberation* (New York: Outerbridge & Dienstfrey, 1971).

ARCHER, JOHN (ed.), *Male Violence* (London: Routledge, 1994).

ARCHER, LOUISE, *Race, Masculinity and Schooling: Muslim Boys and Education* (London: HMSO, 2003).

ARMSTRONG, JAMES D., 'Homophobic Slang as Coercive Discourse among College Students', in Livia and Hall, 1997: 326–34.

AWKWARD, MICHAEL, *Negotiating Difference: Race, Gender and the Politics of Positionality* (Chicago: University of Chicago Press, 1995).

BADINTER, ELISABETH, *XY: On Masculine Identity* (New York: Columbia University Press, 1995).

BARKER-BENFIELD, G. J., *The Horrors of the Half-Known Life: Male Attitudes toward Women and Sexuality in Nineteenth Century America* (New York: Harper & Row Book, 1976).

BELTON, DON, *Speak my Name: Black Men on Masculinity and the American Dream* (Boston: Beacon Press, 1995).

BENEKE, TIMOTHY, *Men and Rape: What They Have to Say about Sexual Violence* (New York: St Martin's Press, 1982).

—— *Proving Manhood: Reflections on Men and Sexism* (Berkeley and Los Angeles: University of California Press, 1997).

BERGER, MARTIN, *Man Made: Thomas Eakins and the Construction of Gilded Age Manhood* (Berkeley and Los Angeles: University of California Press, 2000).

BERGER, MAURICE, WALLIS, BRIAN, and WATSON, SIMON (eds.), *Constructing Masculinity* (New York: Routledge, 1995).

BERGMAN, DAVID, *Gaiety Transfigured: Gay Self-Representation in American Literature* (Madison: University of Wisconsin Press, 1991).

BERKOWITZ, ALAN D., *Men and Rape: Theory, Research, and Prevention Programs in Higher Education* (San Francisco: Jossey-Bass, 1994).

BOONE, JOSEPH A. and CADDEN, MICHAEL (eds.), *Engendering Men: The Question of Male Feminist Criticism* (New York: Routledge, 1990).

BORDO, SUSAN, *The Male Body: A New Look at Men in Public and in Private* (New York: Farrar Strauss & Giroux, 2000).

—— 'Pills and Power Tools', *Men and Masculinities* 1/1, (July 1998), 87–90.

BOSWELL, JOHN, *Christianity, Social Tolerance and Homosexuality* (Chicago: University of Chicago Press, 1980).

BOURDIEU, PIERRE, *Masculine Domination* (Stanford: Stanford University Press, 2001).

BRAUDY, LEO, *From Chivalry to Terrorism: War and the Changing Nature of Masculinity* (New York: Alfred Knopf, 2003).

BRITTAN, ARTHUR, *Masculinity and Power*, (London: Basil Blackwell, 1989).

BROD, HARRY (ed.), *The Making of Masculinities: The New Men's Studies* (Boston: Allen & Unwin, 1987).

——. (ed.), *A Mensch among Men: Explorations in Jewish Masculinity* (Berkeley, Calif.: Crossing Press, 1988).

—— and KAUFMAN, MICHAEL (eds.), *Theorizing Masculinities* (Thousand Oaks, Calif.: Sage Publications, 1994).

BROUGHTON, TREV, *Men of Letters, Writing Lives: Masculinity and Literary Auto/Biography in the Late Victorian Period* (New York: Routledge, 1999).

BUTTERS, GERALD, *Black Manhood on the Silent Screen* (Lawrence: University of Kansas Press, 2002).

CARNES, MARK C. and GRIFFEN, CLYDE (eds.), *Meanings for Manhood: Constructions of Masculinity in Victorian America* (Chicago: University of Chicago Press, 1990).

CHAPMAN, ROWENA, and RUTHERFORD, JONATHAN (eds.), *Male Order: Unwrapping Masculinity* (New York: Routledge, 1988).

CHRISTIAN, HARRY, *The Making of Anti-sexist Men* (London: Routledge, 1994).

CLARIDGE, LAURA, and LANGLAND, ELIZABETH (eds.), *Out of Bounds: Male Writers and Gender(ed) Criticism* (Amherst: University of Massachusetts Press, 1990).

CLATTERBAUGH, KENNETH, *Contemporary Perspectives on Masculinity: Men, Women, and Politics in Modern Society* (Boulder, Colo.: Westview Press, 1990).

COHEN, THEODORE F. (ed.), *Men and Masculinity: A Text Reader* (Belmont, Calif.: Wadsworth Publishing, 2000).

CONNELL, ROBERT, *Masculinities* (Berkeley and Los Angeles: University of California Press, 1995).

CONNELL, R. W., *Gender & Power* (Stanford: Stanford University Press, 1987).

CORNWALL, ANDREA and LINDISFARNE, NANCY (eds.), *Dislocating Masculinity: Comparative Ethnographies* (London: Routledge, 1994).

CRAIG, STEVE, *Men, Masculinity, and the Media* (Newbury Park: Sage Publications, 1992).

DELLAMORA, RICHARD, *Masculine Desire: The Sexual Politics of Victorian Aestheticism* (Chapel Hill: University of North Carolina Press, 1990).

D'EMILIO, JOHN, and FREEDMAN, ESTELLE B., *Intimate Matters: A History of Sexuality in America* (New York: Harper & Row, 1988).

DIGBY, TOM, (ed.), *Men Doing Feminism* (New York: Routledge, 1998).

EASTHOPE, ANTONY, *What a Man's Gotta Do: The Masculine Myth in Popular Culture* (Winchester, Mass.: Unwin Hyman, 1986).

FALUDI, SUSAN, *Stiffed: The Betrayal of the American Man* (New York: William Morrow & Co., 1999).

FARRELL, WARREN, *The Liberated Man: Beyond Masculinity. Freeing Men and their Relationships with Women* (New York: Random House, 1974).

FASTEAU, MARC FEIGEN, *The Male Machine* (New York: Dell Publishing Co. Inc., 1975).

FERBER, ABBY L., *White Man Falling: Race, Gender and White Supremacy* (New York: Rowman & Littlefield Publishers Inc., 1998).

FERGUSON, ANN ARNETT, *Bad Boys: Public Schools in the Making of Black Masculinity* (Ann Arbor: University of Michigan Press, 2001).

FORD, DAVID, and HEARN, JEFF (eds.), *Studying Men and Masculinity: A Sourcebook of Literature and Materials* (Bradford: University of Bradford Press, 1988).

FRAIMAN, SUSAN, *Cool Men and the Second Sex* (New York: Columbia University Press, 2003).

FRANKLIN, CLYDE W., III, *Men & Society* (Chicago: Nelson-Hall Publishers, 1988).

GARDINER, JUDITH KEGAN (ed.), *Masculinity Studies and Feminist Theory: New Directions* (New York: Columbia University Press, 2002).

GAY LEFT COLLECTIVE (eds.), *Homosexuality: Power and Politics* (London: Allison & Busby, 1980).

GERZON, MARK A., *A Choice of Heroes: The Changing Face of American Manhood* (New York: Houghton Mifflin, 1982).

GIBSON, JAMES WILLIAM, *Warrior Dreams: Violence and Manhood in Post-Vietnam America* (New York: Hill & Wang, 1994).

GILMORE, DAVID D., *Manhood in the Making: Cultural Conceptions of Masculinity* (New Haven: Yale University Press, 1990).

—— *Misogyny: The Male Malady* (Philadelphia: University of Pennsylvania Press, 2001).

GUTMAN, MATTHEW, *The Meanings of Macho: Being a Man in Mexico City* (Berkeley and Los Angeles: University of California Press, 1996).

HABEGGER, ALFRED, *Gender, Fantasy and Realism in American Literature* (New York: Columbia University Press, 1982).

HADLEY, D. M., *Masculinity in Medieval Europe* (London: Longman, 1999).

HALLEY, JANET E., 'The Construction of Heterosexuality,' In Michael Warner (ed)., *Fear of a Queer Planet: Queer Politics and Social Theory* (Minneapolis: University of Minnesota Press, 1993), 82–102.

HARPER, PHILLIP BRIAN, *Are We Not Men? Masculine Anxiety and the Problem of African-American Identity* (New York: Oxford University Press, 1998).

HARTSOCK, NANCY, 'Masculinity, Heroism, and the Making of War,' in Adrienne Harris and Ynestra King (eds.), *Rocking the Ship of State: Toward a Feminist Peace Politics* (Boulder, Colo.: Westview Press, 1989), 133–52.

HAWKESWOOD, WILLIAM G., *One of the Children: Gay Black Men in Harlem* (Berkeley and Los Angeles: University of California Press, 1996).

HEARN, JEFF, *The Gender of Oppression: Men, Masculinity, and the Critique of Marxism,* (New York: St Martin's Press, 1987).

—— and MORGAN, DAVID, (eds.), *Men, Masculinities & Social Theory,* (London: Unwin Hyman, 1990).

HOCH, PAUL, *White Hero Black Beast: Racism, Sexism and the Mask of Masculinity* (London: Pluto Press, 1979).

HOCQUENGHEM, GUY, *Homosexual Desire* (London: Allison & Busby, 1978).

HOOKS, BELL, *We Real Cool: Black Men and Masculinity* (New York: Routledge, 2004).

HORROCKS, ROGER, *Masculinity in Crisis: Myths, Fantasies, Realities* (New York: St Martin's Press, 1994).

JACKSON, DAVID, *Unmasking Masculinity: A Critical Autobiography* (London: Unwin Hyman, 1990).

JARDINE, ALICE, and SMITH, PAUL, (eds.), *Men in Feminism* (New York: Methuen, 1987).

JARVIS, CHRISTINA S., *The Male Body at War: American Masculinity during World War II* (Dekalb: Northern Illinois University Press, 2004).

JEFFERS, SUSAN, *Hard Bodies: Hollywood Masculinity in the Reagan Era* (New Brunswick, NJ: Rutgers University Press, 1994).

JOHNSON, CHARLES, MCCLUSKY, JOHN, and MCCLUSKEY, JOHN Jr. (eds.), *Black Men Speaking* (Bloomington: Indiana University Press, 1997).

JOHNSON, SALLY, and MEINHOF, ULRIKE (eds.), *Language and Masculinity* (London: Blackwell Publishers, 1997).

KATZ, JONATHAN NED, *The Invention of Heterosexuality* (New York: Dutton, 1995).

KAUFMAN, MICHAEL, (ed.), *Beyond Patriarchy: Essays by Men on Pleasure, Power and Change* (New York: Oxford University Press, 1987).

KIMMEL, MICHAEL S. (ed.), *Changing Men: New Directions in Research on Men and Masculinity* (Newbury Park, Calif.: Sage Publications, 1987).

—— *The Gendered Society* (New York: Oxford University Press, 2000).

—— (ed.), *Men Confront Pornography,* (New York: Crown Publishers, 1990).

—— *Manhood in America: A Cultural History* (New York: The Free Press, 1996).

—— (ed.), *The Politics of Manhood: Profeminist Men Respond to the Mythopoetic Men's Movement (and the Mythopoetic Leaders Answer)* (Philadelphia: Temple University Press, 1995).

—— and MESSNER, MICHAEL A. (eds.), *Men's Lives* (Upper Saddle River, NJ: Pearson Allyn & Bacon, 6th edn., 2003).

—— and MOSMILLER, THOMAS E., (eds.), *Against the Tide: Pro-feminist Men in the United States, 1776–1990: A Documentary History* (Boston: Beacon Press, 1992).

KING, THOMAS A., *The Gendering of Men, 1600–1750: The English Phallus* (Madison: University of Wisconsin Press, 2004).

KINSMAN, GARY, *The Regulation of Desire: Homo and Hetero Sexualities* (Montreal: Black Rose Press, 1996).

KOESTENBAUM, WAYNE, *Double Talk: The Erotics of Male Literary Collaboration* (New York: Routledge, 1989).

LEAP, WILLIAM L., *Word's Out: Gay Men's English* (Minneapolis: University of Minnesota Press, 1996).

LEFLOWITZ, BERNARD, *Our Guys: The Glen Ridge Rape and the Secret Life of the Perfect Suburb* (Berkeley and Los Angeles: University of California Press, 1997).

LEVERENZ, DAVID, *Manhood in the American Renaissance* (Ithaca, NY: Cornell University Press, 1989).

LEVIN, JAMES, *The Gay Novel: The Male Homosexual Image in America* (New York: Irvington Publishers, 1983).

LILLY, MARK, *Gay Men's Literature in the Twentieth Century* (New York: New York University Press, 1993).

LINDSAY, LISA A., and MIESCHER, STEPHAN (eds.), *Men and Masculinities in Modern Africa* (Portsmouth, NH: Heinemann, 2003).

LIVIA, ANNA, and HALL, KIRA (eds.), *Queerly Phrased: Language, Gender and Sexuality* (New York: Oxford University Press, 1997).

LOMBARD, ANNE S., *Making Manhood: Growing up Male in Colonial New England* (Cambridge, Mass.: Harvard University Press, 2003).

LOUIE, KAM and LOW, MORRIS (eds.), *Asian Masculinities: The Meaning and Practice of Manhood in China and Japan* (London: Routledge, 2003).

MAAS, JAMES, *Speaking of Friends: The Variety of Man-to-Man Relationships* (Berkeley: Shameless Hussy Press, 1985).

MACINNES, JOHN, *The End of Masculinity: The Confusion of Sexual Genesis and Sexual Difference in Modern Society* (Buckingham: Open University Press, 1998).

MCLAREN, ANGUS, *The Trials of Masculinity: Policing Sexual Boundaries, 1870–1930* (Chicago: University of Chicago Press, 1997).

MARRIOTT, DAVID, *On Black Men* (New York: Columbia University Press, 2000).

MESSNER, MICHAEL, *Power at Play: Sports and the Problem of Masculinity* (Boston: Beacon Press, 1992).

—— and SABO, DON (eds.), *Sport, Men and the Gender Order: Critical Feminist Perspectives* (Champaign, Ill.: Human Kinetics Books, 1990).

METCALF, ANDY and HUMPHRIES, MARTIN (eds.), *The Sexuality of Men* (London: Pluto Press, 1985).

MILLER, TOBY, 'A Short History of the Penis,' *Social Text*, 13 (1995), 1–26.

—— *Sportsex* (Philadelphia: Temple University Press, 2002).

MORGAN, DAVID, *Discovering Men* (New York: Routledge, 1992).

MORGAN, THAIS, *Men Writing the Feminine: Literature, Theory, and the Question of Gender* (Albany: State University of New York Press, 1994).

MURPHY, PETER F. (ed.), *Fictions of Masculinity: Crossing Cultures, Crossing Sexualities* (New York: New York University Press, 1994).

—— *Studs, Tools, and the Family Jewels: Metaphors Men Live By* (Madison: University of Wisconsin Press, 2001).

—— 'Toward a Feminist Masculinity: A Review Essay,' *Feminist Studies*, 15 (Summer 1989), 351–61.

MURRAY, JACQUELINE, (ed.), *Conflicted Identities and Multiple Masculinities: Men in the Medieval West* (New York: Routledge, 1999).

NARDI, PETE M., *Gay Masculinities* (Thousand Oaks, Calif.: Sage Publications, 2000).

NELSON, DANA D., *National Manhood: Capitalist Citizenship and the Imagined Fraternity of White Men* (Durham, NC: Duke University Press, 1998).

NELSON, MARIAH BURTON, *The Stronger Women Get, the More Men Like Football* (New York: Harcourt Brace, 1994).

NICHOLS, JACK, *Men's Liberation: A New Definition of Masculinity* (Harmondsworth: Penguin Books, 1975).

PALEY, MAGGIE, *The Book of the Penis* (New York: Grove Press, 1999).

PERRIAM, CHRIS, *Stars and Masculinities in Spanish Cinema: From Banderas to Bardem* (New York: Oxford University Press, 2003).

PFEIL, FRED, *White Guys: Studies in Postmodern Domination and Difference* (New York: Verso Press, 1995).

PLECK, ELIZABETH, and PLECK, JOSEPH (eds.), *The American Man* (Englewood Cliffs, NJ: Prentice-Hall Inc., 1980).

PLECK, JOSEPH, *The Myth of Masculinity* (Cambridge, Mass.: MIT Press, 1981).

—— and SAWYER, JACK *Men and Masculinity* (Englewood Cliffs, NJ: Prentice-Hall Inc. 1974).

PORTER, DAVID (ed.), *Between Men and Feminism* (London: Routledge, 1992).

PRONGER, BRIAN, *The Arena of Masculinity: Sports, Homosexuality and the Meaning of Sex* (New York: St Martin's Press, 1990).

RAPHAEL, RAY, *The Men from the Boys: Rites of Passage in Male America* (Lincoln: University of Nebraska Press, 1988).

REYNAUD, EMMANUEL, *Holy Virility: The Social Construction of Masculinity* (London: Pluto Press, 1983).

ROPER, MICHAEL, and TOSH, JOHN (eds.), *Manful Assertions: Masculinities in Britain since 1800* (New York: Routledge, 1991).

ROSEN, DAVID, *The Changing Fictions of Masculinity* (Urbana: University of Illinois Press, 1993).

ROTUNDO, E. ANTHONY, *American Manhood: Transformations in Masculinity from the Revolution to the Modern Era* (New York: Basic Books, 1993).

RUTHERFORD, JONATHAN, *Men's Silences: Predicaments in Masculinity* (London: Routledge, 1992).

SABO, DON, and RUNFOLA, ROSS (eds.), *Jock: Sports & Male Identity* (Englewood Cliffs, NJ: Prentice-Hall Inc., 1980).

SAVRAN, DAVID, *Taking it Like a Man: White Masculinity, Masochism, and Contemporary American Culture* (Princeton: Princeton University Press, 1998).

SCHWENGER, PETER, *Phallic Critiques: Masculinity and Twentieth-Century Literature* (London: Routledge & Kegan Paul, 1984).

SEGAL, LYNN, *Slow Motion: Changing Masculinities, Changing Men* (New Brunswick, NJ: Rutgers University Press, 1990).

SEIDLER, VICTOR, (ed.), *The Achilles Heel Reader* (London: Routledge, 1991).

—— *Recreating Sexual Politics: Men, Feminism and Politics* (London: Routledge, 1991).

—— *Rediscovering Masculinity: Reason, Language and Sexuality* (New York: Routledge, 1989).

—— *Unreasonable Men: Masculinity and Social Theory*, (London: Routledge, 1994).

SHAMIR, MILETTE, and TRAVIS, JENNIFER (eds.), *Boys' Don't Cry?: Rethinking Narratives of Masculinity and Emotion in the U.S.* (New York: Columbia University Press, 2002).

SIMPSON, MARK, *Male Impersonators: Men Performing Masculinity* (New York: Columbia University Press, 1994).

SINCLAIR, PETER (ed.), *King, Warrior, Magician, Weenie* (Freedom, Calif.: The Crossing Press, 1993).

SMITH, PAUL, 'Men in Feminism: Men and Feminist Theory,' in Alice Jardine and Paul Smith (eds.), *Men in Feminism* (New York: Methuen, 1987), 33–40.

SNODGRASS, JON (ed.), *For Men against Sexism: Essays on Sex and Justice* (Portland, Ore.: Breitenbush Books, 1989).

SONKIN, DANIEL J., and DURPHY, MICHAEL *Learning to Live without Violence: A Handbook for Men* (San Francisco: Volcano Press, 1982).

STAPLES, ROBERT, *Black Masculinity: The Black Male's Role in American Society* (Oakland: The Black Scholar, 1982).

STEARNS, PETER N., *Be a Man! Males in Modern Society* (New York: Holmes & Meier Publishers Inc.1979).

STECOPOULOS, HARRY, and UEBEL, MICHAEL (eds.), *Race and the Subject of Masculinities*, (Durham, NC.: Duke University Press, 1997).

STEPHANSON, RAYMOND, *The Yard of Wit: Male Creativity and Sexuality, 1650–1750* (Philadelphia: University of Pennsylvania Press, 2003).

STOLTENBERG, JOHN, *The End of Manhood: A Book for Men of Conscience* (New York: Dutton, 1993).

—— *Refusing to Be a Man: Essays on Sex and Justice* (Portland, Ore.: Breitenbush Books Inc., 1989).

SUMMERS, MARTIN, *Manliness and its Discontents: The Black Middle Class and the Transformation of Masculinity, 1900–1930* (Chapel Hill, NC.: University of North Carolina Press, 2004).

TEAL, DONN, *The Gay Militants: How Gay Liberation Began in America, 1969–1971* (New York: St Martin's Press, 1971).

TOLSON, ANDREW, *The Limits of Masculinity: Male Identity and Women's Liberation* (New York: Harper & Row, 1977).

TRIMBERGER, ELLEN KAY, 'Feminism, Men and Modern Love: Greenwich Village, 1900–1925,' in Ann Snitow (ed.), *Powers of Desire: The Politics of Sexuality* (New York: Monthly Review Press, 1983), 131–52.

WALLACE, MAURICE, *Constructing the Black Masculine: Identity and Ideality in African American Men's Literature and Culture, 1775–1995* (Durham, NC.: Duke University Press, 2002).

WEEKS, JEFFREY, *Coming Out: Homosexual Politics in Britain from the Nine-teenth Century to the Present* (London: Quartet Books, 1977).

—— *Sex, Politics and Society: The Regulation of Sexuality Since 1800* (London: Longman, 1981).

—— *Sexuality and its Discontents: Meanings, Myths and Modern Sexualities* (London: Routledge, 1985).

WHITEHEAD, STEPHEN, *Men and Masculinities* (Cambridge: Polity Press, 2002).

—— and BARRETT, FRANK J. (eds.), *The Masculinities Reader* (Cambridge: Polity Press 2001).

WOODS, GREGORY, *A History of Gay Literature: The Male Tradition* (New Haven: Yale University Press, 1998).

YOUNG, ALLEN, *Allen Ginsburg: Gay Sunshine Interview* (Bolinas, Calif.: Grey Fox Press, 1973).

Index